IN SEARCH OF ANNIE DREW

In Search of Annie Drew

JAMAICA KINCAID'S MOTHER AND MUSE

Daryl Cumber Dance

UNIVERSITY OF VIRGINIA PRESS • *Charlottesville & London*

University of Virginia Press

Printed in the United States of America on acid-free paper

First published 2016

9 8 7 6 5 4 3 2 1

Library of Congress Cataloging-in-Publication Data
Names: Dance, Daryl Cumber.
Title: In search of Annie Drew : Jamaica Kincaid's mother and muse / Daryl Cumber Dance.
Description: Charlottesville : University of Virginia Press, 2016. | Includes bibliographical references and index.
Identifiers: LCCN 2015043814 | ISBN 9780813938448 (cloth : alk. paper) | ISBN 9780813938462 (pbk. : alk. paper) | ISBN 9780813938455 (e-book)
Subjects: LCSH: Kincaid, Jamaica—Family. | Novelists, Antiguan—Family relationships. | Novelists, Antiguan—20th century—Biography. | Drew, Annie, -1999. | Mothers and daughters—Antigua and Barbuda—Antigua.
Classification: LCC PR9275.A583 K56434 2016 | DDC 813.54—dc23
LC record available at http://lccn.loc.gov/2015043814

To the mothers who passed our stories on to me,
Sallie Corona Brown Bell Brown (1875–1952)
and
Sallie Veronica Bell Cumber (1911–1996),

and to the line of sons and daughters to whom I entrust them,
Warren Carlton Dance Jr.
Allen Cumber Dance
Daryl Lynn Dance
Tadelech Edjigu Dance
Yoseph Carlton Dance
and
Veronica Cumber Dance

CONTENTS

ACKNOWLEDGMENTS

My thanks first of all to Jamaica Kincaid for the brilliant body of work that motivated this project. I am grateful to her also for inviting me to her home to discuss it, giving me a tour of her gardens, sharing her photos and mementos with me, and providing names of people who knew her mother well.

My very special thanks to the late Annie Victoria Richardson Drew, whom I never met, but whom I now regard as an unforgettable companion on this journey. The effort to elucidate her life has been a struggle, but I thank her for the extraordinary story she left behind for me to attempt to revisit and reconstruct. Because of her I have a greater appreciation of Alice Walker's postscript to *The Color Purple:* "I thank everybody in this book for coming. A. W., author and medium."

I am also grateful to Ms. Kincaid's assistant, Amber Lee, who helped me arrange accommodations in Bennington, secured critical information and materials from Ms. Kincaid's files, helped me set up my recording equipment, took a photo for me, and assisted in other ways too numerous to mention.

I am indebted to a wide range of individuals who provided crucial support in this project, some of whom I never actually met, but their prompt e-mail or "snail mail" responses to my requests for assistance, their cheery voices on the telephone, and, oftentimes, their enthusiasm for this project endeared them to me. I regret that I did not record all of the names of such supporters, but I am pleased to acknowledge the following.

For help in planning my trip to Antigua, I thank Beryl Riley, Dr. Gregson Davis, Joanne Hilhouse, Dr. John Rickford, Dr. Arnold Rampersad, Dr. Sele Adeyemi, Dr. Bernard Moitt, Clive Wong, and Dr. Carmen Wong.

I am grateful to the following agencies that provided assistance in planning my trip and/or locating important documents: the Government of Antigua and Barbuda Consulate General Office in New York; the Embassy of Antigua in Washington; the Office of the Registrar, Antigua High Court; the Government of Antigua Barbuda National Archives; and the Vermont State Archives and Records Administration.

For help in contacting family and associates of Annie Drew and Jamaica Kincaid, I thank Dr. Moremi Adeyemi, Barbara Arindell, Pamela Arthurton, Joy Bramble, Amy Cherry, Dr. Carole Boyce Davies, Winston Derrick, Joseph Drew, Gordon George, Michelle Henry, Verne Lake, Reverend Rosa Lee, Michelle Lightfoot, Susan Matthias, Dr. Ermina Osoba, Samuel Raphael, and Dame Gwendolyn Tonge.

For sharing memories of Annie Drew and/or her family, I am grateful to Sharon Chacko, Dr. Carole Boyce Davis, Vincent (Tubby) Derrick, Winston Derrick, Joseph Drew, Gordon George, Dr. Catherine John, Reverend Rosa Lee, Conrad Luke, Phyllis Mayers, Dr. Ermina Osoba, Ivor (Splif) Philip, Connie Rabinowitz, Sir Dr. Prince Ramsey, Jocelyn Reid, and Dame Gwendolyn Tonge. I am grateful also to several individuals who spoke with me but will remain anonymous.

I am especially indebted to Verne Lake and Vincent (Tubby) Derrick, who responded to my pleas for assistance with this project on the ground in Antigua after I had returned to Virginia. Their support was critical.

I am obliged for various acts of kindness to more people in Antigua than I can mention. In addition to those mentioned above, I wish to thank the staff and personnel at the Siboney Hotel for providing comfortable accommodations and facilitating my project in every way possible, including providing computer assistance. I am grateful to the gentleman, who will remained unnamed, who provided reliable taxi service and made every trip an educational tour. I thank Yolanda Goodwin for her help in scanning and mailing information to me. Everywhere I went, Antiguans were generous and helpful. When I approached a man on the street to ask for directions, he walked seven or eight blocks with me to be sure I arrived at my destination. When I inquired in my hotel lobby about a market, a lady walked me there and helped me bring my groceries back. When I couldn't find Reverend Lee's house, a gentleman called her on his cell phone and then rode with me to her house. When I was leaving a market, a taxi driver insisted on taking me the short distance to my hotel at no charge because I had heavy bags. Though I know they existed and to some degree still exist, nowhere did I see the Antigua or the Antiguans of *A Small Place.*

The University of Richmond provided generous support throughout this project. A sabbatical allowed the time for me to do the research and writing. A travel grant helped to finance my travel to Vermont and Antigua. The Boatwright Memorial Library Staff provided crucial support, especially Betty B. Tobias, Interlibrary Loan Associate; Dr. Marcia E. Whitehead, Humanities

Librarian; and the late James Gwin, Head of Collections Development. I am grateful to several individuals in Academic Technology Services for frequent support, especially Dr. Kenneth Warren for ongoing assistance with technology that made it possible for me to record and transfer interview videotapes, recordings, and pictures. Thanks to everyone at the Computer Help Desk, whose services were graciously provided throughout the time I worked on this project, especially Ellis Billups, Stephanie Charles, John Hurst, Alfra Moody, and Orlanda Stevens. Special kudos are due Wendy Levy and Emily P. Tarchokov in the English Department and Debbie Govoruhk in the History Department for their assistance. I am grateful for the encouragement and support of Dr. Andrew F. Newcomb, former Dean of the School of Arts and Sciences, and Dr. Suzanne Jones, former Chair of the English Department.

I wish to acknowledge also the support of the Library of Virginia, especially their Archives Division.

I thank the editors at the University of Virginia Press for recognizing the promise in this project and working with me to bring it to fruition: Cathie Brettschneider, Ellen Satrom, Morgan Myers, and Susan Murray.

I am grateful to Jared Della Rocca at the Crossett Library (Bennington College) for assisting me in determining the location of some of the homes that figure into Kincaid's works.

I thank all of my sister writers in the Wintergreen Collective for their constant support and encouragement.

I thank all of my sisters in my varied civic and social clubs for delightful reprieves from the pressures of this project.

As usual, I thank my children and grandchildren (Warren Carlton Dance Jr., Tadelech Edjigu Dance, Allen Cumber Dance, Daryl Lynn Dance, Yoseph Warren Dance, and Veronica Cumber Dance) for their support and encouragement. I owe special thanks to my middle child, Allen Cumber Dance, who pays the price for being the only offspring living in the area and the only one who is a computer specialist. He responded regularly to my desperate calls for emergency assistance for a range of computer problems. His patience with his technologically challenged mom has no boundaries. And, whenever he came, his sunny disposition and comic personality lifted the problems of the world off my shoulders and left me renewed to tackle this project again.

ABBREVIATIONS

The following abbreviations and shortened titles are used in citations of the works by Jamaica Kincaid:

AC	"Antigua Crossings: A Deep and Blue Passage on the Caribbean Sea"
AF	*Among Flowers: A Walk in the Himalaya*
AJ	*Annie John*
AT	*At the Bottom of the River*
Auto	*The Autobiography of My Mother*
"Biography"	"Biography of a Dress"
Kin/Dance	Jamaica Kincaid interview by Daryl Cumber Dance
MB	*My Brother*
MG	*My Garden (Book):*
MP	*Mr. Potter*
NY	"Jamaica Kincaid's New York"
See	*See Now Then*
SP	*A Small Place*

INTRODUCTION *Filling In the Gaps*

> What is left out is as important as what is there.
> —Toni Morrison, "Rootedness: The Ancestor as Foundation"

> What you see on the page is only part of the story.
> —Olive Senior, "An Interview with Olive Senior"

She was a peasant girl born in Dominica who, when she was sixteen, ran away to Antigua, where she subsequently found herself a single mother. She finally married a carpenter and raised four children. She was a hardworking housewife and a devoted churchgoer. She made two trips to the United States to visit her daughter, her only travels outside her two tiny islands. This is not the stuff of which biographies/autobiographies/histories/literary studies are usually made. Such individuals never make the newspaper or the local evening television news unless they are the victims of some violent crime; no line is given to them in a magazine or a book; they are lost in the invisible masses who do not warrant close attention. They are like Roland in Jamaica Kincaid's *The Autobiography of My Mother:* "He did not have a history; he was a small event in somebody else's history" (167), "no history yet written had embraced him" (176); and like Mr. Potter: "the world did not pause when [he] was born, and the world did not ignore his birth, the world was only indifferent to it" (*MP* 61). And so it would seem to be with Annie Victoria Richardson Drew, who was, Kincaid writes after providing a few of the details of her life, "without interest in the world" (*MP* 138).

Despite the ordinariness of Annie Drew's life, there is perhaps no other flesh-and-blood individual who has ever been so constantly and obsessively featured in the full canon of any writer as the mother of Jamaica Kincaid—not William Faulkner's Civil War general grandfather, representing as he did the Old South, with which Faulkner was obsessed; nor Ernest Hemingway's father, whose suicide was to forever haunt and perhaps finally destroy his son; nor Henry James's adored cousin, whose early death is commemorated over and over in his portraits of beautiful but doomed young heroines; nor James Baldwin's brutal stepfather, whose approval and acceptance the bastard child sought for a lifetime. None of these appears so persistently in those novelists' works as does Annie Victoria Richardson Drew (by some part of that name or some other name) in the works of Jamaica Kincaid. Indeed, one might argue that everything Kincaid has written is about her mother. Whether her subject is ostensibly herself (*At the Bottom of the River, Annie John,* and *See Now Then*), her father (*Mr. Potter,* his actual name), her brother (*My Brother,* the most directly autobiographical and the least fictionalized of her works), her employers (*Lucy*), her home nation (*A Small Place*), a precolonial world (*Annie, Gwen, Lily, Pam and Tulip*), or her gardening (*My Garden (Book):* and *Among Flowers: A Walk in the Himalaya*), the real subject is her mother. And whatever her plot *seems* to be—a brother's death from AIDS, a father's desertion, a young girl's maturity, her shattered marriage—the real issue underlying everything appears to be Kincaid's efforts to free herself from her mother. The mother is indeed, as Kincaid writes in *Mr. Potter,* "the central figure in my life" (153). This mother may go by slightly different names, and a few details in her life may vary from story to story, but in fact Kincaid aficionados immediately recognize her in story after story. She is unforgettable. Kincaid seems preoccupied by, even obsessed with, a series of events involving Annie Drew or involving Annie Drew and herself, and she reworks them over and over throughout her oeuvre.

Oddly enough, given the prominence that the mother has in Kincaid's works, she is never the admitted focus, not even in that oddly and contradictorily titled *The Autobiography of My Mother,* where Xuela Claudette Richardson, the figure who might arguably be said to be her mother and who bears her mother's surname, is less like the actual mother than most of the mother figures in the rest of Kincaid's canon. Though Kincaid directly told Robert Birnbaum that she attempted in *The Autobiography of My Mother* to write an autobiography of her mother (173), it is apparent that Xuela is often more like Jamaica than like Annie. Kincaid, who lamented, "I am my mother" (Dance/Kin), leads us to see Xuela as a combination of mother and daughter when she ends her story: "This account of my life has been an account of my mother's life as much as it has been an account of mine, and even so, again it is an account of the life of the children I did not have" (227). The fact that in this novel, as is so often the case, the daughter and mother are indeed one helps to explain the oft-noted incongruity of the title, for the "autobiography" of her mother seems truly her own autobiography.

Since Kincaid has never written a novel or a memoir or a biography tellingly titled *My Mother,*[1] I project here reflections of her mother that grow out of Kincaid's writings, my own exploration of the life of Annie Drew, and even my speculations on the inner workings of her mind and emotions—speculations arising from my own experience as a woman, wife, mother, and daughter and from my empathetic association with her in certain instances. While these reflections seek to evoke the flesh-and-blood woman who was the loving mother of the renowned author, they also find much of their substance in the hated "character"/"monster"/"demon"/"jablesse" (*AT* 8–12)"/"god" (Goldfarb 95; Kincaid, "The Estrangement" 40)/"god Cronus" (Haber)/"Mrs. Judas" (*Lucy* 130)/"serpent" (*AJ* 52)/"crocodile" (*AJ* 84), "ball of fury" (*Lucy* 150), and "hypocrite" (*AJ* 133) passionately and bitterly sketched in minute detail in myriad accounts in the Kincaid canon. Thus, instead of focusing on any one work, I read Kincaid's works intertextually. I take my cue and find my justification for this reading in two other of my favorite writers, Toni Morrison and Olive Senior, as well as in some "cues" from Kincaid herself.

Nobel laureate Toni Morrison frequently talks about the reader's obligation to fill in the gaps in the novels she writes. In "Rootedness: The Ancestor as Foundation," she discusses her goal "to have the reader work *with* the author in the construction of the book," adding that "What is left out is as important as what is there" (341). A characteristic of Black literature, like other Black art forms, is that it seeks to elicit and incorporate audience response, and Morrison strives to have her works, like the Black sermon, move the reader to "join . . . in the sermon, . . . to stand up and to weep and to cry and to accede or *to change and to modify—to expand on the sermon*" (341; emphasis mine). She seeks what she calls, in *Playing in the Dark,* "response-ability," noting that "readers and writers both struggle to interpret and perform within a common language shareable imaginative worlds. And although upon that struggle the positioning of the reader has justifiable claims, the author's presence—her or his intentions, blindness, and sight—is part of the imaginative activity" (xii). Morrison's goals as a writer, detailed in "Rootedness," are remarkably similar to Kincaid's: to pass on the historical and archetypal stories (folklore, oral literature); to tell an individual story (autobiography) that is also a group story (history); to reflect the culture out of which she writes; to retain the presence of the ancestors ("timeless people whose relationships to the characters are benevolent, instructive, and protective" [343]); and to include in the book "discredited knowledge," that is, "[other] ways of knowing things," "superstition and magic" (342).[2] (Though I provide generic designations parenthetically here, it should be noted that Morrison and Kincaid, as well as several other Diasporic writers, often deny the validity of these generic distinctions.)

Thus I assume what Morrison calls the reader's "response-ability" to assess Kincaid's "blindness, and sight," to fill in the gaps and make the changes and modifications that seem necessary in a reading of Kincaid's mother. I trust that after my argument the reader may acknowledge, in the words of Antonia S. Byatt in a different context, "that we *shall know* the writing differently or better or satisfactorily." "In these readings," Byatt continues, "a sense that the text has appeared to be wholly new, never before seen, is followed, almost immediately, by the sense that it was *always there,* that we, the readers, knew it was always there, and have *always known* it was as it was, though we have now for the first time recognised, become fully cognisant of, our knowledge" (*Possession,* qtd. in Morrison, *Playing in the Dark* xi–xii).

I find further support for my reading of Kincaid in comments by the noted Jamaican short-story writer Olive Senior regarding her own oeuvre: "What you see on the page is only part of the story. The inexplicable, the part not expressed, the part withheld is the part that you the reader will have to supply from your emotional and imaginative stock. . . . I believe it's my job as writer not to say it all, for I am only one-half of the equation—reader-writer—and that the work becomes complete only when it is read, when the reader enters the world I have created. I therefore tend to leave a lot of my work open-ended" (Rowell 483).

Kincaid voices a similar sentiment in her interview with Susan Walker when she talks about the horrors unleashed by Europeans: "All of these things I knew when I wrote (Mr. Potter [*sic*]), but *I would never put them in a book. It interests me to have a reader discover them, not to tell them*" (E04; emphasis mine). Such cues exist throughout Kincaid's works, and I highlight them as entrées to the readings I offer of her canon. Throughout are some of the details that I believe beg to be discovered, filled in, and corrected—and I shall do it! I shall, in other words, try to do for Annie Drew what Toni Morrison does for the similarly silenced and vilified African Americans in her study of early Anglo-American fiction, *Playing in the Dark: Whiteness and the Literary Imagination*—tell the half that has never been told, that has indeed often been intentionally unseen, ignored, concealed, repressed, distorted, and misrepresented.

I therefore propose in this study of Annie Drew to enter not only the actual worlds of Antigua and Dominica but also Kincaid's literary world, bringing to the latter, in the words of Senior, my "emotional and imaginative stock" in order to "complete" Kincaid's canon. I do this keeping in mind that her work begins with her mother's stories, which Kincaid often reminds us are probably colored by her mother's imagination. I would add that they are perhaps also colored by the mother's motivation in sharing a particular story with her child—to instruct, discipline, govern, and/or coerce. Kincaid does not make much of this usual motivation for the stories our ancestors tell us, but we know that folklore is often designed to teach. Kincaid brings to bear her own imagination and needs and motives as she refashions those stories. In *My Brother,* she notes that even when she was a child, when her mother would omit details in her account of something, "I filled them in" (75). Jamaica Kincaid always had a remarkable memory. It is surely the author herself speaking when she has Xuela declare, "I always looked back" (*Auto* 139).

Her mother was once proud of Jamaica's ability to fill in details she might have missed as she recounted an event. As Jamaica got older, however, her mother hated this because her daughter would remind her of things she preferred to forget. Kincaid clearly remembers the moment her mother harshly reprimanded her for remembering too much: "You mine [*sic*] long, you know" (*MB* 75). (It's very likely that Annie Drew did not consider that rather mild "You mine long, you know" to be the vicious repudiation that her daughter imagined it.) Kincaid told Brad Goldfarb that she is enraged when she hears her mother's accounts of things: "Her telling of it is always so different from how I remember it" (98). She explains that her mother "plays with memory"—she's not so much telling a lie as remembering "something quite the way it did not happen" (Goldfarb 98). Their varying "memories" reinforce Paul Eakin's definition of memories as "perceptions newly occurring in the present rather than images fixed and stored and in the past and somehow mysteriously recalled to present consciousness" (Rice 26).[3]

The accounts of Kincaid or the Kincaid persona are often not just her current perception of a past event, but a conscious revision of those past events, a revision designed to achieve her own personal goals. Thus even as a schoolgirl writing an essay to be read in class about an event that occurred when her mother took her swimming, the Kincaid persona Annie John provides a fictional ending, noting: "I didn't exactly tell a lie about the last part. That is just what would have happened in the old days. . . . I couldn't bear to have anyone see how deep in disfavor I was with my mother" (*AJ* 45), clearly establishing a pattern we see in many of Kincaid's works wherein she manipulates events apparently because of some concern about her own image. She writes all of her brothers out of the otherwise autobiographical story of her childhood in *Annie John* and allows her employer Mariah to believe the Kincaid persona Lucy was an only child in the autobiographical *Lucy.* Always the reader must seek to uncover the revisions, interpret their significance, and determine the actual truth. As Kincaid has said, although her work is autobiographical, "it wouldn't hold up in a court of law" (qtd. in Simmons, *Jamaica Kincaid* 5). Elsewhere she has explained: "You can't trust [memory]. For one thing, the thing that is happening to you might be so unpleasant, you may need to subtract from it or add to it so that in the retelling, you can manage it" (Headlee).

While there are admittedly changes from the actual events in the Kincaid plots, many of them filtered through her mother's experience and imagination and some of them revised to serve the author's purposes, there is no doubt that Kincaid is committed to writing autobiography: she has insisted that there is no reason for her to be a writer without autobiography (for similar assertions about the autobiographical nature of her writing, see Ferguson, "A Lot of Memory" 176; Cudjoe 227; Gilmore, "Endless Autobiography" 213; Vorda, "An Interview" 16; and Muirhead 45). When asked how much of her work is autobiographical, her stock response is, "All of it, even the punctuation" (Gilmore, "Endless Autobiography" 213). She told Hannah Levintova, "Everything I write is autobiographical." Kincaid informed Donna Perry that she didn't know how to write a story about something that hadn't happened to her (495). When Brad Goldfarb asked about the people she wrote about, she replied, "Well, I've only ever written about my family" (99). In the interview with Emily Listfield, she insisted that she had never written about anyone except her mother and herself (82). She has frequently reaffirmed that the basic plot in several of her works comes from her own experience: she said that nearly all of *Annie John* comes directly from her own life (Cryer B4); and of *Lucy,* she declared, "I really was an *au pair,* . . . I was writing about my own experience" (Perry 506–7). Jane King has maintained that "it is impossible not to feel that in reading about Annie or Lucy we are reading about Jamaica, or rather the formation of Jamaica; more correctly, that we are reading about Elaine [Kincaid's given name]" (887). Thus whether the central character is called Mignonette in "Antigua Crossings"; Annie in *Annie John;* Lucy in *Lucy;* Xuela in *The Autobiography of My Mother;* Jamaica in *A Small Place, My Brother, Mr. Potter, My Garden (Book):,* and *Among Flowers;* Jamaica Sweet in *See Now Then;*[4] or is unnamed as she is in the stories in *At the Bottom of the River* and "the Biography of a Dress," the protagonist inevitably represents familiar aspects of the character and conflicts of Jamaica Kincaid or a blending of Kincaid and her mother. Thus to avoid confusion in this study, I sometimes refer to the protagonist/narrator in the fiction simply as the "Kincaid character" or "Jamaica character."

Kincaid's body of autobiographical literature, some presented as fiction, some as memoir, some as autobiography, some as essay, has been characterized by Leigh Gilmore as serial autobiography: "It is not that Kincaid is writing the same book over and over; rather, she is adding volumes to a series" ("Endless Autobiography" 214). Jana Evans Braziel has also commented on what she calls Kincaid's "autobiographical ambivalence" (7): "Autobiography, for Kincaid, is entangled with myth and history; and this aesthetic knot imbues all of Kincaid's writings, particularly her philosophical engagements with genre" (6). Ultimately, she concludes, what Kincaid is writing is "alter-biography," "texts . . . *not* essentially about an individual life, or even a group of individual lives, but rather—more abstractly, but with material ramifications—about the national-textual problematic of identity in diaspora" (8).

Kincaid makes it clear that she gave little time to research in writing *Mr. Potter,* the biography of her father: "No, no research, . . . I don't believe in that. Then I would have to actually write one of those conventional things" (Jones D1); "Always I'm writing about these actual people in my past. I don't write about them to know them in any biographical way. I like to think of them in some sort of existential way" (Walker). In *My Brother,* as she explains some of the things she told the people among whom she was living in the United States about her mother, she declares that what she told them was a combination of fact and fiction, but she insisted that both the parts she made up as well as the actual facts were true (119). She told Moira Ferguson that the events in her work are "true to me. They may not be true to other people" ("A Lot" 176). Kincaid probably was following the precept of the sage who said, "Never let what really happened get in the way of the truth."[5] Kincaid's truth is thus a complex blending of facts, fiction, memories, ego, goal, imagination, and artistic construction. Like Derek Walcott, Wilson Harris, and several other African Diasporic writers, Kincaid refuses to acknowledge the purity of genre, to accept the absolute separation of history, biography, autobiography, memoir, mythology, folktale.[6] Kincaid fudges those lines throughout her work and ends up to some degree reinforcing Walcott's insistence that autobiography is a form of fiction, and "I myself am a fiction" (qtd. in Baugh 50). Of Kincaid, Walcott told Leslie Garis: "As she writes a sentence, the temperature of it psychologically is that it heads toward its own contradictions.

. . . Her work is so full of spiritual contradictions clarified that it's extremely profound and courageous" (Garis 80).[7]

All of these contradictions often lead to recurrent portrayals of her mother in stories usually motivated by her mother. In fact, she told Kay Bonetti: "If I had had another kind of life I would not have been moved to write" (133)—thus for good or for bad, she would not have been a writer except for her mother. And writing, she has often said, has been her salvation: by writing about her own life, she saved her life; by writing about her dying brother, she avoided perishing with him (cover of *MB*). And in *The Autobiography of My Mother,* Xuela declares that she probably saved her life by writing letters (22).

Marie-Hélène Laforest emphasizes what every Kincaid scholar acknowledges: "Her mother's body is . . . preserved in her daughter's words" (26). However, Kincaid's acknowledged difficulties in her trip to the Himalayas might be used to explain her problems with portraying her mother: "Not ever did I become accustomed to the vast difference between my expectation, my perception, and reality; the way things really are" (*AF* 143).

The goal of this study is to provide at least one mirror that provides a fuller, fairer, and more evenhanded reflection of this mother, one not restricted to the daughter's expectations and perceptions, one that might even reveal, not just Jamaica's mother, but Annie Victoria Richardson Drew. I try to complete Kincaid's portrait of her mother, not by fantasizing some created events but by filling in some of the blanks Kincaid leaves and perhaps correcting some of the misrepresentations she makes. In doing this I am presumptuous enough to hope to allay her lament, "I don't know her really" (Cook 20), and to help her (as well as Kincaid aficionados and even casual readers) to know the mother she leaves in the shadows (Morrison would say in the dark) and seems fearful to fully portray, perhaps unable to move beyond some of the traumatic events in their relationship. I recognize more than ever after working on this biography that Kincaid was quite right when, reflecting on the man who was the previous owner of her house in Vermont, she declared that "no one can ever be really known" (*MG* 48). I recognize more than ever as well that to write about Annie Drew is inevitably to write about Jamaica Kincaid. Like the author who often agonizingly recognizes that she can never separate herself from her mother ("I am my mother" [Kin/Dance]; "I was not like my mother—I was my mother" [*Lucy* 90]), I learned during this study that to unearth Annie, I had to write about, with, and through her alter ego. To paraphrase Xuela, the Kincaid character in *The Autobiography of My*

Mother, this telling of Annie Drew's life is as much an account of her daughter's life as it is of Annie Drew's.

Nevertheless, I hope, too, to provide some balance by giving some indications of the views of the flesh-and-blood Annie Drew, to achieve that balance that Kincaid insists should obtain in an honorable world in which each person "must be considered with the utmost seriousness, the same seriousness with which we consider our own lives" (*MG* 47). I hope to realize something of what is achieved by Rosellen Brown in her *Autobiography of My Mother,* an interesting parallel not so much to Kincaid's work of the same name but to Kincaid's whole canon. Brown, too, pictures a mother and daughter with serious conflicts and differences and inabilities to understand and communicate with each other; the key difference, however, is that Brown relates her story from both points of view, alternating between the mother (Gerda) and daughter (Renada).[8]

I hope that this study of Annie Drew will not be perceived as an attack upon Kincaid's works, each of which I, a shameless Kincaid devotee, regard as a magnificently achieved masterpiece, and each of which I acknowledge represents Kincaid's own truth.

In the interest of full disclosure, I must admit, too, to having an intensely emotional response to Kincaid's work. Her conflicts with her mother are something about which I know a great deal. While I won't attempt another biography/autobiography/memoir/confessional here, I must note that I, like Kincaid, experienced an occasionally tumultuous relationship with a mother who on one level made every sacrifice and provided every opportunity for me at the same time that she resented me for the choices I made and the independence I asserted; who at one and the same time took great pride in and expressed great jealousy of my successes. However, our battles were minor compared to those of Kincaid and her mother: Our moments of not speaking were infrequent and short; our separations were rare and short-lived; our communication was better; we forgave (though I'm not sure either of us ever apologized enough to please the other); we enjoyed many happy times together throughout her life; and each of us always knew the other had her back when either one of us was sick, in need, or under attack by someone—*anyone*—else. I am vain enough to believe that I understand my conflicts with my mother better than Kincaid understands hers and that I have more empathy for my mother's behavior and motivations. I am vain enough to believe that Kincaid may need me to "ente[r] the world she created" and provide "the inexplicable, the part not expressed" that will give fullness to the portrait of Annie Victoria Richardson Drew. And in doing this, I hope to help Kincaid achieve the victory that she never experienced in her battle with her mother. My presumptuousness here is to some degree prompted by Kincaid's expressed hope that whenever she writes something it will change her, make her into something not herself. The change never happens, she has said, but she keeps attempting it (Alleyne).

The last word that Kincaid presumes to offer as writer with the power of words is never the last word when those words deal with a superhuman mother who still, even from the grave, dictates everything she writes.

I was particularly pleased that, as I began this study, Kincaid herself was very enthusiastic about it, declaring the project a fascinating idea and expressing delight that her mother was of interest to scholars. Kincaid enthusiastically shared with me pictures of the family, of her grandparents, her Aunt Mary's baptism, her Aunt Mary's wedding, of her brothers, all of which she promised to scan and send to me, pictures that she said she just took from her mother. Unfortunately, as this study neared completion, Kincaid decided that I was taking possession of something that was, in fact, hers (e-mail, March 30, 2009). She never sent the pictures.

There has certainly been a substantial body of work treating Jamaica Kincaid's issues with her mother. Scores of postcolonial critics have provided important studies allegorizing the mother as representative of the colonial motherland (see Paravisini-Gebert 27; Ferguson, "A Lot" 1; de Abruna 173; and Jackson 310). Ramon E. Soto-Crespo, in "Death and the Diaspora Writer: Hybridity and Mourning in the Work of Jamaica Kincaid," views the spreading of AIDS through Devon's body as analogous with the spread of colonialism through the West Indies. Others have effectively provided psychoanalytical interpretations: Bryant Mangum, in one of the earliest critical essays on Kincaid, "Jamaica Kincaid," presents a Freudian analysis of *At the Bottom of the River* and the stories that would soon appear in *Annie John;* J. Brooks Bouson, in *Jamaica Kincaid: Writing Memory, Writing Back to the Mother,* "read[s] her works through the lens of contemporary shame and trauma theory" (5); while H. Adlai Murdoch, in "Severing the (M)other Connection," defines Annie John's quest for identity as "mediated primarily by the Lacanian paradigm of the alienated subject" (325), and sees a "possible efficacy" of reading the narrative "through the prism of . . . the Freudian oedipal paradigm" (327). Giselle Liza Anatol, in "Speaking in (M)other Tongues," provides a linguistic reading, focusing on the "mother tongue." Louise Bernard's "Countermemory and Return: Reclamation of the (Postmodern) Self in Jamaica Kincaid's *The Autobiography of My Mother* and *My Brother*" provides one of a number of postmodernist readings. Giovanni Covi combines feminist, postmodern, and postcolonial approaches in her *Jamaica Kincaid's Prismatic Subjects.* Several others, too numerous to mention, have offered important feminist or womanist readings.

Earlier in her career, when Kincaid was confronted with such postcolonial, psychoanalytical, feminist, modernist, postmodernist, and even Africanist readings of her works, she rejected membership in any kind of school, declaring that she doesn't want to be considered a feminist and cannot bear to be in any kind of category or group or school (Cudjoe 221). She even rejected Cudjoe's characterizing of her mother's stories as folklore, insisting that she wouldn't call it folklore; she would simply describe it as her mother's "experience with life" (231). As time passed, however, Kincaid tended to point to some of the postcolonial implications of the mother figure. When Gerhard Dilger asked about her relationship with her mother in 1992, she said that earlier in her career, she could have discussed the immediate mother and daughter, but that now she is writing about the mother country, the powerful and the weak, something much broader (23). In a 1994 interview, she similarly declared: "I used to think I was writing about my mother and myself. Later I began to see that I was writing about the relationship between the powerful and the powerless. . . . And then it became clear to me . . . that the mother I was writing about was really Mother Country" (Ferguson, "A Lot of Memory" 177).

Kincaid parodies Freudian interpretations in *Lucy:* when the Jamaica character tells her employers, Lewis and Mariah, her dream, Mariah said, "Dr. Freud for a Visitor," confusing Lucy, who did not know who Freud was. Lucy is upset by their laughter because she had shared her dreams with them, something she did only with people who were important to her (15). Clearly the theory prevented them from understanding Lucy and her realities, something like the problem that the novelist Buchi Emecheta experienced: "I chronicle the little happenings in the lives of the African women that I know. I did not know that by doing so I was going to be called a feminist" (175). Giovanna Covi concisely reinforces Kincaid's position regarding theoretical interpretations of her work: "She constantly warns us against grounding her discourse upon any presumed external foundation . . . [and] makes clear that Western culture is not adequate to understand her" (91).

Many other African and African Diasporic writers also seek to distinguish and distance themselves from the old prescribed Western male-dominated theories that have not reflected *them,* their lives, and their works, often viewing Western criticism as another imperialist project. Audre Lorde warned in her memorable speech at the Second Sex Conference in New York on September 29, 1979: *"The master's tools will never dismantle the master's house"* (112, emphasis in original). Barbara Christian, in her 1987 "The Race for Theory," argued that the popular linguistic jargon of Western critics was designed to silence Black women writers. Opal Palmer Adisa has accused that these "theories, . . . rather than illuminating the works under exploration, obfuscate and problematize these works so that students are rendered speechless, [one telling me,] 'I can't talk that talk, so I end up not saying anything'" (103). Toni Morrison's *Playing in the Dark* is motivated by her interest "in how agendas in criticism have disguised themselves and, in so doing, impoverished the literature it studies"; she continues, "It is important to see how inextricable Africanism is or ought to be from the deliberations of literary criticism and the wanton, elaborate strategies undertaken to erase its presence from view" (8–9).[9]

That the Kincaid character is similarly silenced by theory when she is concerned about her individual relationship with her mother is aptly illustrated in Lucy's discussion with her employer, Mariah, who is pained by Lucy's difficult relationship with her mother: "Mariah wanted to rescue me. She spoke of women in society, women in history, women in culture, women everywhere. But I couldn't speak, so I couldn't tell her that my mother was my mother and that society and history and culture and other women in general were something else altogether" (*Lucy* 131–32).

Mariah nonetheless goes out and comes back with a large book on women, which she opens to the first chapter and hands to the Kincaid character, who painfully realizes that Mariah cannot understand her dilemma, which was "more simple and more complicated" than these theoretical explanations: she was mourning "the end of a love affair, perhaps the only true love in my whole life I would ever know" (*Lucy* 132).

In a similar way, when Mariah tries to console her on the death of her father by saying that nobody thinks about the fact that their parents will die, Lucy is once again annoyed at her for talking about "everybody" when she (Lucy) was talking only about herself (139).

This study does not repeat the important allegorical readings of Annie Drew; it is not about "everybody"; it is not about "other women in general";

it is not about "women everywhere." It is about the flesh-and-blood individual who was Jamaica's mother ("my mother was my mother")—or at least as much about her as I can glean from my sources, from Kincaid's writings, and from my own experiences as a woman/mother/daughter, inspired by the spirit of this fascinating mother who has been inhabiting my being since 2007.

1

BEGINNINGS IN DOMINICA

> My mother['s] . . . story of leaving Dominica . . . is my favorite of all her stories.
> —Jamaica Kincaid, "Antigua Crossings"

Our story of Annie Victoria Richardson Drew begins in Dominica, the largest and most mountainous of the Windward Islands. It is also, according to Lizabeth Paravisini-Gebert, "the most unspoiled of all the Caribbean islands," with its "luxuriant tropical vegetation, steep green cliffs, sulfuric springs, and boiling fountains" (147). In *The Autobiography of My Mother,* Kincaid, too, evokes the magnetic, even magically beautiful landscape with its green hills, golden fields, and magnificent sea. Dominica is also proud of its reputation of having some of the longest-living people on earth—a boast that I heard from several Dominicans. It seems to be something the Dominicans celebrate as the Barbadians celebrate their being the most British and the best educated of Caribbean people.

Though Columbus explored Dominica in 1493, it was the last of the islands to be colonized by Europeans because of the determined resistance of the Carib Indians, who had conquered the Arawak Indians before the arrival of the Europeans. Both Britain and France claimed Dominica, but their settlements continued to be attacked by the Caribs. A French settlement was finally established in 1727, and France became the dominant power for a while until the British attacked in 1761. The defeated France ceded possession to Great Britain in 1763 but made several attempts to reclaim the island, succeeding only in burning much of Roseau to the ground in an 1805 invasion. The British began producing sugar in Dominica but never developed the large slave plantations there that were to be found in other Caribbean nations. Slavery was abolished in 1834, and Dominica later became the only British colony in the Caribbean to have a legislature controlled by Blacks. When White planters protested, however, the British government diminished the power of the legislature. In 1967 Dominica and the other Windward Isles became self-governing members of the West Indies Associated States. In 1978 Britain granted independence to the Commonwealth of Dominica. Two years later Dominica elected Mary Eugenia Charles the first female prime minister in the Caribbean. She served from 1980 to 1995. Dominica still has around three thousand Carib Indians, the only pre-Columbian population remaining in the area. It remains part of the Commonwealth of Nations, which is officially headed by the United Kingdom's Queen Elizabeth II.

Annie Victoria[1] was born in Mahaut, in St. Paul Parish of Dominica (*MP* 131), on September 15, "probably 1919," Kincaid told me, a year that I was able to confirm in her mother's medical records and her death certificate. She had always believed her mother was younger because her mother used to tell her a later date.

Annie Victoria's mother, Ma Chess, was a mysterious and sometimes terrifying figure who exerted a powerful and enduring influence on her daughter and granddaughter. I was unable to find anyone who knew her real given name, not even Kincaid.[2] She was a Carib Indian who is described in "Antigua Crossings" as "very tall and very dark and very fierce looking" (48). Though Mignonette, the Kincaid character in "Antigua Crossings," notes that Ma Chess became a Christian to please her husband, she insists that Ma Chess still "hunts agouti and I know that she has not forgotten the history of her ancestors and it makes me glad" (48). Every evening as the sun was setting, Ma Chess sat on a bench and silently gazed intently at the sea (48), an apparently simple action that has great significance in this study. Most of the nations of the Caribbean are surrounded by the sea. A source of great pleasure and livelihood, the sea is also a source of fear and destruction. It is all encompassing, ever-present in the lives of the people and in their literature. Their history begins with the Middle Passage, and their future is predicated on the journey away from their island home. The impact of the sea in Kincaid's life and works will be apparent throughout this volume and stands as one other indication of her separation from Caribbean life and culture.[3] The image of this iconic, ancestral figure, Ma Chess, sitting each day as the sun set and gazing at the sea is one that is replete with significant reverberations in the Kincaid canon.

Annie Victoria's father, Alfred John Richardson (probably named after Alfred the Great and John of Lackland, the English king from 1199 to 1216), but better known as Pa Chess, was of mixed Scottish and African ancestry (Bouson 210). He was a policeman from Antigua. Given that policemen were rarely allowed to serve in their own island, he was sent to St. Kitts and then later to Dominica, where he met Ma Chess. Kincaid told me that he very likely had children in St. Kitts. She also said that he "became sort of corrupt [after he went to Dominica]. He had nothing, and he acquired things." Despite his wildness during his early years, he later became a pious landowner and lay minister in the Methodist church. Other than Kincaid, the only individual I could find with any knowledge of Pa Chess was a Dominican businessman whose ninety-year-old father-in-law knew him well. According to the businessman with whom I spoke on the telephone, his father-in-law, also a policeman, said that "Richie" (as he called him) left the police force because of controversy surrounding his homosexuality, and noted that "though Richie was married and had children, everyone knew he was a homosexual" (May 30, 2009).[4] On July 8, 2009, I talked with the father-in-law, who seemed reluctant to discuss Mr. Richardson's alleged homosexuality, but he noted that Mr. Richardson walked and spoke in an effeminate way and there were rumors about him. Nonetheless, he said that Mr. Richardson was a well-respected colonel. He described Mr. Richardson as brown, "not light-skinned," adding that he did not have straight hair, but the kind of hair mixed people have and that he was medium size, around five foot ten. This description varies from fictional portraits of a fair Mr. Richardson, but it is consistent with the photograph on the cover of *Mr. Potter,* which Kincaid told me was really a picture of the Richardson family. The policeman who worked with Pa Chess never met Mrs. Richardson or their children.

Both Ma and Pa Chess were literate, though it is quite likely that Ma Chess was not as educated as her husband. According to Kincaid, they had three children, whom they named after British royalty: John (who was ten years older than Annie Victoria), Annie Victoria, and Mary Elizabeth. Annie Victoria's oldest son, Joseph Drew, however, recalls that his mother had *two* other sisters, Louisa Green and Virginia Coffee. They do not figure in the Kincaid canon.

By all accounts, the Richardsons were something of a dysfunctional family, perhaps in part because of the early death of the only son in the family, a death that fascinates Kincaid and appears in one form or another in almost all of her novels. Annie Victoria, who, of course, told Jamaica about "Johnnie," loved her brother very much, indeed "worshipped" him (*AJ* 69) and described in detail the nature of his extended illness and the arguments the parents had about how he should be treated. When he became ill, the doctors were perplexed by his illness, but the Obeah woman knew what it was: Kincaid told Selwyn Cudjoe, "He was possessed, and something was set on him" (226). However, Pa Chess insisted that he be treated by a medical doctor rather than the Obeah woman, whom Ma Chess preferred—and he prevailed. In *Annie John,* the narrator tells us that Uncle Johnnie remained in bed for two years, looking rosier and rosier every day; on the day he died, he looked better than ever. Upon his expiration, a big worm dug its way out of Johnnie's leg and died (125). Pa Chess arranged Johnnie's funeral and preached the sermon, but Ma Chess did not attend. After Johnnie's death, Ma Chess never said another word to Pa Chess; she retreated into her own world, actually moving out of the house she had shared with her husband and no longer cooking for or relating to him. She wore only black for the rest of her life (125).

A similar situation is pictured in *The Autobiography of My Mother.* Here the brother dies, but though, like Pa Chess, the "father held the beliefs of the people who had subjugated him" (108), the protagonist's stepmother is allowed to try to cure her child with Obeah. He was wrapped in rags designed to protect him, and Obeah men and women were called in from Dominica and Guadeloupe. However, the outcome was similar: when he died, pus flowed out of his body and a big worm bored its way out of his leg (111). Similar deaths of young men whose festering bodies seep pus and/or who have a worm crawling out of their legs are found in "At Last" (*AT* 16) and *Mr. Potter* (47). Though there is no worm associated with the death of Kincaid's brother Devon Drew, we are reminded of the loathsome nature of these earlier deaths when Kincaid describes the sores that covered his penis, the fungus-like white substance on those sores (*MB* 91), and the yellow pus that flowed from his anus (*MB* 138).

Kincaid told me that her mother frequently spoke of Johnnie as if he were still alive and she had recently seen him, noting that even now she (Kincaid) still doesn't think of Uncle Johnnie as dead. Given her fascination with the stories about Johnnie and her mother's love for him, it is no surprise that she gave her heroine in *Annie John* the name Annie John. Kincaid saw the combination of the two names as a reflection of the psychological relationship Annie Victoria had with her brother, even suggesting that her marriage to a sick man whose last name was John was a way of caring for her brother again.

Unlike many fathers of the time, Pa Chess insisted that Annie Victoria and her sister go to school. Kincaid does not claim to know why he was so committed to having his daughters educated, but our conversation and her stories suggest that after Johnnie died, he may have transferred to the daughters the dreams that a Caribbean father of the time would have had for his son. Kincaid portrays both Pa Chess in *Mr. Potter* and Xuela's father in *The Autobiography of My Mother* as insisting on their daughter's education, possibly to indicate that even these tainted fathers recognized the importance of an education for their daughters, while Annie Victoria (as we shall see) forced her daughter, Jamaica, to drop out of school to help raise her brothers and care for the family, an action for which her daughter could never forgive her.

Annie Victoria was fluent in English, French, and patois. She undoubtedly was required to speak proper English in her home, especially with her father, which would have been complicated for her since almost everyone in Dominica spoke a French patois. Even after she had lived in Antigua most of her life, she still spoke English with a Dominican accent, her daughter told me.

Though young Annie Victoria went to school and lived in a family a step above most Dominican peasants, she presumably still had to work hard. The Richardsons lived on a large estate on which they grew coffee, bananas, plantains, oranges, grapefruits, limes, nutmeg, cloves, cassavas, dasheen, green figs, coffee, and almonds some distance from their house. They would go "up to ground," the area where their crops were raised, and sometimes spend a few days there cultivating their land and harvesting some food to bring back to the house. It was hard work, as Annie Victoria's accounts frequently suggest. In one of the few quotations from her not filtered through her daughter, she told Mariana Cook, author of *Generations of Women,* in 1996: "I was raised by my father in Dominica. If I had been raised by my mother, I wouldn't be so rough, but I wouldn't have been able to storm through life; no work was too hard for me" (20).

Several of Annie Victoria's tales focused on her walking miles with a bunch of plantains (sometimes figs) on her head, which she discovered when she arrived home held a long black snake (AC 50; *AJ* 68–69).[5]

Annie Victoria's sister was also educated, but she did not make much of her education, having married an "inappropriate man," according to Kincaid; a man whose last name was Pacquet, according to Joseph Drew—the name that Kincaid gives Xuela's sister's husband in *The Autobiography of My Mother.* When they were children, Annie Victoria complained that Mary Elizabeth was "soft" and did not have to work as hard as she did. The two sisters' disagreements and quarrels persisted all of their lives. Kincaid declared that they argued all the time, most of their disputes being carried on in an exchange of letters sent on the *M. P. V. Rippon,* the ship that plied between Antigua and Dominica. In *Annie John,* the narrator mentions the quarrels carried on through letters and indicates that her mother would call her sister a "barren, crippled, interfering idiot" because she frequently told Annie Victoria how she should raise her daughter (122–23). Some of their conflicts may have stemmed from the fact that Mary was not as intelligent, hearty, independent, or beautiful as her sister. Mary had the gray eyes and the red hair so characteristic of most descriptions of the Richardsons, but her hair was kinky while her sister's was straight.[6] She was an example of what African Americans call "Yellow gone to waste"—one who is fair in complexion but has "nappy" hair.

The Annie Victoria character pictured in *Annie John* had been a shy girl who covered her mouth when she laughed.[7] She always obeyed her mother, Ma Chess (perhaps this was emphasized, or even exaggerated, in her recollections to her daughter to encourage her to be more obedient). Annie Victoria loved her mother but was somewhat in awe of her; indeed, in some accounts, the Annie Victoria character fears her mother. Ma Chess was, after all, according to Kincaid, a bit fierce-looking and very tall: when the Kincaid character in *Annie John* says she towered over her mother, she notes that she was almost as tall as her grandmother (128), so Ma Chess must have been over six feet. (However, if the picture on the cover of *Mr. Potter* indeed shows Ma Chess, as Kincaid told me, she does not appear to be so tall; we must keep in mind that Kincaid's memories are those of a child.)

Ma Chess was a powerful Obeah woman! Annie Victoria embraced her mother's Obeah beliefs, as did Kincaid, who wrote approvingly of her grandmother's traditional beliefs and practices (AC 48; *Annie John* 123–27). Certainly Annie Victoria's embracing of Obeah was an indication of her rebellious nature, for it was a rebellion against her father as well as against colonialism, which feared and instituted the harshest of sanctions against African beliefs and practices such as Obeah. Though many accounts suggest that it was her father Annie Victoria was escaping when she left Dominica for Antigua, in Cook's *Generations,* Kincaid writes that her mother was so afraid of her mother (Ma Chess, the most powerful of all women) that she could not possibly live on the same island with her (9).

Early on it was clear that Annie Victoria had inherited some of her mother's fierceness. If anyone annoyed her in school, a family member told me, she waited afterward to settle the score, give them some words, physically attack them, or take something from them (January 20, 2009). Joseph Drew told me that when her sister once snatched a chair from under her as she was about to sit down, Annie Victoria grabbed a mallet and slammed her on the head (January 15, 2009). Those who knew her even then knew that you didn't mess with Annie Victoria. Yet, as was evident throughout her life, she reacted to a wrong, but she did not nurse a grudge. She might curse the person out or give him/her a blow, but then it was over. Reverend Lee, Annie Victoria's minister, told me: "Because whenever I saw that she was getting off the handle, you know, I just stopped, just listened to her. I wouldn't argue with her. And then she might stay away for a little while, and then afterwards she would come back. She doesn't stay mad with you for long. Which is not nice anyway. You know she gets off the handle, but she comes back down. But still not everybody can take that kind of behavior."

Annie Victoria's lifelong love of the sea and her remarkable swimming skills developed in Dominica, where she lived not far from the mouth of the Mahaut River. I learned from a source close to the family that many years later, she reminisced about that love with one of her granddaughters. When Kincaid visited Mahaut, she was amazed to see that everybody could swim; she watched in awe as they would dive in and swim out to sea.

Annie Victoria cherished many other pleasant memories of Dominica, especially of some of the foods there, many of which Ma Chess continued to pack in baskets and send to her in Antigua. The Annie Victoria figure in "Antigua Crossings" declared that everything in Dominica was better than things in Antigua (50).

Annie Victoria left Dominica as a young woman (the age ranges from sixteen to twenty-three in varied accounts): her daughter observes, "I pointed out to her that she changed her age everytime [*sic*] she tells this story" (AC 50). In *Annie John* (105) and *Mr. Potter* (132), she is sixteen. According to Annie's son Joseph, she came to Antigua in 1942, which would make her twenty-three.[8]

As previously noted, Annie Victoria's reasons for leaving vary from work to work, but it seems clear that her departure was related to her conflicts with Pa Chess. In *Mr. Potter,* Kincaid tells us Annie Victoria left Dominica after violently quarreling with her father "over the direction her life should take" (118) and "over the way she should pursue her unfolding future" (131). In *Annie John,* Kincaid indicated that although her mother never told her the details, she had pieced it together and determined that Annie Victoria had left because her father wanted her to live at home while she wanted to live alone (105). According to the fictionalized account in "Antigua Crossings," her father was upset that she was leaving so soon after her brother's death and that she was dressed in a flashy red dress that looked like she was going to a big dance (AC 50). On the day she left, every sign looked ominous to the annoyed and worried father, even the falling of the rain and the tolling of the church bells.

This conflict between father and daughter has remained a puzzle for Jamaica Kincaid. There are a few hints that have led me to speculate that it may have resulted from some sort of sexual abuse. It is clear that for many years Ma Chess lived apart from Pa Chess and had nothing to do with him. In *Annie John,* Annie John says they didn't speak but continued to live in the same house (105), but in our interview Kincaid explained that Ma Chess moved out of the main house and lived in a different little shack on the property; the daughters lived in the house with the father,[9] and Mary did the cooking. Such situations have been known to lead to a man's selecting a convenient substitute for sexual relief, which might explain Annie Victoria's insistence on moving out of the house. (*Annie John* leaves open the possibility that she at first planned to live elsewhere in Dominica.) My admittedly far-fetched theory gains a little reinforcement from Kincaid's somewhat vague and yet suggestive declaration to me that "they [Pa Chess and Annie Victoria] seemed to have had a particularly close relationship *or something.*" Further, Kincaid added that she thought it strange that Pa Chess gave Annie Victoria Ma Chess's wedding ring before Ma Chess died. Even though Ma Chess had stopped wearing it, Kincaid found it odd that he would give his daughter a wedding ring. Since Annie Victoria gave the beautiful yellow gold ring with flowers in it to Jamaica, perhaps she did not treasure it. When I asked Jamaica if she ever wore it, she recoiled, explaining that she never wears it because it seems like a chain to her. One might interpret Kincaid's comments as reflecting suspicion (perhaps subconscious) that her mother was sexually abused, something that would explain Annie's lifelong bitterness toward her father. Kincaid commented that she hadn't written about the ring, perhaps suggesting her difficulty in facing some of the implications of this relationship. Given Annie Victoria's ferocious protectiveness of her daughter, Jamaica, one might infer she would not have allowed Jamaica to visit Pa Chess at home if he had been a sexual abuser. On the other hand, though, when Jamaica went to Dominica, she stayed in the separate house with Ma Chess and slept with her in her bed. Could this have been the assurance that Annie Victoria required before she allowed her daughter to visit the Richardsons?

It is, of course, quite likely that there was no sexual abuse of Annie Victoria and that her alienation from her father resulted from the rebelliousness of a daughter who resented the restrictions this stern man placed on her. Perhaps Annie Victoria, like her own daughter (Kincaid), continued to nurse childhood conflicts and never forgave her parent for something that to others seems rather insignificant, such as objecting to a dress she selected or a young man she wanted to date or requiring her to go up to ground and work when she had other plans or when Mary Elizabeth wasn't required to do so. We shall never know for sure. But we do know that Kincaid probably represents her own feelings when she has the narrator of "Antigua Crossings" declare that the story of her mother's leaving Dominica "is my favorite of all of her stories" (50), one that is detailed in *Annie John.*

As the mother character in *Annie John* prepared to leave home, she purchased a large wooden trunk in Roseau, the capital of Dominica and its largest city. She spent a lot of time preparing it for her trip, obviously decorating it to express the bright and free new life she anticipated: she painted it yellow and green and lined it with wallpaper featuring pink roses (19–20).

She was as nervous as she was excited about her trip. She had never, after all, been anywhere away from her home. Pa Chess took her to Roseau to spend the night before the crossing with a relative, and Annie Victoria experienced thoughts similar to those of the Jamaica character, Annie John, when she was about to depart Antigua many years later: despite her anxiety as she was about to embark on her first trip away, she was looking forward to never again having to walk for miles with heavy plantains on her head (AC 50).[10]

The day she left, it was raining as it so often did in Dominica: the Annie Victoria figure in "Antigua Crossings" declares that it always rains in Dominica while the sun always shines in Antigua (50). She boarded an unseaworthy sailboat, passing through the Windward Passage and its turbulent winds, heading for Antigua, the land of her father's birth. Ordinarily, the trip would have taken only a day and a half, but the ship was caught in a hurricane, blown off course, and practically destroyed. A few travelers and some cargo were lost overboard. Annie suffered from seasickness the whole time—five days—throwing up all over her beautiful dress (AC 50). Finally, she arrived in Antigua, which she had despaired of reaching during that harrowing ordeal. Also safe was her trunk, which would become a central icon and symbol in her daughter's life.

Pa Chess had arranged for her to have a room in Antigua in the house of good friends whom the Richardsons had known in Mahaut, but who were not such nice people, Annie later tells her daughter without any further elaboration (AC 50).

Annie Victoria did not return to Dominica for many years; one reason that she offered was that she couldn't face that turbulent passage by ship again, but, as previously noted, Kincaid suggests in Cook's *Generations* that she feared her mother too much to live on the same island (9), and the Kincaid character in "Antigua Crossings" affirms that it was because she didn't get along with Pa Chess (50). Her continuing antipathy toward her father is reflected in the fact that she never found it in her heart to have any sympathy for him, no matter how grave his suffering. Many years after she left home, the Annie Victoria figure in *Annie John* takes great pleasure in receiving notice in a letter from her sister that her father is so infirm that he must rely on others to help him get around; she shares the news with her husband, triumphantly declaring: "So the great man can no longer just get up and go. How I would love to see his face now!" (78). In "Antigua Crossings," the news of Pa Chess's problems is communicated by Ma Chess, who writes that Pa Chess is suffering from constipation, causing the Annie Victoria character to laugh, "So the great man can't shit" (50). Kincaid changed this line to make it acceptable to the *New Yorker* when she wrote "Columbus in Chains," which later became a part of *Annie John* (Perry 496–97).

Just as Mr. Potter would later disinherit Jamaica after he visited her in the United States, Alfred John Richardson "made [Annie Victoria] dead in the realm of fatherly love, he disinherited her" (*MP* 131; see also Cudjoe 218).

2

FREE AND SINGLE IN ANTIGUA

> My mother [was] a whirlwind of sex and passion and female beauty.
> —Jamaica Kincaid, *Mister Potter*

Annie[1] had left "a small place" (Dominica is 29 miles long and 16 miles at its widest point, encompassing 291 square miles) for an even smaller place (Antigua is 14 miles long and 11 miles wide, encompassing 108 square miles, but it is the largest of the English-speaking Leeward Islands).[2]

Antigua's history is not unique. From about 2400 BC Antigua was inhabited by a series of Native Americans, beginning with the Siboneys and later the Saladoids. The Arawak Indians replaced the earlier inhabitants around AD 1200, and finally, by 1500, the island was inhabited by Carib Indians, whose superior weapons and sea vessels made them the most powerful force in the Caribbean before the arrival of the Europeans. Christopher Columbus landed in Antigua in 1493 and named the island after the Church of Santa María de la Antigua in Seville, Spain. The Caribs' fierce resistance prevented the Europeans from settling there until 1632, when England succeeded in establishing a colony. African slavery was introduced, and after disappointing efforts at raising tobacco and a variety of other crops, Antigua became noted for its sugarcane.

One of the most personal accounts of Antiguan slavery was provided in 1833 by Mary Prince, who was a house slave in the town of St. John's, where she was charged with being the nursemaid and laundress. Though she suffered serious illnesses exacerbated by her work and violent and severe punishments, she was shocked on a visit with her master and mistress to the country (Date Hill) to see how hard the field Negroes worked from before daybreak until after dark and how little they were fed. She concludes, "Will not God call the Buckra men to answer for this on the great day of judgment?" (16).

During the eighteenth century, the British Royal Navy Caribbean fleet was headquartered in Antigua, making it a major port in the Caribbean.

Slavery was abolished in 1834, and here Antigua was unique. The August 1, 1834, Emancipation Act allowed for a four-year apprenticeship of laborers, in effect continuing slavery for all slaves in the British West Indies, except those under six years of age, until 1838; Antigua was one of the few islands that escaped that apprenticeship process and immediately freed all slaves. Most Antiguans, however, continued to work on plantations, albeit as wage earners who were free to move about as they pleased. Antigua was still a British colony, and the racial stratification was similar to that during slavery, with Whites at the top, mulattoes in the middle, and Blacks at the bottom (Goveia 160–62). As in most of the Americas, the Native American population in Antigua did not survive conquest, slavery, and European and African diseases.

Antigua became a member of the West Indies Federation in 1958 and then, in 1967, entered into a free association with Great Britain. Thus, when Jamaica Kincaid was growing up in Antigua from 1949 to 1965, it was still a British colony. In 1981 the islands achieved independence as the nation of Antigua and Barbuda. It remains part of the Commonwealth of Nations with Queen Elizabeth II as its official head.

When Annie moved to Antigua, she lived in a room in a house in Grays Farm in St. John's Antigua (*MP* 132–33). She held a variety of domestic jobs—housecleaner, washing woman, babysitter—before she was able to find employment with an unnamed physician who was a friend of her father's and later with another physician, Dr. Zoltan Weizenger, a refugee from Prague, Czechoslovakia (*MP* 8, 14), by way of Greece, Singapore, Shanghai, and Sydney (*MP* 11), who practiced both dentistry and medicine, and whom Mr. Potter (Kincaid's father) had chauffeured upon his arrival in Antigua. She was an all-purpose medical assistant, and though she considered Dr. Weizenger an ignorant man, she learned a lot about illnesses while working for him. Kincaid emphasizes his ignorance in *Mr. Potter* by using the term "little knowledge" three times to describe his understanding of dentistry and medicine and by noting that he could not "properly" speak English (*MP* 134–35). Kincaid often writes of his disdain for Antiguans (see *SP* 28).

Annie was a beautiful young woman. The striking figure that she cut as a young girl was reinforced by those who observed her throughout her life. Kincaid's friend Connie Rabinowitz, who did not meet Annie until 1983 or 1984, declared: "First of all, she was tall, slim, and she had that gorgeous posture that Antiguans have. I've never seen such excellent carriage." One of Annie's best friends recalled, "She was pretty too—what they called a butter-skin girl" (January 21, 2009). Only two people with whom I spoke in Antigua did not find her attractive: Splif (Ivor Philip) and Dame Gwendolyn Tonge agreed she was "tall and lanky" but "not really attractive."[3]

Annie was also a very animated and often charming personality with a great sense of humor, this latter attribute one to which acquaintances testified throughout her life. Rabinowitz, who did not meet Annie Drew until she was at least sixty-four, observed of her: "Yeah, she had a twinkle in her eye—Annie had a *real* twinkle in her eye. I mean she just had that!" One of Annie's relatives recalled: "She had a sense of humor. Every once in a while she give a little joke" (January 20, 2009). Reverend Lee affirmed: "She was fun to be around. She would say things that make people laugh. She would get a joke out of them." Interviews with Annie's friends, neighbors, and family suggest that she was a very social person, not at all the individual that Antonia MacDonald-Smythe perceives from *Annie John:* "Annie's mother is isolated in her domestic realm. There are no gatherings of women, none of the rambunctious energy that Paule Marshall [captures] in her depiction of her mother's kitchen" (48). True, in *Annie John* we are given only those scenes with the mother that include and are of significance to her daughter (domestic scenes); however, the many allusions to her friends, their deaths, their illnesses, their children, etc., indicate that there are many interactions to which we are not privy. Accounts from Jocelyn Reid, Reverend Rosa Lee, Dr. Ermina Osoba, and others, which I detail later in this study, certainly reveal lively exchanges not unlike those in Marshall's work. It should be noted that the active *political* side of the mother is not seen in *Annie John,* either; we later learn a little about this in *A Small Place, My Brother,* Kincaid's interviews, and Tim Hector's writings.

Other aspects of Annie's character that people who knew her through the years from her youth to her death mentioned included forthrightness, honesty, verbosity, outspokenness, irreverence, rambunctiousness, irascibility, and profanity, with her "forthrightness" being described with particular frequency. The Antiguan political activist Vincent Derrick declared to me: "She was well admired among her friends and so on for her forthrightness. She was a sincere woman. I mean, if she liked you, she liked you, and if she didn't like you, she, well, you know, she let you know. And that was it. She was not a woman to hold back things and hold on to any sort of ill will and that type of thing, you know. She dealt with matters as she saw them, and that was it." Conrad Luke, a prominent Antiguan and one of the founders of the United Progressive Party, concurred: "Annie was quite cantankerous. She was sharp with her tongue. She let you have it if she became upset with you. Despite that, those who really knew her had high regard for her. She was honest and forthright."

Pastor Lee also highlighted Annie Drew's problems with her temper: "Well, she was a kind-hearted woman, but she was quick-tempered as well. If you interfered, you know, crossed her, sometimes she would get a little insulting; some people didn't understand her, but *underneath* that outburst, she was a lovely person."

The major characteristic that stood out for one relative who had lived with Mrs. Drew was that "she was straightforward. She would tell you exactly how she feel" (January 20, 2009). Everybody recalled her outspokenness. Vincent Derrick averred that "Mr. Drew was a quiet person compared to Annie. You know Annie, she ruled the roost." Dame Tonge said: "There was a roughness about her. She was a little loud. She talked a lot." Dame Tonge and Splif laughingly declared her "mouthie, mouthie," that is, a gossiper, a big talker. Winston Derrick, who grew up in the same neighborhood, knew her well when he was a child: "Annie was always a feisty lady—her husband was more calm. If she were upset, she spoke her mind. If she thought you needed cussing, she did that too. She was vibrant. Everyone knew her. She would be very loud whether she was calling out a hello or yelling at you to correct you. I don't want to call her a busybody, but she was something of that. If you were taking plums from someone's tree, she would sound the alarm."

Several remembered her occasional profanity: Vincent Derrick recalls, "She was a woman who was not afraid to use bad language." When I asked for examples, he responded: "Well, she had her vocabulary [laughter]. She had her vocabulary. I couldn't exactly get down there; I'm not sure if I could remember exactly the language she used, but it was crude language."

Everybody agreed that she was opinionated: Vincent Derrick declared: "Well, she had an *opinion.* She knew where she wanted to go to, you know what I mean, that type of person, and she really didn't take no for an answer."

All who knew her knew that Annie did what she wanted to do. Pastor Lee asserted: "She does not take anything from anybody. Even though it's a policeman, and she's standing there, and they are going to tell her to move, and she doesn't feel to move, she's going to tell ya she na move. She's that kind of person. She has her self—if she doesn't feel that she should do anything."

What Senator/scholar Tim Hector described as her "combativity" (14) came, he suggested, from the warlike Caribs from whom she descended: "No one, just no one, was going to walk over Annie Drew, in no circumstances, on no condition. She fought like a tiger, or rather, like a true Carib" (14)—and as Kincaid has insisted, the Caribs survived because they were fierce (Ferguson, "A Lot of Memory" 174). Observing one woman crying about her marital situation, the Jamaica character, Lucy, declared that had any man caused her mother to cry so much, he would have suffered immediate demise (*Lucy* 113).

Annie's enemies considered her a wicked person. Reverend Lee told me: "But people always heard she was wicked. I remember one day I was walking with her—I had been at her house and she was following me home, and we were passing by the police station, and I remember a police called out, 'Sister Lee, don't walk wid dat woman, you know, she's a bad woman. Don't let nobody see you keeping company.' [laughter]"

Almost everyone agreed, however, that she was a loving and devoted mother who would do anything for her children, a kind and helpful person who would take care of those in need, an involved person who looked out for her neighborhood. A child in her family told me, "She was sweet" (January 16, 2009). "She was," Pastor Lee insisted, "a nice person." Winston Derrick concurred: "She was a very pleasant person. People liked her." Another friend declared: "Annie Drew was a nice woman—courageous, always looking out for her children. She brought [Jamaica] up properly. I was amazed at the bitterness [Kincaid expressed toward Annie]" (January 21, 2009).

Of course, Annie was never one-dimensional. She could be as innocent, reverent, quiet, and demure as the occasion demanded, but the real Annie was someone you didn't mess with. If she were provoked, she could be mean, loud, and violent. Rabinowitz recalls mentioning Annie to a mutual friend as "such a quiet lady," whereupon the friend roared: "Quiet! She's one of the toughest, feistiest women I know!" When I asked Rabinowitz if she ever saw that side of Annie, she responded: "Never. No. I think that was a class thing. I really do." Dame Tonge told me that Annie and her family were quite poor: "They were humble people," whereupon Splif declared, "She wasn't really humble. She was like an open book. She didn't pretend."

Some sources, including Kincaid's writings, suggest the likelihood that the young Annie, newly arrived in Antigua and reveling in her new freedom and independence, rebelled against everything her parents had insisted upon and may even have embarked on a lifestyle of uninhibited sex as the Kincaid character is portrayed as doing a generation later when she fled to America. In America, the Kincaid character, Lucy, discovers her erotic nature and enters into several casual sexual relations (see *Lucy* 67, 83, 97, 116). For just one example, after buying a camera from one Roland, she spends the rest of the day and half of that night in his bed (116). Lucy often failed to protect herself during sexual encounters and only later recognized the possibility of pregnancy and sexually transmitted diseases. Kincaid herself has declared in "Putting Myself Together" that the list of those with whom she had intimate relations is so long that she would no longer be able to identify all the faces (94), and she concludes, "My youth was exhausting, it was dangerous, and it is a miracle that I grew out of it unscathed" (101).

Annie was certainly aware of her beauty as a light-skinned woman ("butterskin girl") with beautiful long black wavy hair. In *Mr. Potter,* Kincaid writes that as a young woman her mother was beautiful, delighted in her beauty, and often flaunted her hair (135). She is clearly the inspiration for Xuela, a striking, tall woman with thin, wide lips (*Auto* 198), who tells us that she knew she was beautiful and that people were excited when she walked in a certain way with her long, thick, wavy hair flowing upon her shoulders (*Auto* 174). Kincaid verifies the attraction that light-skinned women hold for some Antiguan males where she notes that during the AIDS crisis in Antigua, men leaving an AIDS lecture still admitted that "Me rather dead dan leave butta women 'lone," that is, the fair-skinned Santo Domingan female prostitutes (*MB* 39).

Kincaid also recalls her mother having said to her in passing, "Well, you know, I used to love mi rum," possibly suggesting that in her day, she was a wild and sexually adventurous woman, completely unlike the mother that the young Jamaica knew, who made sex seem like something one should never do (Kin/Dance).[4] It is important to note that in her later years, according to Jocelyn Reid, Annie might have a little brandy now and then with her meal, but she was not someone who drank to get drunk (April 26, 2009).

It is clear that, like Xuela and other "butterskin girl[s]," Annie was very attractive to Caribbean men. Perhaps like Xuela, Annie seduced or allowed herself to be seduced by married men, selfishly seeking her own gratification without regard to others whom she may have hurt. There are hints in *The Autobiography of My Mother* that Xuela has an affair with the husband of her half sister Elizabeth (128). At the time Xuela lived with and worked for a White European doctor, Philip, and his wife, Moira, she went to Philip for an examination and aroused him by telling him that her breasts were in a constant state of sensation that could be relieved only by a man's sucking them. He then comes to her room that night, presumably to bring her a book (151), and when he walks in she continues masturbating. Their affair begins, and she ultimately marries him after his wife's convenient demise. Then she discovers an exact opposite of Philip, a Black stevedore named Roland by whom upon her first glance she is so titillated that, despite the fact that he is talking with another woman (likely his wife), she yells out her name to him and declares, “I love you,” something she had probably never truthfully said to any other person. Obviously, here this “love” is pure passion, for it is clear that Roland is very much one of the men she elsewhere excoriated for taking pride in the number of women they impregnated. Nonetheless, she continues to declare she loves Roland. Their union, as she had anticipated, is so fulfilling that she declares that she was embarrassed to derive so much pleasure from it (168). Xuela is attacked by Roland’s wife as “a whore, a slut, a pig, a snake, a viper, a rat, a lowlife, a parasite, and an evil woman” (171), an attack that fuels her passion for him: she declares that his love for other women made her love him even more (171).

Eight or nine years after her arrival in Antigua, the twenty-five-year-old Annie, whom Kincaid describes as “a whirlwind of sex and passion and female beauty and . . . narcissism and vulnerability” (*MP* 141), had likely developed something of a reputation as a loose woman. A young woman in a strange country with no family or friends was certainly vulnerable, as Kincaid has noted. Indeed, the author was to find herself in a comparable position in America, when she writes that having no money and being unable to pay her rent and buy food, she exchanged sex for meals (“Putting” 94).

It was at this time, when she was twenty-five, that Annie met Mr. Roderick Potter as he stood near the car he drove, we are told in one account (*MP* 141–42); in another, we are informed that she met him in Mr. Shoul’s household, where she worked as a nursemaid (*MP* 162).

Kincaid’s biography of her father, *Mr. Potter,* gives us the details of his family history, some of which may be fictionalized.[5] He was born January 7, 1922 (177). His father was Nathaniel Potter (99), a fisherman (36), who was also the son of a fisherman (41). Nathaniel, who fathered twenty-one children by different women, knew only eleven of them (38). They were all illiterate (40), including Mr. Potter, the last of his children (36). Nathaniel, who had ancestors from Africa, Spain, England, and Scotland, died at the age of forty-seven of a curse, which turned him black and caused boils to appear on his body and leak pus (47). Mr. Potter’s mother was Elfrida Robinson (97), who was sixteen when he was born. His mother named him after “the English maritime criminal George Brydges Rodney” (64). When he was young he was called Drickie (81). When Mr. Potter was five or so, Kincaid explains, his mother, having tired of her son, gave him to a woman and drowned herself in the sea (70).

When Annie met Mr. Potter, the handsome and self-assured young man worked as a chauffeur for Mr. Shoul. One can imagine that the mere fact that he drove a car made him attractive to a poor girl in Antigua in 1944, though Kincaid insisted to me that her mother was not the sort of person to have been attracted to him for anything material. Certainly his dapper image helped to make him stand apart from those who worked and sweated for a living and dressed as laborers. Drickie was always dressed in a nice clean shirt (washed and ironed by one of his many women [*MP* 118]), neat tie, and well-pressed trousers, with his shoes carefully polished (indeed, "gleaming" [148]), his *tightly* curled hair dressed to lie flat on his head (118), and his cap adding the final touch to his remarkable attire (89, 104). He had a special "stylish" walk, and called himself *Mr.* Potter (89). Further, he had many women who loved him and had children by him, though he loved neither the women nor their daughters (120). Perhaps at first this "popularity" attracted Annie to him; winning him might have been a challenge to her as winning Roland was to Xuela, who would never have loved him so much had he not loved other women (*Auto* 171).

Annie moved in with Mr. Potter in a one-room house at Points (*MP* 142). We know nothing about their relationship except its bitter ending. We might assume that there were some romantic times. They probably made an attractive and stylish couple, he a confident young man maneuvering his car through the streets of St. John's, stepping out with Annie on his arms, all heads turning to look at this tall and striking woman with her light complexion and her beautiful long, wavy black hair, and Mr. Potter in his clean and well-pressed shirt, his polished shoes, and his tie, moving with his bebop strut, what Kincaid describes as "that jaunt of his" (122).

Kincaid suggests that Annie enjoyed parading her beauty as she walked down Scot's Row with her beautiful hair apparently carelessly piled on her head (135). No doubt Mr. Potter was proud to have her on his arm, and, Kincaid tells us, he was proud to see his face reflected in her hair. He loved the hair, even though Kincaid suggests that he didn't really love Annie (163). They were planning for the future, and either he or they were saving so that he could stop driving someone else's taxi, buy his own car, and go into business for himself. He was, Kincaid told me, apparently tight-fisted. Thus, it was likely that he might have viewed having a child to support as an impediment to achieving his goals. But over the course of the fourteen years she had been in Antigua, according to Kincaid, Annie found herself pregnant five times, and despite her success in aborting four prior pregnancies, she was not able to abort the fetus that would become Jamaica Kincaid, conceived when Annie was twenty-nine.

When Annie was seven months pregnant, the couple's relationship ended, leaving both parties full of hatred and bitterness, and Kincaid's writings suggest that this hatred and bitterness is all Annie shared with her daughter about her parents' relationship. Or it may be—and this is probably the most likely—that this is what Jamaica remembers of what her mother told her about the relationship. Or perhaps, yet again, it is only this that Jamaica chooses to write about the relationship, since it is this, interpreted in a particular way, that helps to explain Jamaica's unrelenting anger toward her mother. That certainly is the view one of Annie's friends, shared with me: "The reason Jamaica doesn't like her mother is because she was not married to her father—her mother did not give her the aura of respectability" (January 21, 2009).

The ending of that relationship is one of the first of the many traumatic events for which Kincaid will never forgive her mother. In Kincaid's account, Annie took all of Mr. Potter's savings and walked out of his life. Kincaid constantly harks back to Annie leaving Potter but never offers any explanation for her leaving beyond the fact that they quarreled (*MP* 142; see also "The Estrangement" 40). Annie's action is portrayed as a "treachery" (*MP* 194) and a theft—she took *his* money and destroyed *his* dreams—"her murderous action . . . taking the money he had saved, with which he meant to make of himself some semblance of a man [left] him to perish again and again each day in the world of Mr. Shoul" (142). Kincaid allows no sympathy for Annie and no consideration that her behavior was less than culpable; indeed, Kincaid complains that Annie's action caused Jamaica to have a line drawn through her[6] and her father to reject her (*MP* 142–43). Kincaid declares of a vacant look on her face in a photo taken when she is seven years old that it is "the absence of Mr. Potter that is written on my face" (145). She never gets over the absence of the father—"My father's absence will forever hang over my present and my present, at any given moment, will echo his absence" (192; see also 170)—and she always holds her mother responsible for that void in her life.

Here and elsewhere, Jamaica shows more sympathy for and forgiveness of Mr. Potter than of Annie. Whether or not we agree with Colbert Nepaulsingh's argument that, in *Mr. Potter,* "Jamaica tries to resurrect her dead fictional father and 'kill' her real but also fictional mother" (218), it is certainly clear that in that book, Kincaid insists that Mr. Potter's treatment of her

(Jamaica) was a direct result of Annie's cruelty to him: "She added to his life an excess of bitterness and ill feeling, so much that he extended it to me" (*MP* 94). Elsewhere she discusses the hatred between her parents, a hatred that caused Mr. Potter to deny his daughter a father's protection (129). Indeed, the account of the father's ignoring the child's requests for money changes frequently throughout *Mr. Potter,* changes that we may attribute to her mother's accounts or to Kincaid's increasing pain and anger. At first, as a four-year-old sent to ask for money to buy a writing tablet, she waves at him and he ignores her. She claims that she remembers his ignoring her only because her mother told her about it—the slights, in other words, are not slights she recalls from her father but rather incidents she remembers only because her mother told her about them in her own words (126). In a later account of what one might assume is the same incident, she asks him for money to buy books; again she informs us that she doesn't remember asking him but only remembers her mother telling her so (154). Of course, here, as elsewhere, Kincaid reminds the readers, "my entire life as I live it is all my mother has told me" (127); and "my mother's tongue and the words that flow from it cannot be relied upon" (154). In her last account of what may be this same incident, he not only ignores her when she requests money to purchase writing paper but slams the door in her face (161). Oddly enough, she claims to have "a vague memory" of this incident (161). It might have been at this time that Annie took Potter to court to sue for support for his daughter. Kincaid recalls that her name was then registered in the court as Potter-Richardson, though she never used the hyphenated name—sometimes, she told me, she was Potter and sometimes Richardson. Potter was required to give the court thirteen shillings every three months; the court kept one shilling and allotted a shilling a week to Jamaica.[7]

It is difficult to understand why Kincaid rarely seems as bitter toward Mr. Potter as she does toward Annie despite the often negative portrayals of Mr. Potter's illiteracy, his lack of awareness of or interest in anything beyond himself, his lack of concern for his illegitimate children, his ignoring Jamaica when she went to ask him for help in purchasing school supplies (126, 154, 161), his failure ever to acknowledge her when she was growing up in Antigua, and his failure to ever speak to her ("He never spoke to me at all" [132]). This latter is an exaggeration, for Kincaid's father visited her in New York, where he bragged about the fact that all of his daughters had his nose. At first the long-neglected daughter, by then a world-renowned writer, was speechless: "And how glad I was to be alive and to hear Mr. Potter say that I was his and my nose was his" (168). But when she finds her voice and asks what she is to call him, she is so overcome with anger that she wishes to kill him. In *Mister Potter,* no other words are said; presumably her fury drives him to leave (169–70). Elsewhere in an account of this confrontation, he responds, "Oh, why, Dad," and Kincaid declares, "We never spoke again" (Jones D1). What is most interesting in this account is her eagerness to forgive and embrace him had he but offered words of apology for the pain he caused her. It is clear that there is the possibility of forgiveness for this cruel and indifferent father—and even, elsewhere, for the colonial conquerors she despises—while there seems no possibility of forgiving Annie.

Though she frequently laments the absence of a father, it is clear that had he been in her life, the character whom she portrays (unworldly, self-centered, licentious, uncaring, incapable of loving, illiterate, proud of his chauffeur's uniform) would clearly have been a blight on her life. Kincaid obviously secures some vengeance for his neglect of her—and all the other unloved girls he fathered by several other women—by visiting a series of horrid punishments on him. In *Mr. Potter,* Kincaid writes a poignant scene in which Roderick as a young boy sees his father for the first time and hears his mother bitterly reproach the father for his inattentiveness to them, a scene that is to be repeated in the next generation with Kincaid as the neglected daughter of that same Roderick Potter. Not satisfied with Potter suffering the loss of a father that she, too, suffered, in *Mr. Potter* she has his mother commit suicide and leave him a pitiful waif without mother or father, left to cry from his birth to his death with no one ever paying any attention to his cries (99–100). Finally she has him marry a woman who is unfaithful and who gives birth to a son (his only son), who is not really his son but the son of an undertaker. Kincaid makes much of the irony that this man who neglected all of his blood children through the years loved only this son, a ne'er-do-well who always finished at the bottom of his class and failed at sports but had plenty of school supplies and food, and, most importantly, the home with a father that Kincaid so longed for (158–59). The son, who lived for forty-five years without ever achieving anything significant (159), is adequate payment for the cuckolded father. It is clear that the calamitous disappointments Mr. Potter endures are the author's vengeance for the pain he caused her.

Despite Kincaid's anger, *Mr. Potter* ends with a long lament, cataloguing the sadness of a life without a mother, without anyone to love him, with his unclaimed children fighting at his graveside, and with his beloved "son" not bothering to come from Canada to his funeral. She shows some sympathy for a man fated to grow old and die with no one to cry upon his death, to be put in an unmarked grave, to remain anonymous, to have his life have no meaning, except that that his rejected daughter brings to it: “Mr. Potter . . . died and will never be heard from again, except through me” (191). Despite her vacillating feelings, a jealous Kincaid relishes her power as a writer to punish those who neglected her. Couldn’t Mr. Potter see that she was the daughter who deserved his love? That same rhetorical question echoes elsewhere through her accounts of her brothers born to Annie and Mr. Drew.

There are, however, subtle reminders that Kincaid on some level recognizes that Annie is not really the villain she often portrays her as being in her relationship with Mr. Potter. Two statements in *Mr. Potter* force the readers to fill in more of an explanation for Annie’s leaving. Kincaid directs us to “Hear the sound of my mother’s wounds as she left the house she shared with Mr. Potter” (194); and Kincaid notes that when she “was not even yet a person, only seven months living in my mother’s stomach, . . . Mr. Potter first abandoned me” (104). Though she does not elaborate these isolated statements, they invite us to consider some of the motivation for her mother’s leaving.

We may certainly assume that by this time, approaching thirty, having worked at numerous jobs and relationships, having had four abortions, Annie was probably desirous of a steady relationship, indeed marriage, and Mr. Potter seemed a promising candidate for a woman who was concerned about image and security. Annie’s usual concoctions of herbs that she prepared herself apparently did not bring about the desired abortion of Jamaica, and being seven months pregnant, Annie needed marriage. To walk out, as she presumably did, could not have been easy, even with the money she took to help her survive.[8] Indeed, Kincaid’s suggestion that Mr. Potter abandoned her (Jamaica) at that time, may even imply that *he* ended the relationship with Annie. All that Kincaid writes about Mr. Potter suggests that he would never have been faithful in the relationship and that he probably was not at that time the marrying type. It is likely that by the seventh month of her pregnancy, Annie recognized that the rake who had likely seduced her and offered her empty promises was neither going to marry her nor put an end to his sleeping around. Perhaps the self-centered Potter had tired of Annie’s complaints about his other women, his lack of attention to her, his postponement of making her a respectable woman. In similar circumstances, many such men might beat the offending woman or kick her out. But in all her references to their parting, Kincaid indicates that Annie took his money and left. And Kincaid firmly rejects the possibility that Potter may have been physically abusive to Annie, declaring that her mother would have killed any man who dared to lay a hand on her. In fact, Kincaid does not believe that her mother wanted to marry Mr. Potter. She told me that Annie felt confident in her ability to manage without a man for support and that she wouldn't have been embarrassed to have a child out of wedlock, characteristics very inconsistent with the mother figures pictured in *At the Bottom of the River, Annie John,* and *Lucy,* or with women of the time generally.

As Annie reflected on her own dilemma with Mr. Potter, she undoubtedly recalled the arguments she had had with her father before she left Dominica (*MP* 118). Clearly her father was upset with her quest for independence and undoubtedly admonished her, as she was later to lecture her daughter, about the calamitous results a young girl would face if she did not follow her parents' warnings.

"Misery don't call ahead."

Now here she was, as he had very likely predicted, a fallen woman about to have an illegitimate child.

"Man no buy cow when he kin get de milk fa free."

Given what we know about Annie's firm belief in Obeah and her frequent consulting of Obeah practitioners, it is very likely that she might have tried Obeah to force Mr. Potter to marry her and to cease his unfaithfulness. Given her character and her bitterness, she might even have tried to have something more harmful visited upon him. Victoria, the Annie character in "Antigua's Crossings," writes to her sister, whose husband is a philandering "louse" (49): "What to do with him? . . . I know only too well, but it's true, as everyone says, that you are by far the nicer sister" (49).

Annie was not in a good position, but she was a woman of strength and perseverance. Her anger and her need for revenge no doubt determined the nature of her leaving. Not only had she probably invested time and emotional commitment in the relationship, but she had probably also contributed to the stash they had hidden away for Drickie to open his business. I expect the disappointed Annie felt perfectly justified in ending this relationship and taking the savings they had accumulated to help her care for herself and the baby she would soon have. The only thing we know for sure is that when Annie left the room she shared with Drickie, she left consumed by a hatred of him that would last for the rest of her life, and she did not leave empty-handed.

Annie returned to her one room at Grays Farm. Perhaps by this time she had recognized the futility of her efforts to abort her fetus. When Jamaica was forty-one, she wrote in *Mr. Potter,* Annie told her daughter about her efforts to abort her (136). Undoubtedly the mother thought that by that time in her own life, Jamaica—who had seen all around her in Antigua the results of giving birth to children that could not be afforded, who knew something of the world and the relationships of men and women, especially poor vulnerable women who were seduced and betrayed—would sympathize with the desperate twenty-nine-year-old Annie. She could not have been more mistaken.

Jamaica was appalled and added the attempt to abort her to the list of affronts she had suffered at the hands of her mother that she would wrestle with in her fiction. In fact, Kincaid told me that her mother never really *told* her that she had had abortions and that she had attempted to abort Jamaica, but that she was simply able to glean it from what she said from time to time. She explained that her first indication of the numerous abortions occurred when Mrs. Drew visited her in Vermont in 1987. Kincaid asked her mother if she could believe that the youthful and sprightly nanny who worked for her had had eleven children, and the competitive Mrs. Drew, every bit as energetic and youthful, though not as young as the nanny, exclaimed that she had had nine. Kincaid, who knew of her efforts to abort Devon, thus deducted that her mother had had four abortions before she was born, thus explaining how it was that Annie was nearly thirty when she had her first child, while, Kincaid declared, women from Antigua usually have children very early. Kincaid had earlier attributed this to her mother's restraint and her management of her life, to her waiting. Now she concluded that she had had a wild life and had simple resorted to abortions.

While Kincaid may be correct in surmising that her mother attempted to abort her, the reader must consider the possibility that this may simply have been one of the things Annie said to needle her daughter, reinforcing their friend and neighbor Jocelyn Reid's assertion that Mrs. Drew "loved rubbing it into Elaine." Often during their bitter conflicts the hostility of the combatants caused each to say unspeakable things to the other, with what Kincaid describes in *Annie John* as frightening black things emanating from each and meeting in lethal combat (101). In fact, it seems hard to believe Annie really wanted to abort Jamaica, given all of her careful planning for her and the intricate clothes she made before she was born. Certainly during much of her pregnancy, she was excitedly looking forward to being a mother.

Though there are few biographical details in *The Autobiography of My Mother* that argue that Xuela, the motherless protagonist, is a portrayal of Annie Drew,[9] and though Xuela is often arguably more consistent with the character of Jamaica Kincaid herself, it is very clear that in this novel Kincaid creates a situation where she in effect punishes Annie Drew, whom Jamaica insists never should have been a mother, by making her (as Xuela) childless. (During a telephone conversation with me on August 5, 2008, Kincaid declared that her mother was a horrible person who should never have had any children.) In a moving passage, Xuela declares that she would never become a mother: "I would bear children, but I would never be a mother to them. . . . I would bear children in the morning, I would bathe them at noon in a water that came from myself, and I would eat them at night" (*Auto* 97). She goes on to imagine the most horrific and monstrous punishments and persecutions she would visit on these children. At the end of the novel as she reflects on her orphan status and her loneliness, she laments her decision not to have children, acknowledging that only becoming pregnant and giving birth would have given her complete happiness (225–26) and concluding that the account in this autobiography is an account of her mother's life, of her own life, and of the lives of the children whose voices she never heard and whose faces she never saw. She acknowledges that in denying those children the opportunity to develop and live, she denied herself the opportunity to become the person she might have been (227–28).

The suffering that Kincaid creates here for Xuela is probably more extreme than that Annie Drew experienced, though, like Gwendolyn Brooks's unrepentant but still sensitive mother in her famous poem "The Mother," Annie must have from time to time, "heard in the voices of the wind the voices of my dim killed / children" (Brooks 4).

Kincaid's vengeance for her mother's abortions extends to the hated Moira in *Autobiography*, the woman who was married to the doctor for whom Xuela served as assistant before seducing him and assisting her in suicide. Moira, too, had a broken womb. Further, Kincaid has Moira, a stereotypical self-centered British colonial who hates Blacks simply because of their color, turn black before she died (207).[10] The series of those hated women who kill their own children include Xuela's sister Elizabeth, her father's daughter by a stepmother who attempts to kill Xuela. When Elizabeth becomes pregnant by her secret lover, Xuela helps her abort the child (114–15), an action for which Elizabeth shows no gratitude, only disdain. Elizabeth ends up disfigured by an accident, unable to walk without limping or to focus her eyes properly

(127), her body covered with scars (126). She marries a man who does not love her and who desires Xuela. The malicious treatment of that character in *Autobiography* reflects Annie Drew's animosity toward the real Elizabeth more than Kincaid's more affectionate recollection of her, but then as Xuela reflects in the previously quoted passage, the autobiography of her life is also the story of her mother's life (227).[11]

The seven-months-pregnant Annie Richardson was alone in Antigua without the support of a husband or parents, but, as previously noted, Kincaid believes that she was neither upset nor embarrassed that she was about to bear a child out of wedlock. Clearly, from all accounts, she was enthusiastically preparing for the birth of her child. As described in *Annie John,* she zealously applied her sewing talents to make elegant outfits for her child. She made a white chemise with scalloped edging around the neck, sleeves, and bottom, and embroidered white flowers on the front (*AJ* 20), which were, unfortunately, not put on perfectly because the Kincaid character was kicking around in her stomach. Her mother later told her, "Even then you were hard to manage" (*AJ* 21–22). It was the first outfit the infant ever wore. Annie made her baby diapers with a special handkerchief hemstitch (*AJ* 20).

Two months after leaving Mr. Potter, Annie went to the Magdalene Maternity Ward at Holberton Hospital, where she gave birth to her illegitimate child. Jamaica later often heard her mother declare of her father, "A line runs through him" (*MP* 101), that is, a line is drawn through the space on his birth certificate where the name of a father should be. Throughout *Mr. Potter,* Kincaid returns over and over to the line drawn through the empty space on the birth certificates for him and for her ("this line that runs through Mr. Potter and that he then gave to me" [100]) where the father's name should be, and she determines that she will never have illegitimate children (101), which to Kincaid is no less ignominious than aborting them. Of the many questions posed in "The Letter from Home," a story in *At the Bottom of the River,* the only one that is set off with quotation marks in the dialogue (which suggests that the protagonist in "Girl," the opening story in the same collection, is now living in the United States) is, "Will [the children] bear their mother's name?" (38).

Jamaica was born on May 25, 1949, at five o'clock in the morning (*MP* 128) and named, she tells us in many accounts, Elaine Cynthia Richardson (and just about every biography and literary study lists her birth name either as Elaine Cynthia Richardson or Elaine Cynthia Potter Richardson). In fact the name listed on her birth certificate is Elaine Potter, and given the fact that the last name of her mother is Richardson, her full legal name would be Elaine Potter Richardson. Annie's address at the time is listed as Grays Farm.

The birth itself offered at least three more affronts to Kincaid, all highly symbolic. First, Kincaid suggests that her birth was the source of the gulf between her and her mother because after her birth, which split her mother open, her mother could never be whole again (*MP* 129). She clearly exonerates Mr. Potter, declaring that he did not cause the gulf (129). Second, upon her birth, she did not cry, and the woman assisting at her birth slapped her, a blow that Kincaid insists was hard to her (*MP* 144), one of the first instances in her memory of pain inflicted on her by or because of her mother, pain that she could not possibly remember, but pain that she has read into her retelling of one of her mother's anecdotes about their life together. Third, though she relishes the "memory" of the first time her mother nursed her, exclaiming, "how she loved me as she fed me" (*MP* 147), as Annie shared with her the only thing she had to offer her, milk from her breast, Jamaica drank and drank until "I sucked her dry" (*MP* 144). Kincaid says her mother told her this story when she was three, five, and seven years old, but later denied that her mother told her the story and that it ever happened (*MP* 144).

The battle of memories had already begun during these first hours in the life of the infant Jamaica.

3

RAISING AN ONLY CHILD

> I loved being an only child. I concentrated all my attention on myself,
> I treasured myself, no hurt directed at me was too small to go unnoticed by me.
> —Jamaica Kincaid, in *Generations of Women*, by Mariana Cook

Annie continued to work for Dr. Weizenger after she gave birth to Jamaica. She continued also to spend whatever time she could find in her hectic days creating beautiful outfits for her daughter, such as a yellow dress with green smocking on the front that she made for her first birthday (*AJ* 20), and the yellow poplin dress with a new kind of smocking that Annie had just learned for her second birthday, a creation that inspired a whole story dedicated to its conception and fashioning, Kincaid's "Biography of a Dress."

Kincaid remembers (or recalls through Annie's stories) many instances of her mother's great love for her as she was growing up, though she sometimes harbors suspicions of a devious underlying motive. Annie was a mother who always did whatever was necessary for her child. She would chew Jamaica's food and put it in her mouth because Jamaica declared that chewing was tiring (*MB* 17; "Biography" 93); she would even draw the mucus out of Jamaica's nose into her own mouth if Jamaica's nose were clogged (*MB* 17). Even after Jamaica could walk, because the child preferred to be carried, Annie would often carry her for long distances in the hot sun, sometimes holding her in her arms, sometimes carrying her piggyback. On Jamaica's second birthday, Annie, after a long day of work that included finishing a dress for her daughter, carried her in the hot sun to the photographer to have her picture taken. The child realized how tired her mother was but noted that she spoke lovingly to her ("Biography" 100). Her mother also marked Jamaica's second birthday by piercing her ears. The pain was so great that Jamaica says she felt she was torn in two, with one part of her observing and the other enduring the painful experience, leaving her wondering if her mother's having her ears pierced was an expression of hostility ("Biography" 97). On her birthday, gold hoop earrings and a pair of silver bracelets were put on her for the picture.

Kincaid's narrator recalls in "At the Bottom of the River" how much she was loved as a child, "how much I loved myself and how much I was loved by my mother" (73). In *Annie John,* the Kincaid character describes being the center of her mother's life and sharing every detail of her day as a paradise (25). In "My Mother," she and her mother are not only together, but they become one person with one voice, achieving a "complete union" (*AT* 60).

Much of the passion in Kincaid's memory of her mother was inspired by Annie's beauty. The narrator in "At the Bottom of the River" recalls her mother's "voluminous skirt" and her "wondrous beauty," declaring, "How I worshipped this beauty" (73). Her mother was so pretty, Kincaid told me, that "I was *ashamed* of how beautiful she was when I was a child, because I thought everyone would know that she might have sex. She was *just* gorgeous—beautiful hair which she wore in a French twist." In *Annie John,* the Kincaid figure imagines how beautiful a child her mother must have been with her two long plaits hanging down past her shoulders (69); and she describes her joy in fondling the strands of her mother's hair when she unraveled her braids (87). Kincaid or the Kincaid character is often fascinated by "beautiful" hair, that is, straight hair, and sometimes comments in derogatory terms about her own unruly hair (*AJ* 27). In *Annie John,* it is clear that her only attraction to Sonia, a retarded playmate, was that this "dunce" had such beautiful "long, thick black hair" (7). In *My Garden (Book):,* Kincaid recalls her envy of the golden-haired girls pictured in the Antiguan magazines she read as a child: she would look at their pictures and wish to be like them, "with hair like that" (57). In "Biography of a Dress," she laments the fact that her skin is not cream-colored and her hair does not have a silken texture like the girl whose picture inspired the dress her mother made for her in an effort, Kincaid believes, to try to make her look like that little White girl (96–97).

This is one of the few suggestions that Annie might have wished that her daughter had had more Nordic features and hair. Unlike many fair Afro-Caribbeans,[1] Annie did not seem to view her color and her hair as something that made her superior to darker people. In fact, as Kincaid pointed out, she was attracted to dark men, such as Mr. Potter and Mr. Drew. "Color," Kincaid told me in 2008, "was never an issue with her." Jocelyn Reid reinforced this: "There was no color complex in the family." In fact, Reverend Lee suggested that Devon might have been Annie's favorite child precisely because he was the darkest.

Kincaid insists that Annie never in any way used her beauty for gain. Though she describes Annie as vain, her vanity seemed to be based upon her pride, her independence, and her work rather than her beauty. Annie always told her that it was better to be a smart woman than a pretty woman (NY 73).

Annie loved to read, mostly nonfiction, according to Kincaid (Cook 20). She read biographies of Florence Nightingale and Louis Pasteur (*MB* 78). Annie also had numerous medical books, which she frequently consulted when her husband or children were ill. She was familiar with all of the tropical diseases, and she knew which foods were required for specific vitamin deficiencies (*MB* 78). She always diagnosed her family's medical problems and devised natural cures (*Talk Stories* 240). As she got older and became a big churchgoer, she limited her reading to the Bible, according to her daughter, an observation reinforced by the fact that Annie is holding a Bible in the photograph in Mariana Cook's *Generations of Women.*

Annie conscientiously passed on her love of reading to her daughter. She taught Jamaica to read when she was three and a half (Cook 20; Birbalsingh 143),[2] and took her to the library every Thursday evening (Paravisini-Gebert 6; NY 72). Kincaid insists that her mother taught her to read so that she could read her own books in peace (Cook 20). Obviously Annie was a good teacher because Jamaica recalls being able to read right away. Her mother would tell her a word, and Jamaica could just go right on and read without effort—"It must have been something she did." Annie was so pleased with Jamaica's reading that when her daughter was seven years old, she gave her a copy of the *Concise Oxford Dictionary,* in which she presciently wrote, "To My Darling Daughter, who will one day make me proud of her" (NY 72). Jamaica was so proud that she took it everywhere with her and read the dictionary like a book, declaring, "I'm hopelessly in love with language" (Jones D-1). "By the age of nine," Paravisini-Gebert writes, "she had already read all the books in the children's section and would borrow her mother's card to choose books from the adult selections" (7).

Their special weekly trips to the library were remembered as a part of that lost paradise she had shared with her mother, a treasured memory of a time when they went everywhere together and people commented on what a couple they were (NY 72).

Kincaid developed a love of the library and books that remains a central part of her life. She recalls that first library as "a splendid library" (*SP* 8), "one of those splendid old buildings from colonial times" (*SP* 9). Mrs. Phyllis Mayers, a retired librarian, recalls Jamaica as "an avid reader" and "a bright child," though she says she doesn't remember Jamaica as well as Jamaica remembers her. She says when Jamaica returned to lecture in Antigua, she told Mrs. Mayers how she used to sneak out books beyond her limit by hiding them in her clothes. Mrs. Mayers wasn't aware that Jamaica kept books she checked out. She remembers Mrs. Drew only because she brought Jamaica to the library, and she doesn't recall Mrs. Drew being someone who used the library a great deal herself. Antigua's failure to restore her beloved library after it was damaged in the 1974 earthquake remains one of Kincaid's major grudges against her birthplace.

Though Annie was an unwed mother, the striking young woman continued to have male suitors. Kincaid shared with me some memories during her early years of "shadowy figures that I called uncle" who she now recognizes were her mother's suitors or sexual partners. She recalls in particular one man, a stevedore, whom she and her mother used to visit and who used to give them sugar. She vividly remembers details of his house, which she still passes by during her visits to Antigua and where she used to play in the portulaca while her mother was inside with him. Kincaid obviously found this man fascinating, since he is the source of the titillating lover in *The Autobiography of My Mother* to whom Xuela was so attracted that she expressed her love to him when she first saw him and whose union with him was, as she had anticipated, so fulfilling that she was ashamed of how much pleasure she felt (168).

Though Kincaid portrays Mr. David Drew as Annie's husband before she is two years old in "Biography of a Dress," she could only recall during our interview that Mr. Drew came into their lives before she started school at the age of three and a half. The known fact is that Annie, at some time between 1951 and 1953, entered into a common-law marriage with Mr. Drew. One of Mrs. Drew's friends told me that the marriage was "engineered" by David Drew's employer at the time (January 21, 2009). Kincaid, who admits that she doesn't remember the marriage, told me that she believes they married when she was around five years old. In all of her writings and interviews she pictures them as married, but the fact is that they did not marry until March 9, 1967, almost two years after Kincaid left Antigua.[3]

Annie, David, and Jamaica lived on Dickensonsbey Street and later Nelson Street (now Charlesworth Ross Street) in a one-room house (*MB* 111) that had no electricity or running water (Garis 42, 44), though the lack of running water was more the result of the Antiguan infrastructure than their means (Paravisini-Gebert 2). A few people, like their next-door neighbors, the Javises, had private water, but the Drews had to get their water from rain tanks or from the public pipe. Jamaica never lived in a house with a refrigerator or a telephone or a television until she came to the United States, if we accept *Lucy* as the autobiographical book she declares it to be (4); it is, however, almost certain that she became familiar with those appliances in Puerto Rico, though that part of her life never enters any of her works.

In our interview, Kincaid pictured Mr. Drew as a confident, handsome, and vain man. None of his children or anyone else with whom I talked seems to have ever seen a photograph of Mr. Drew, who, like Mr. Potter, had had many female conquests. His previous lovers sometimes physically attacked Annie and her daughter. He had fathered several illegitimate children, some of whom he didn't even know. Occasionally one would come to their house and introduce her/himself, but sometimes it took quite a bit of prodding to make Mr. Drew remember his visitor's mother. Jamaica recalls the very first of his children, born to a woman named Sylvia; she assumes that Mr. Drew and this woman must have had a romantic relationship because they named their son and daughter after themselves, though she adds, after reflection, that two other women also named their sons David after him. She told me that Mr. Drew's daughter Sylvia turned out to be a public alcoholic whom they often saw on the streets and occasionally when she showed up at their house drunk. She recalled running into either the son or grandson of the first son named David when she visited Antigua recently, and added, "I run into people in Antigua all the time who are my relatives." Bearing a strong resemblance to her father's family (the Potters), she is often approached on the street by offspring of her philandering father as well.

In *Lucy*, Kincaid writes that her mother was young and her father was old when they married, a situation that suited them both since marriage afforded her mother some respect and provided her father someone to care for him in his old age (80–81). In *Annie John*, the husband is thirty-five years older than Annie, and he had two children four and six years older than his wife. However, the Drews' actual marriage certificate indicates that at the time of their betrothal, Mr. Drew was sixty-one and Annie was forty-one, both ages probably erroneous. In fact, assuming other records are correct, Annie was forty-seven and Mr. Drew was sixty-six when they married on March 9, 1967; their sons were nine, six, and four; Jamaica was seventeen and would turn eighteen in two months.

Despite his earlier philandering, Kincaid often pictures Mr. Drew as a committed and faithful husband, though she also suggests his faithfulness was attributable to the debilitations of old age.

A very talented carpenter, Mr. Drew could, Kincaid told me, replicate any piece of furniture that he saw in a book. He was, she has insisted, the best carpenter on the island except for the man to whom he had been apprenticed and who had died before Jamaica was born (*Talk Stories* 237). Mothers constantly came to their home, appealing to him to take their sons on as his apprentices (*Talk Stories* 221–22). He built houses, including the house they lived in during her childhood, and made furniture. Mr. Drew is pictured in *Annie John* as a hard worker who built a house and all of the necessary furniture for his family. In "Antigua Crossings," however, Annie has to nag him to make the necessary repairs to their house (49). In one "Notes and Comment" piece, we are told that Annie Drew kept asking him to make some of the beautiful furniture he made for other people for their house, but he did not, explaining that he had loaned furniture to the widow of the man to whom he had been apprenticed and he would get that back for them. He never did, and Annie Drew was often furious and embarrassed by their lack of appropriate furniture (*Talk Stories* 238–39; *MG* 42; Kin/Dance), though he did, Kincaid told me, make the furniture for her that she describes in *Annie John* (bed, bureau, washstand, desk, chair) and a crib for her brothers.

Another source of friction in their marriage, according to Kincaid, was the fact that Mr. Drew was a daydreamer who wasted much of his time sitting around in his little shop, smoking, talking with his friends, and doing very little work, often spending a day carving one leg of a chair. One of the quarrels that Kincaid recalls her parents having occurred when a young carpenter moved next door and opened up a little shop that did great business, with people constantly coming in to order things like cribs and chairs. Annie reprimanded Mr. Drew, "You could be doing that!" But Mr. Drew lacked ambition, Kincaid told me.

It is clear everywhere that he was a man of a few words. Jamaica writes in "Notes and Comments" that Annie Drew's rows were with "herself, for my father never quarreled with anyone—not even his wife" (*Talk Stories* 239). Everybody remembered Mr. Drew as a quiet man. Jocelyn Reid said of him: "Mr. Drew didn't argue. He was very quiet. All the children loved him. He never hit them." Vincent Derrick recalled that "Mr. Drew was a quiet person compared to Annie." In "The Fourth," Kincaid portrays him as dignified and critical, a man who rarely said anything much (*Talk Stories* 58). It does appear, however, that there were times when he (or the Kincaid father figure in the fiction) drew the line and asserted his authority in his house. In

Lucy, the mother enjoyed a friendship with one Sylvie, who had been sent to jail because of a fight she had had with another woman over a man, but the mother had to keep this friendship secret and could not have Sylvie in her home when her husband was present (24–25). He also forbade visits from Obeah doctors when he was home.

Mr. Drew had other faults. In "Antigua Crossings," Annie seemed to be always correcting her husband's manners and was disturbed that he kept his hat on and whistled at the table, but he paid no attention to her (50). He was also such a heavy chain smoker of Lucky Strikes that his fingers were stained brown (*Talk Stories* 238). When he was diagnosed with a heart problem, Annie Drew looked up heart diseases in her medical books and declared that his illness resulted from his chain smoking (*Talk Stories* 240). Though many of Kincaid's other writings suggest something less than the romantic idyll she paints of their marriage in *Annie John*, where the husband and wife always seem eager to please each other, all accounts suggest Annie Drew was a most attentive and loving wife, pampering her husband with all kinds of special porridges, milk drinks, custards, and other specially prepared foods when he was sick (see *Talk Stories* 240–41; *MG* 146).

Though Jamaica recalls her stepfather as old and unattractive (made especially so by his false teeth that clopped like a horse trotting in the street [*AJ* 32]), her many narratives of him suggest that she had a good relationship with him: She frequently speaks of his kindness to her, and notes that they were very close. Despite their warm relationship, she told me that she did not regard him as her father—"I thought of myself as fatherless." Later Kincaid contradicted herself, telling me, "I thought of him as my father." She also declares in *My Brother* that Mr. Drew was her father (103). She and her brothers, like everyone else, always called him "Mr. Drew." He had a shop, presumably connected with the house, and she would go in and watch him work, and he would tell her about his life, mainly about his being a cricketer (*Talk Stories* 238). Thus, despite Kincaid's jealous attachment to her mother, Kincaid recalls only pleasure in Mr. Drew's being a part of their family.

Once when he was advised to rest because of heart and digestive tract problems, Jamaica developed hookworm (because, her mother said, she walked around barefooted), and she and her father spent their days together, eating a delicious and nourishing breakfast cooked by Mrs. Drew and lying silently on their backs in his bed with their feet on the windowsill in the sun when Annie wasn't looking. Jamaica, who would spend these days reading, looked back on their sickness as "a delicious time" (*MG* 145–46). Annie came in regularly to check on them, made them take their feet out of the windowsill, gave them special preparations to speed their healing, and kissed them on their foreheads, while affectionately addressing them as her "two invalids" (*Talk Stories* 240–41). After they had a delicious lunch, father and daughter would walk to the Botanical Gardens and sit under the rubber tree (*MG* 146).

These sick-together episodes were to be repeated over and over as Mr. Drew was sick during most of Jamaica's childhood, and she suffered a variety of illnesses: typhoid fever, measles, chicken pox, whooping cough, and "some other terrible thing that you now never hear of." When she was around seven she almost died with the whooping cough, the basis, she told me, of her account of washing the photographs and of Ma Chess's visit in *Annie John,* where she presents herself as fifteen years old. In the Donna Perry interview, she says everything in *Annie John* happened, though she may have changed the time a little. In real life, her illness was whooping cough and she was seven, eight, or nine (depending upon the source); the bathing of the photographs happened when she was nine, she told Perry (494). In the *Annie John* account of the illness, the mother carefully pampered her, bathed her, prepared her food, soothed and comforted her, and sought every possible cure for her illness. In the afternoon, she would pick elderberries with her father and sit under a rubber tree in the Botanical Gardens,[4] where he would tell her stories about his own father, who had left him to work on the Panama Canal, leading Kincaid to think for many years that her stepfather's father "had built the Panama Canal single-handed except perhaps with the help of one or two people" (*Talk Stories* 241).

Even when he wasn't sick, Mr. Drew regularly took Kincaid for walks to the Botanical Gardens, and sometimes to the jetty, where he would chat with some of his friends. He also took her to performances of the Gilbert and Sullivan Society, which were the only cultural events she remembers going to. Perhaps her comments about him in *My Brother* say more about their relationship than any other: not knowing her biological father, she grew up regarding Mr. Drew as her father: "To me he was my father. He was a man I loved and had known very well, better than his own children knew him" (*MB* 103). This absolute declaration of love for Mr. Drew can be fully appreciated only when we understand that Kincaid often seems unable to determine whether she loves or hates most people in her life. Only her husband (before their divorce) and her children has she unequivocally said she loves.

Kincaid informs also that Mr. Drew worked as a carpenter on the American base in Antigua during World War II,[5] and he told her stories about the

Americans, picturing them as a "great" people who were smart, funny, and attractive. She says that from the time she was nine until she left Antigua, she started ending her prayers with "And please, God, let me go to America" (*Talk Stories* 58). This fascination with America was enhanced by her sense (at the time) that "any place that Negroes are is cool" (58).

Several of Kincaid's accounts of Mr. Drew reveal also her or the Kincaid character's empathy for the pain of his childhood. In *My Garden (Book):*, she says his mother left him when he was small and went to England and he never saw her again. She sent him a pair of shoes, but they were too big, and when he tried them again they were too small (147). His father went off to build the Panama Canal. The same account is given in *Lucy,* where he was five when she left, twelve when she sent the shoes, and seven when his father went off to build the Panama Canal (124). In *Annie John,* the parents left him to go to South America. In *Lucy* and *Annie John,* she gives the account of the grandmother who took care of him dying when he, then eighteen years old, was sleeping in her bed (*Lucy* 125; *AJ* 23). In *Annie John,* the Kincaid character is so distraught by what happened to him that she cries and cries, thinking that no one should have had to endure the suffering he did and noting that she loved him so much that she wished she had a mother she could give to him (24).

Mr. Drew was obviously a calm and comforting influence in the household, both for his stepdaughter and the three sons who would soon be born. Joseph, the oldest son, reminisced during our interview about the good relationship he and the other children enjoyed with their father.

Kincaid enjoyed constant physical expressions of love when she was growing up. Mr. Drew held her hand on their regular walks and often bent down to kiss her forehead when she was younger; later she grew so tall that she would have to bend down so he could reach her forehead (*AJ* 104). Every story, every lesson, every event was accompanied with hugs and kisses from her mother. When her mother told her stories, Jamaica would sit at her side and lean against her or crouch on her knees behind her mother and lean over her shoulder, her head leaning on her neck, enjoying the scents of her mother and the soft texture of her hair. We are led to believe that what cures the severe and long-lasting bout of depression that the Kincaid character suffers in *Annie John* after her mother insists that she is too big for some of the pampering to which she was accustomed is the arrival of her grandmother, Ma Chess, with whom she slept nestled like a little comma in her embrace (*AJ* 125–26). One might argue that Jamaica was always trying to recapture the emotional comfort of that fetal position, which is even suggested in the photographs with her daughter, Annie, in Cook's *Generations of Women,* where she nestles her head under her daughter's neck and on her shoulder.

When she was not employed outside the home, Annie Drew was a busy housewife and an immaculate housekeeper (*MB* 90). Her day started before dawn, but Annie *loved* the early morning. It was always reassuring to her to wake up in her own house, her husband softly snoring beside her and her daughter sleeping quietly, projecting an angelic image that denied the hobgoblin that possessed her body during her waking hours. She thrilled, too, to wake up to the Antiguan morning breeze wafting through her open windows, the Antiguan sun about to begin its journey through the sky, and the sounds of the Antiguan morning, entering one by one like the instruments in an orchestra warming up for an eagerly anticipated performance. She felt the thrill of a music aficionada in a concert hall when she heard first the crowing of her rooster—all day she thought she should get rid of that good-for-nothing rooster who did nothing but pick at her flower garden and annoy her hens, but she couldn't imagine not hearing his signal of a new day, the first sound of the morning's orchestra. The morning had quieted again when the northern flicker began hammering on the wood of the tree near her garden. Annie would smile at the industry of this little woodpecker. A new thrill emanated with, first, the tinkling sound of Mr. Jarvis driving his goats to pasture, and second, his whistling, which became audible as he passed by her house. She knew then without looking at the clock that it was 5:30. The next sound that entered the harmonies of the morning emanated from the home of her next-door neighbor, Mr. Gordon, who, as soon as Mr. Jarvis passed, opened his windows and doors and turned his radio on to a station playing American country-and-western music. Annie loved country-and-western—and Hank Williams, her favorite, was often singing.[6]

Every morning after Annie arose, got dressed, washed her face, brushed her teeth, and gargled (*AJ* 131), she went outside to prepare water for her family's baths, to which she would add oils, barks, flowers, and leaves that she had boiled in a large cauldron. She built a fire to heat Jamaica's water, but Mr. Drew preferred his bathwater with the chill of the morning. Every morning when she walked outside, she was reminded why she stayed in Antigua: if it were summer, the bright-yellow sun was already peeping through the black, black skies (no skies could be as black as Antigua's), turning them all orange and red, a spectacular vision on the world stage that seemed orchestrated for her alone. Before this enchanting view, she daily had to pause and say a little prayer for all of God's blessings and sometimes softly sing a few lines of "How

Great Thou Art," acclaiming the awesome wonder of the stars, the birds, the rolling thunder, the mountains, the wondrous universe that God had created and that she was blessed to enjoy each day.

At this moment when the rising sun painted variegated pictures in the morning sky, she knew she was the luckiest person in the world. She felt sorry for the people who didn't witness this glorious panorama. It was the highlight of the opening concert of her day. She was glad she wasn't one of those spoiled women who lived in the mansions hidden behind the hedges where she had sometimes cleaned, who screamed to a maid to close the shutters to keep the sun out of her bedroom, pulled the blanket over her eyes, and went back to sleep, all unaware of the drama she was missing.

Annie then took a minute to see what new miracles had unfolded in her garden. There was always some new flower blooming, adding to the magnificent colors she orchestrated in her garden. Just as certain was the appearance of a weed that needed to be plucked out (many years later a family member recalled that "she liked to pull up weeds" [January 16, 2009]). She might stoop for a whiff of her new flower or simply to admire its beauty. With no one else in the yard or stirring in her house, the world was Annie's, and she relished this feeling of a universe displaying its wonders only to and for her, still singing "How Great Thou Art!"

She was delighted to hear the house wren add his notes to the morning's orchestra, for she knew he would eat the garden pests that might otherwise destroy her flowers. She looked up at the cheeky bird, whose yellow breast and black top reflected the contrast of the sun and the still, black sky. Their songs brought the morning's orchestra nearly to its full complement.

Inspired, Annie went back into her house, set out Jamaica's vigorously polished shoes, and her painstakingly starched and pressed gray linen school uniform,[7] and bent down to lovingly awaken her daughter. Though it took some effort to coax her daughter out of the bed, Jamaica insisted that she had actually been aroused by Mr. Jarvis and his goats and the sound of her mother gargling. (In fact, Kincaid notes in one account of her Antiguan mornings [*Talk Stories* 92] that she still wakes up at five thirty.) If her daughter had wet the bed, Annie grabbed the sheets and put them to soak in a pot of water. If there were evidence that someone had tried to put an Obeah curse on her and Jamaica—evidence such as freshly dug-up dirt around their house, or bottles around the house with something in them—she would first have Jamaica wash her feet in the urine in her nighttime potty; then she would put Jamaica's urine in the pot with her parents' urine, bathe her own feet in it and then dribble it down the steps of the house (Cudjoe 229).

Annie cajoled her dawdling daughter to bathe and dress. Jamaica, who longed for the days when her mother bathed and dressed her, was at least grateful that after all of these grown-up changes she deplored, Annie would still magically reappear at just the necessary moment to wash her back for her.

After arousing her daughter, Annie then took her husband's bathwater in to him, pecked him on his forehead, and dashed off to the grocer to buy fresh bread and cheese.

Now that Mr. Drew and Jamaica were awake, Annie could sing along with the radio as she prepared a substantial breakfast for her family, so when she heard Hank singing "Your Cheating Heart," she chimed in ". . . will tell on you," and it was a duet all the way. She emoted dramatically when they sang "cry and cry," pain reverberating through her voice. The wide-eyed glares from her husband and daughter, clearly questioning her sanity, caused her to collapse with laughter but not to stop singing.

All the time, she was cutting and squeezing oranges for fresh juice or grating cheese and spreading it on their freshly baked bread. Eggs would be cooked to order for her husband and daughter. Fresh fruit or oatmeal might also be served. This would be finished off with chocolate milk made from the fresh milk that she had delivered to their house each morning and the chocolate that Ma Chess had made from the beans she grew. Annie insisted that breakfast was the most important meal of the day, and she was determined that her husband and daughter would begin their day with a nutritious and satiating repast. If it were a Sunday breakfast, or some other special day, Annie might also fix salt fish and antroba[8] and souse (*AJ* 135). If Jamaica and/or Mr. Drew were feeling ill, some special dish designed to cure their ailment would be prepared.

At seven o'clock, the last sound of the morning completed Annie's morning symphony: the Anglican church bell rang. That was the signal for Annie to turn on the BBC news and for the family to sit down to breakfast (*Talk Stories* 89–91). Breakfast, like every other meal, was a relaxed family affair, with everyone taking time to observe the appropriate manners. Jamaica had been taught to eat in the proper English manner, the food carefully balanced on the fork held in the left hand and the knife held in the right. However, when no one was looking, she ate the way she preferred—with her fingers ("On Seeing England"). Immediately after breakfast, Mr. Drew would leave for work.

Annie's care in preparing her daughter's breakfast was one of the many indications of her determination to provide the most healthful diet for Jamaica. She never allowed her to drink Coca-Cola, instead preparing fresh orange juice and lemonade with just a tiny bit of sugar. She made her eat lots of vegetables and gave her a purgative every Saturday. The only sweet Jamaica was allowed was an ice cream cone every Saturday night—"That was the *only* sugar I had." Annie knew the nutritional value of the breadfruit and was determined that her daughter would eat this fruit that she—and, according to Kincaid, every Antiguan child—hated (*MG* 44). (Elsewhere Kincaid insists, "No West Indian that I know has ever liked it" [*MG* 135].) Determined to get her daughter to eat breadfruit, Annie disguised it in different ways, making it at one time look like rice (*AJ* 84). "She used to have all these ideas about how you [maintain] strong teeth," Kincaid told me. "Actually everything she said is what a doctor would say now." Further, she not only insisted that her daughter eat healthful food and eat it properly but also that she chew each mouthful thirty-two times (*AJ* 136). And, finally, she fed her a daily teaspoon of cod-liver oil ("Biography" 96).

After she sent Jamaica off to school, Annie washed the dishes, made the beds, swept the yard, fed the chickens, gathered the eggs. If it were Monday, she washed her white clothes by hand, starched them, and carefully stretched them out on a stone heap to bleach in the sun. The stones would often fall down and have to be restacked (*MG* 43), causing additional work for the busy housewife. On Tuesdays, she washed her colored clothes and hung them on her clothesline. On the days that she ironed, she kept four irons heating over the fire to meticulously iron her husband's shirts and pants, her daughter's dresses, her sheets and linens. A latrine in the yard would be emptied on Wednesday night by the night-soil men, and the loud clapping of their horses and their loud talk would disturb everyone's sleep. They would also trample on things and leave the yard a mess that Annie would have to tidy the next day (*MG* 43).

Annie always managed to finish her morning chores in time to prepare lunch for her daughter, which included fresh milk brought by Miss Henry. Once Jamaica was sent back to school, Annie might do some shopping or help out a sick or needy neighbor before she picked up some fresh buns to serve her husband and daughter for afternoon tea.

Somehow she also found the time to make the clothes she and her children wore, to make their sheets and curtains, to embroider designs on their spreads (*AJ* 133), and to mend their clothes, never allowing anyone to go out with a missing button unreplaced or a drooping hem unrepaired. All this she would do as she sat on the sill of the doorway ("Biography" 96). The busy housewife looked forward to snatching an hour—or even a half hour—somewhere in the day, when she could sit in the shade of her trees or lie in her hammock and read the latest book she had gotten from the library. At some point during the day, this devoted gardener would find some time to plant, seed, or weed some part of her garden, delighting in the feel of the cool soil on her hands. Insisting on the healthiest and freshest of foods for her family, Annie might cut some vegetables and gather needed herbs for dinner. Then she tried to decide whether to kill a chicken and dress it to cook for her family's dinner or to purchase fish from the neighboring fishermen when they got back to shore, in which case she would select for each member of her family his or her preferred fish. She often paid a neighborhood boy to climb the tree to get a coconut for coconut milk. Then, with her daughter who had arrived from school following behind her, she would cook dinner outside in a clay pot over a hot fire. When I visited Kincaid's home in Bennington, she showed me the kind of clay pot in which Annie cooked. For a while Kincaid's family in Vermont would put charcoal in it, cover it with a wire, and use it to barbecue, but they stopped using it because the pots, which fall apart after a while, are no longer made in Antigua.

As soon as Mr. Drew arrived home, Annie would serve dinner, wash the dishes, check her daughter's homework, put her daughter to bed, polish her husband's shoes (*MG* 147, with some details from other works), put out a fresh glass of water for her husband's false teeth, which she was certain caused his digestive problems (*MG* 147), and massage her husband's aching limbs. As Mr. Drew's illness progressed, she had to gather herbs and barks and boil them in water for him since he preferred them to the prescriptions from the doctor (*AJ* 132).

Many of Annie's tasks were extremely difficult in a tropical region and in a home with no refrigerator or stove, no electric washing machine, dryer, iron, sewing machine, vacuum cleaner, can opener, juicer, knife, blender, or mixer. Kincaid asserts that her mother never stood still (*AJ* 25). And yet, Kincaid insists that though what she did was difficult, "she never made it seem hard." Finally, with all the day's tasks completed, she brushed her hair, cleaned her teeth, gargled her throat, washed her face, slipped into a fresh nightgown, and joined her "husband" in bed, ready to joyfully review the day with him—and provide other wifely duties if he were so inclined. She sought his advice on purchases she wanted to make or problems she was having with Jamaica; she shared some neighborhood gossip with him; she laughed at his accounts of his day, especially his problems with his ever-incorrigible partner, that "big oaf" (Kincaid's words) Mr. Otie; she whispered sweet nothings in his ear; she made him rejoice anew that he had won this beautiful, industrious, and sexy lady. She snuggled up close to him and immediately fell into a deep sleep, never stirring until it was time to begin a new day—unless she had a migraine, the only ailment suffered by this busy woman.

Annie's migraines were so terrible that they frightened her daughter, whose misbehavior and impertinence usually precipitated them. Kincaid often speaks of her fear when she was young that her mother might die while suffering an attack of one of her terrible headaches occasioned by something her miscreant daughter had done. One headache in particular was brought on when, during an argument about the Jamaica character's first communion in *Annie John,* she told her mother she wished she was dead. Annie Drew suffered such a bad headache that the usual remedies did not help and she was forced to walk the floor moaning all night. The young daughter suffered as much as her mother, fearing, whenever her mother was quiet, that she had died (*AJ* 118–19). Exactly the same incident is recalled by Lucy in *Lucy* (93–94), and appears in the introduction to Cook's *Generations of Women* (10).

While Annie carefully planned to find the time to provide every service to her family, there was one duty she farmed out. Jamaica was sent to a neighbor (Miss Roma) to have her hair braided. One wonders whether Annie, who was so attentive to her daughter, sent her because she simply didn't have the time needed to braid Jamaica's hair in the morning, or because, with her own straighter hair (the folk would say "good hair"), she did not know how to care for her daughter's less manageable hair (the folk would say "bad hair"). It may simply have been one onerous task that Annie preferred to avoid. Given her daughter's tendency to complain about any discomfort or inconvenience, it is quite possible that Jamaica squawked and squirmed throughout the ordeal and ended up being angry with whoever combed her hair and caused her the unavoidable pain. Kincaid insists that Annie was not prejudiced toward people with darker skin and kinkier hair, but numerous dark girls with kinky hair recognize the disappointments of their Anglo-appearing mothers that they did not inherit their "finer" features. Kincaid, or the Kincaid character, who "worshipped" (*AT* 73) her mother's beauty (this usually focuses on hair, lips, nose), often speaks of her own big nose and African features, and the Lucy character notes that the first time she ever considered that she "might" be beautiful was quite some time after her arrival in America (133).

Jamaica was also teased about and ashamed of her height as an adolescent: in *Annie John,* the Kincaid character wants her father to make a set of clamps that she could screw herself into to impede her growth (27).

Though Annie was ever the devoted housewife, whose husband was never expected (or ever known) to perform any domestic task (*MG* 147), she was never the intimidated wife. Once when she had a quarrel with Mr. Drew, he was so angry that he threw the food she had prepared for him on the ground and walked away. Imagine his shock when he came to the table for his next meal and uncovered a plate with that same food that she had picked up off the ground. She enjoyed sharing her account of this incident with her friends, describing her husband's consternation when he uncovered his dinner plate and laughing heartily at his shock. It was an oft-repeated tale that infuriated Mr. Drew and delighted Annie. For the most part, Annie and David Drew were probably the example par excellence of what Tim Hector called Antigua's "funny patriarchal society" where men rule but women run things (12).

Kincaid often talks of being involved in all of the household tasks with her mother, but accounts differ as to how much she really did. Annie Drew told Mariana Cook: "I would do everything and she would get the time to read. I don't know if she can still play music, but I sent her to learn to play. I didn't have anybody to raise me the way I did her, but it is to my own interest now that I'm old, because she's my support" (20).

Annie did indeed involve Jamaica in all of her activities, both as a part of her education and in an effort to be sure the child felt important and independent; to further those goals, Annie did assign her some minor responsibilities. Jamaica recalls in the interview with Leslie Garis that she went every Wednesday to register their outhouse at the Public Works Department, that she went each morning and evening to draw pails of water for their house, she wiped the soot from the lampshade and trimmed the wick of their kerosene lamp at night, and she went to buy more kerosene as needed. Elsewhere she recalls that each morning she swept the yard (*Talk Stories* 36) and went to the grocers to buy fresh bread, butter, and cheese (*Talk Stories* 91). Kincaid rarely mentions these minor tasks in her fiction. It seems clear that Jamaica was raised (at least until her brothers were born) as a pampered child.

Kincaid recalls these early days with her mother as heavenly: she relished having her mother feed her delicious, specially prepared foods (Annie was a superb cook); having her mother give her special baths; and following her mother around; and she delighted in the admiration people in the community showed for her mother. Annie made Jamaica feel so cherished and so important, including her in everything she did. She would give her a taste of what she was cooking and ask her opinion about it; she would ask Jamaica to get her some herbs from her garden when she was preparing a meal; she would have Jamaica carry the clothespins for her when she was hanging her wash on the line; she would have Jamaica help her clear the table after meals. And one of Jamaica's greatest pleasures was simply looking adoringly at her mother's beauty, caressing her, leaning over her shoulder and smelling her varied pleasant scents (lemon, sage, roses, bay leaves, etc.).

Unlike what many Western observers would conclude, Jamaica's early childhood was pleasant, even paradisiacal. Her little one-room house seemed very big to her when she was a child (*MB* 111), and yet she acknowledges in *My Garden (Book):* that every room in her Vermont house is larger than the house she grew up in (40). At first, as noted, they cooked their meals outside on the coal pot. Then, she writes, the family grew a little more prosperous and acquired a kerosene stove (*MG* 42). She said when they did things inside their house it was regarded as pretentious (43).[9] When Jamaica was ten she came into contact with cold air for the first time when a friend's parents got a refrigerator; she put her hand in the freezer, whereupon she concluded thenceforth that cold air is not natural but connotes man-made prosperity (*MG* 71).[10]

When Jamaica was growing up, her mother gave her her own little chicken. When the hen was ready to set, Annie put Jamaica's name on an egg under the hen, and the chicken that was born from that egg was hers; when her chicken grew up and laid eggs, her mother would say to her when she was eating, "And that's your egg." Finally, when it was time to kill the hen, that would be Jamaica's job.[11]

In her yard were a soursop tree, a clump of sugarcane that her mother tried to destroy with hot water, a dumps tree, a pawpaw tree, a breadfruit tree, a coconut tree, and a squash vine (*MG* 44). Reverend Lee noted that Mrs. Drew "planted things that would last and didn't require much care" and laughed about the fact that her breadfruit tree "turned out to be a breadnut tree. I think she cut it down after a while because something went wrong."

In contrast, the richer people in Antigua who lived in houses with more than one room had flower gardens; this ability to devote their backyards to "the sheer beauty of things" rather than feeding their families was a clear indication of their wealth, Kincaid explains in *My Garden (Book):* (133). One such family, she notes, had a casuarina tree that they decorated with colored lights at Christmas, something that fascinated Jamaica (*MG* 133). She recalls once when her family had a small amount of money they also had "a Christmas tree, a lonely spindly branch of a willow tree sitting in a bucket of water in our very small house" (*MG* 134).

Annie was a remarkable storyteller. Indeed, Tim Hector insists that Annie, whom he describes as "guardian of the memory of the clan," had an "elephantine" memory and that, as a storyteller: "I thought she was better than her daughter. . . . Annie Drew was a griot" (15). She would tell her daughter stories as she went about her daily activities. Nowhere is Chinua Achebe's assertion of the significance of the storyteller more prophetic than it would prove to be with Annie and her daughter: "It is the storyteller, in fact, who makes us what we are, who creates history. The storyteller creates the memory that the survivors must have—otherwise their surviving would have no meaning" (qtd. in Moyers 337).

Clearly some of Annie's stories were designed to teach her daughter a lesson, as when she told about throwing stones for a few days at a monkey who finally caught a stone and threw it back at her, leaving a scar on her face (*Lucy* 54; other versions are in *AJ* 70, and *AT* 44). Some stories were an effort to influence her daughter's behavior, such as when she tried to cajole Jamaica into revealing where her forbidden marbles were hidden by telling a story about walking miles with a snake concealed in a heavy load of figs she was carrying on her head, or when she told Jamaica how as a child she [Annie] obeyed her mother unquestioningly. Many of her stories were devised to get her to eat something Annie considered good for her such as telling her about the man who ate cornmeal every day and when he died at almost a hundred years old, he looked rosy and new and his insides were a beautiful yellow like boiled cornmeal ("Biography" 94). Others were simply a sharing of her history, her family, her relationships, and events regarding Jamaica. One of Kincaid's fondest memories is of her mother regularly going through the trunk she had brought with her from Dominica, in which she now had carefully packed mementos of her daughter's life: her crib sheets, the beautiful clothes she had made for her, her first hat, her first basket, her first notebook, the photographs she had had made, the school report cards and certificates of merit, etc. The Jamaica character in *Annie John* observes: "No small part of my life was so unimportant that she hadn't made a note of it, and now she would tell it to me over and over again" (22). Not only did Kincaid relish her mother's stories, she absolutely "loved the sound of her voice."

Another aspect of Annie's stories that had an impact on her daughter was that her stories were true: "They were never—again something that I perhaps owe her—they were never pure invention. They were always grounded in something true. And the only thing that was elaborate was the way she told it, transmuting it, transforming it, but it was always essentially true." Though there was nothing particularly dramatic about Annie's choice of words or even her delivery, there was nonetheless a certain drama to her stories, Kincaid told me: "I don't remember her being a person of incredibly dramatic gestures, though she did things—they seemed—they had drama to them, but they weren't made up, they were just really her. She really was a kind of grand person in a kind of Greek literature way."

Her mother's favorite anecdotes (of her brother John's death, of her confrontation with a monkey, of the snake in the basket on her head, of leaving Dominica and sailing to Antigua, of Mr. Potter's dereliction, of the efforts of one of the women who had borne a child for Mr. Drew to kill them [Annie and Jamaica], of Jamaica's bedwetting, and of countless other events in Jamaica's life) appear over and over in Kincaid's fiction. Her mother's tales are clearly the source of her literature. During an interview with Selwyn Cudjoe, Kincaid recounted a story her mother had told her, concluding, "If I haven't [written about it], I will have to write about it" (230). Kincaid has often acknowledged her mother's influence on her, declaring on one occasion, "The way I became a writer was that my mother wrote my life for me and told it to me" (O'Conner 6); and she told Cudjoe, "The way I am is solely owing to her" (219); "the fertile soil of my creative life is my mother" (222). In "What Have I Been Doing Lately," the Jamaica character thinks about saying in response to the question, "And just what have you been doing lately?," "I have been listening carefully to my mother's words, so as to make a good imitation of a dutiful daughter" (*AT* 43).

Indeed, it sometimes seems as if this is what the author has been doing throughout her career. And yet often Kincaid denies that Annie had any influence on her development as a writer and attributes her success rather to Michael O'Donoghue, George W. S. Trow, and William Shawn.

Though Jamaica's accounts of these early years before her brothers' births were largely paradisiacal, there is much to suggest that everything was not quite as much a paradise for the mother, who was very protective of Jamaica, responding vehemently to any threat to her recalcitrant daughter, as illustrated in this anecdote Kincaid related to me:

> I think I told this story of getting home late from school, and to hide that I had been doing something she didn't want me to do, I made up a story that

> the science teacher had threatened me with a beating for something. And my mother didn't say anything. But the next day she insisted on walking me to school, and she took me to the science lab, and there was poor Mr. Flaxen [?], and she said to him, "This is my daughter. If you *ever* lay a hand on her (and she took a cutlass out of her bag and said), I'll cut off your legs." And then just walked away. [laughter].

Jocelyn Reid also recalls a similar incident, telling me that once Jamaica came home from school and told her mother that Mr. Maynard had kicked her: "Ms. Annie went to school and kicked Mr. Maynard on *his* leg" (January 16, 2009). Dame Gwendolyn Tonge, who told me she taught Jamaica at St. John's Girls Government School when she was in the third standard, said that Jamaica was "very bright," but she really didn't remember many details about her: what she did remember was that "the mother [Mrs. Drew] used to come up to the school and quarrel. She took her out of that school and enrolled her in a private secondary school—T. O. R. Memorial High School."[12]

Jocelyn Reid, insisting, "Ms. Annie would always stand up for Elaine," recalled an incident when Jamaica and her friend Rosita went to the home of a Black lady who gave Jamaica a U.S. dollar to divide with Rosita. However, when they got back home, Jamaica told Ms. Annie something, and Ms. Annie grabbed a stick and hit Rosita, hurting her so badly that she had to go to Barbados to keep from losing her eye. Jocelyn wasn't sure what Jamaica told Ms. Annie, "but whatever Elaine said, Ms. Annie always took her side" (January 16, 2009).[13] She went on to note that "if someone reported something bad Jamaica had done, Ms. Annie would beat a pillow and tell Jamaica to cry, so that the tattletale would think she was being punished."

Despite her reliance on her medical books and her focus on the use of diet to cure illnesses, Annie Drew continued to believe in and turn to Obeah to provide additional protection for her daughter. When either Annie or Jamaica was threatened by one of Mr. Drew's former women, when some sore wouldn't heal, when something bad or unexpected happened, Annie would often prepare a special bath with all sorts of herbs and concoctions that her Obeah woman had recommended or that she had learned from Ma Chess. When her daughter was suspected of having weak kidneys, she took her to swim in the sea to remedy the problem (*AJ* 42). When her daughter was ill, as described in "The Long Rain" section of *Annie John*, she consulted the local Obeah woman, Ma Jolie, who had to come when Mr. Drew was away because he did not sanction Obeah (*AJ* 110). Ma Jolie made cross marks on varied areas of the child's body, lit special candles over the head of her bed, burned incense, and placed smaller candles and scraps of paper with the names of people who might have tried to harm her in a basin of oil. She pinned a sachet in the child's nightie and left some vials of fluids to be rubbed on her body. Her mother at first put them on the shelf with the prescriptions from the medical doctor, but noting her husband's disapproval, she later put them behind the doctor's medications (*AJ* 116–18).

Finally Ma Chess, who knew ten times more than Ma Jolie, had to be sent for. The fact that she arrived on a day when there was no steamer due and left in the same way bespoke her power. The details of her Obeah treatment are not given in *Annie John.* We are only told that she slept with the child, either on the floor or in her bed, where she lay curled like a bigger comma into which the child fit. She did all of the personal caring for the child that her mother used to do. With Ma Chess, the Jamaica character again enters the protective womb, surely the Eden that she desires to return to with her mother. The long rain finally stopped, the child recovered, and Ma Chess left. When the Jamaica character is about to leave Antigua at the end of the novel, her mother sends her underclothes and her jewelry to the Obeah woman so that she could do something to protect her from evil spirits or any other calamity she might encounter in her travels (134).

As Jamaica got older, her mother shared other Obeah cures with her. In *My Garden (Book):*, Jamaica notes that her mother and her friends used the white-head bush in potions they used for abortions (119). Her mother also told her that years ago the cancanberry bush (which Jamaica called a chinaberry) was used to make a paste to cure children's thrush (*MG* 137). Clearly Mrs. Drew, like Toni Morrison in "Rootedness," values "discredited knowledge, . . . other ways of knowing things . . . superstition and magic" ("Rootedness" 342)

Annie Drew's folk belief in signs was something of a shock to Connie Rabinowitz during her first visit with Annie. When a grasshopper hopped into the room, Annie observed, "You know, if it's green it's money; and if it's brown it's death." "She had this way of talking," Rabinowitz observed. It is important to note that while Annie believed in Obeah, sought help from Obeah practitioners, and was careful to avoid actions believed to have dire consequences, she was not, like her daughter, traumatized by bad signs. When, for example, the two of them were in the graveyard in 1993 seeking Mr. Drew's gravesite and a lizard jumped on Annie Drew's skirt and started climbing up, she nonchalantly brushed it off, calmly noting that she hoped it wasn't a dead person trying to tempt her to join him, and declaring, "Dem people no get me, you know." Observing, a terrified Kincaid was ready to scream and run away (*MB* 123–24).

One might argue that Kincaid was introduced to superstitions, to Obeah, to alternate belief systems before she was born. Annie taught her daughter early on to observe proper caution regarding the dead, warning her about people she knew who had been followed by dead people who wanted the living to join them. When the Jamaica character in *Annie John* views the body of a humpbacked girl she had known, she curled her fingers up tight because she knew that if she made a mistake and pointed at the corpse, her fingers might immediately "rot and drop off" (11). After viewing the humpbacked girl, she rushed home envisioning frightening scenes of the humpbacked girl appearing to her and tempting her to go swimming or to have some delicious fruit, thus causing her own death (12).

Even as a mature writer in the United States, Kincaid still accepts that the dead reappear. Comparing the neat graveyard in New England with graveyards in Antigua, she writes: "Death is just another way of being, and the dead will not stay put, and sometimes their actions are more significant, more profound than when they were alive, and so no square structure made out of concrete can contain them" (*MG* 69). She insists that though Dr. Woodworth (who owned the house she and her husband purchased in North Bennington and was always remembered for chopping wood to burn in a fireplace) does not haunt the house or the room in which he died, which is now her study, every winter the smell of smoke occurs in his room (*MG* 41). In "Holidays," the speaker (evidently the adult Kincaid in New York) concludes: "I have many superstitions. I believe all of them" (*AT* 31).

Annie John pictures the Kincaid character's stepfather, like her grandfather, as one who rejected Obeah. When Ma Chess came to assist in her granddaughter's cure during her illness in *Annie John,* the father kept out of Ma Chess's way—not because he didn't like her but because they had different views of the world (126). However, it appears that as time passed, Mr. Drew came to have more faith in Obeah than in medical science. In at least one account, the stepfather takes the medicine from the doctor only because his wife insisted, and he preferred a preparation made from elderberries (*Talk Stories* 241). Later, when he became ill in *Annie John,* he chose to drink the herbs his wife boiled for him rather than take the doctor's prescriptions (132). And when he was ill, Kincaid tells us in *My Garden (Book),* he went to the Botanical Gardens and picked several plants to treat his illness (147).

It was very important for Mrs. Drew to give her daughter the best education possible. She would have preferred private school and did indeed enroll her in a couple of private schools, such as Mr. Henry's School, but only for brief periods, because she could not afford the tuition. Kincaid has complained that her mother would send her to certain schools and then be unable to buy her any schoolbooks, adding that by borrowing other girls' books, she still managed to come in first (Cook 20). Thus, for the most part, Jamaica went to public schools, though because she was illegitimate, she could not attend the Antigua Girls High School. Indeed (though Kincaid never mentions this), illegitimate children could not even be baptized on the days legitimate children were baptized in most Antiguan churches. Though at that time 80 percent of the children in Antigua and Barbuda were born out of wedlock, it was not until 1986 that, thanks to Prime Minister V. C. Bird, himself born illegitimately, laws were passed to provide illegitimate children equal rights. As a result of these laws, Antiguan men can now easily acknowledge their illegitimate children, who can then inherit from their father's estates and enjoy other rights previously denied them (see Lazarus-Black).

Jamaica has often told of how her mother sent her to the Moravian School when she was only three and a half years old, directing her to say she was five. She was supposed to come home after a half day, but she was so troublesome when she came home that her mother soon was compelled to leave her at school all day (Cudjoe 217). From there she went to Points School. Then, in 1956, Jamaica was enrolled in the Antigua Girls School (not to be confused with the unattainable Antigua Girls High School) and then the Ottas School, in the village of Ottas. She later came in second on the island examination and won a scholarship to Princess Margaret School (Cudjoe 217), which had been established by V. C. Bird to provide a good education to children who were smart but were also illegitimate.

Annie went to great pains to prepare her daughter for school. If it were a new school, her mother would take her for a visit before the school year began so that she could meet her teachers and would be familiar with her new school. Before school she would be given a large, healthful breakfast. Annie made her school uniforms, and Jamaica began each year with a new uniform, hat, shoes, book bag, notebook, and books (except when finances did not allow the purchase of books). At lunchtime a specially prepared meal was waiting for her. If anything about Jamaica's health suggested a need for some special treat during the day, her mother would prepare it and bring it to her at school. When the Jamaica character in *Annie John* asked for glasses, falsely complaining that her eyes felt weak because she wanted to emulate a girl about whom she had read in the *Schoolgirl's Own Annual,* the doctor insisted that she didn't need glasses but that carrot juice would strengthen weak eyes; her mother every day grated and squeezed carrots and brought a glass of juice to her at school during her recess (*AJ* 141).

Kincaid's brilliance was apparent throughout her schooling, and her mother was proud of her achievements. She would show her report card to people but was always so ashamed of the fact that "'If only she would behave' was always at the end of it." Sometimes the mother in *Annie John* was so upset at accounts of such poor behavior in school that she could not flaunt her report card among her friends and would burst into tears (*AJ* 79).

It is clear from all accounts that Annie Drew very meticulously planned to properly teach and raise her daughter, providing her an education that extended beyond the schools. Much of this raising was based upon her own upbringing. Kincaid notes in *My Garden (Book):* that her mother trained her to do things as she had been taught to do them (43). She sent her to learn to sew, actually apprenticing her to a seamstress, Miss Doreen (called Miss Dulcie in *Annie John* [138]), more, it seems, to be sure that she would know how to sew, make clothes for herself, and items for her household than to prepare her for a vocation. She also sent her to take piano lessons and to be trained in proper etiquette. She later made her take typing and shorthand for two years, insisting, "You never know when it might come in handy" (NY 72). When her daughter was six, the mother began her training in financial matters, taking the daughter to the bank to open her own account with the sixpence she had received for her birthday. Every Saturday thereafter she was given money that she would take to the Barclays Bank and deposit in her own account.

Jocelyn Reid also reinforced the fact that Ms. Annie always wanted the best for Elaine. Jocelyn used to go to sewing class: "I could sew, and my mother planned to get me a sewing machine. She told Ms. Annie about it. Ms. Annie went and got a sewing machine for Elaine, even though Elaine could not sew. So Elaine got her sewing machine before I got mine" (January 16, 2009).

Annie's efforts initially seemed to have ended in failure. Most of Jamaica's time with Miss Doreen was spent cleaning up and running errands; the piano teacher sent her home after she caught Jamaica stealing her plums (*AJ* 28; Kin/Dance); the etiquette instructor sent her home when she made farting sounds when practicing curtsies (*AJ* 28); Jamaica never learned how to type or take shorthand, both of which she hated. All of these special efforts at refining and enriching her daughter's life and possibilities ended, at least from Jamaica's perspective, as the brothers took precedence in her family's life.

As a mother and wife, Annie was very concerned about projecting the image of a proper British family. At home the daughter was required to speak the King's English. Kincaid said in an *Essence* interview: "I was brought up to be sexless and well behaved [exasperated]. I was supposed to be full of good manners and good speech. Where the hell I was going to go with it I don't know" (90).

Perhaps Annie Drew knew, though. It was precisely that training that impressed Michael Arlen and his wife, who hired Jamaica as their au pair and made it possible for her to later move comfortably in elite circles in the United States and Antigua, according to someone who knew her when she was with the Arlens (April 23, 2009). Annie's efforts, which Kincaid clearly viewed as a foolish elitist endeavor to model her after the British colonial power, were probably the sort of thing Rabinowitz had in mind when she talked of Mrs. Drew's snobbishness. Dr. Ramsey was more generous in his description of such behavior: "Probably she desired to elevate herself." He went on to describe for me the woman who works as his maid and messenger, who does not want anyone to know about her job: "She has a boyfriend and she said this guy doesn't want to marry her because she's a cleaner, and therefore she tries to conceal what she does from others." Jocelyn Reid told me that she did not find Ms. Annie uppity, clearly contradicting the fictional portrayal of her in "The Red Girl," where the mother does not allow her daughter to play with the poor, dirty, and unkempt Red Girl, based on this same Jocelyn Reid (January 16, 2009).

The ever-perceptive mother in *Annie John* noticed immediately when her daughter's first period came. She calmed Jamaica's concerns, lightheartedly told her about her own first period, assured her that this was a normal step in growing up, and showed her how to prepare and wear the necessary cloth between her legs. Thus Kincaid set off to school, admittedly a bit uncomfortable with her cloth growing heavier and heavier during the day, but confident enough to educate her classmates about what was happening to her. Her experience was mercifully different from that of many young girls, who are frightened, ashamed, and completely unaware of what is happening to them when they see the blood. Undoubtedly Annie had told her beforehand what to expect and had explained that she should come to her at the first sign of her period. When the daughter went home from school, the concerned mother rushed to meet and embrace her (*AJ* 51–53).

Annie not only prepared her for her period, but she also explained to her how to bring about a missed period, though she would not admit that she was giving her directions for aborting: the Jamaica character in *Lucy* explains that her mother gave her information designed, she said, to help her strengthen her womb, but that both of them knew that it wouldn't really be a weak womb that she would need to treat if she missed a period (*Lucy* 69–70).

Certainly, most important on Annie's agenda was preparing her daughter to *avoid* pregnancy. Jamaica was not allowed to date, and the only young man who was allowed to visit her was Lindsay, a friend who liked to read and with whom she exchanged books. It wasn't long, however, before Annie became suspicious of him and prohibited his visits, ordering him to go to the library for his books (*MB* 135). Annie no doubt felt herself doubly justified when Lindsay, whom she suspected of trying to seduce Jamaica by pretending to want to borrow books from her, ended up in the AIDS ward with her brother Devon (*MB* 136–37). Kincaid told me that had she stayed in Antigua, she would have had a boyfriend whom she sneaked out to see and by whom she would probably have become pregnant; she and her child would have ended up living at her parents' house; "and then it would have been a *horrible* time together!" Kincaid's oldest brother, Joseph, insisted his mother's strictness in raising Jamaica and not allowing her to have boyfriends is the reason she is now regarded as such a "decent and respectable person."

Kincaid was adamant in her emphasis of her mother's protection of herself and her daughter from any kind of abuse or sexual molestation, declaring: "My mother would kill a man who laid a hand on her. *Never*! Oh, my god, no, no, she'd never put up—and she would never put up with anyone hurting us!" The only incident Kincaid remembered that hinted at any kind of unwanted sexual misbehavior toward her took place when she visited with the daughter of her mother's friend who lived in the country:

> Kincaid: Anyway this friend had a daughter. The daughter and I slept in the same bed, and one morning, the father in that house got into bed with us and pressed himself against me—and I can still remember the feeling of his erect penis against my bottom—it didn't penetrate or anything. But, I *told* my *mother*! and she never spoke to them again. [pause, reflecting] And I don't remember what she said to me, but I knew that it wasn't something I should be ashamed of or it wasn't *my* fault or anything. I just told her.
>
> Dance: She would never have allowed you to be exposed again.
>
> Kincaid: Never, never!

In fact, Jamaica was so unaware of the realities of sexual molestation that she has the Jamaica character envy a childhood friend who was being regularly molested by Mr. Thomas, one of the fishermen who used to bring her family fish: she is disappointed that Mr. Thomas chose her friend Myrna rather than her to put his finger in her vagina. The Jamaica character would gladly have given him coins for the privilege rather than take coins from him as Myrna did (*Lucy* 105). Kincaid's writings provide no indication that she was ever sexually exploited by the men in the families for whom she worked. Rather, if we accept her frequent assertions that her writings are autobiographical, the men were probably more likely to experience sexual advances from Kincaid or the Kincaid character than the reverse. Xuela routinely seduces the husbands of the families with whom she lives and works, requiring sexual acts that Kincaid characters prefer, such as sucking her breast and cunnilingus. She tells us she would stand naked and "order" Philip to get on his knees and perform cunnilingus until she was completely satisfied (*Auto* 145). Lucy shocks Lewis and Mariah by telling them of her dream that she was naked and Lewis was pursuing her throughout the house (*Lucy* 14–15).

Annie Drew's efforts to protect her daughter from sexual molestation and early pregnancy were neither unfounded nor uncommon. The history of Caribbean women is one of sexual violation beginning with the early colonizers, an issue treated extensively in Patricia Joan Saunders's *Alien-Nation and Repatriation,* where she notes terms such as "conquering 'virgin territories'" and "'penetrating' deep into the 'heart of darkness'" (91), which, in her words, "testify to the historical connections between women's bodies and the landscape under siege" (91–92). She goes on to point to seventeenth-century legislation that "enacts the 'efficient management' of rebellious blacks through the forceful invasion of women and children who are singled out as the recipients of any treatment that is the 'pleasure and will' of those exercising the law" (92). Unfortunately this casual exploitation of Black women continued to be common in West Indian society long after the end of slavery and even colonialism, resulting in a society, at least among the lower classes, in which young women were routinely impregnated by White military men and tourists, by upper-class White and Black men for whom they worked, by adult males in their homes and neighborhood, and/or by young males in their neighborhoods, and then left to fend for themselves and their children.[14] So common was the dilemma that one of the best-known Caribbean sociological studies is titled *My Mother Who Fathered Me* (by Edith Clarke). Clearly, as is attested to by a large portion of the body of West Indian literature and folklore, one of every West Indian mother's primary goals was to protect her female child from being another victim of this horrendous situation, the irony of which is frequently noted by Kincaid and others. Kincaid asserts in *My Brother* that Antiguans are at one and the same time puritanical and promiscuous: they will praise a young girl for being a virgin at the same time that they will not ostracize her for having ten children by as many different men (*MB* 41; Annie would often pride herself in protecting her daughter from having ten children by ten different men). Later Jamaica Kincaid would understand her mother's fears for her daughter and her efforts to protect her from selfish men whose only goal was to use young women for sexual satisfaction, men who would have been a grave danger to her (*MB* 69). As appalled as she is at the notion of such men, Kincaid's main response here is not gratitude that her mother helped to save her from a danger but anger that her mother's cautions prevented her from developing a healthy and normal sexuality, a problem that she says persists until today (*MB* 69).

Later, in the United States, when the Kincaid character in *Lucy* worries about the possibility of becoming pregnant, she knows she couldn't go to her mother for help, declaring that she preferred death to having her mother see her unmarried and pregnant (70).

One of Kincaid's harshest satires of her mother's efforts at raising her daughter is "Girl," her first published story and the opening story of *At the Bottom of the River,* which consists entirely of the mother's cautions to her daughter, many of them containing the usual warnings and directions for a daughter: how to wash the clothes, how to cook, how to keep herself clean, how to dress, how to walk and talk and act like a lady, how to avoid associating with the wrong males, how to sew, how to iron a man's clothes, how to clean a house, how to entertain (including setting a table for tea) and socialize, how to avoid Obeah spells, how to avoid the wrong kind of males, how to love a man, how to bully a man, how to abort a child, and how to allocate funds (5). Constantly in these warnings is the harsh suggestion that the daughter seems bent on becoming a "slut" and not the proper lady her mother is determined to make of her.

"The Letter from Home" is reminiscent of "Girl" except that the speaker here seems to be an adult Kincaid, now herself a mother cataloguing her jobs similar to those that her mother had taught her in the earlier story: milking cows, churning butter, storing cheese, baking bread, brewing tea, laundering clothes, caring for children, shedding her skin, the latter of which suggests that the Kincaid character has become the soucouyant (*AT* 37).[15] Other lines that recall her earlier upbringing allude to chewing her food thirty-two times, and express the fear that the children will bear their mother's name (38).

One of the most painful episodes for the daughter in *Annie John* occurs after she, taking the long way home, walks through town and bumps into a group of boys who tease her in the malicious way that adolescent boys often taunt girls. Among them she recognizes the son of one of her mother's friends with whom she used to play when her mother and her friend got together; so to relieve her embarrassment she walks up to him, offers her hand, and begins a polite conversation, as his friends continue to laugh at her. She offers her hand again as she walks away, evoking even more malicious laughter from the boys. When she gets home, her mother asks her why she is late, and she makes up a lie about being kept after school to prepare for her final exams. Her mother explodes at this lie, declaring that she had witnessed her acting like a slut with the boys, and she keeps repeating the word "slut" over and over until the daughter retorts, "like mother like daughter" (102). Their bitter quarrel leaves both of them pained and broken, suffering the divide that has come between them and that neither can ford.

Kincaid's writings suggest that the mother had some reason to fear that her daughter might become what she called a "slut": At fourteen, the Jamaica character in *Lucy* sucks the tongue of a boy named Tanner (43). Later she encourages him to suck her breast (49–50). Then she regularly meets another boy in the library and they pet (50–51). She discloses that Tanner was the first boy with whom she did everything that it was possible do with a boy (82). In "Putting Myself Together" she says that on her twenty-sixth birthday she "felt old and used up" (93). At the time she "slept with a man who used to buy me dinner" (94); she adds that after that the list of men she kissed and did other things with became long (94)—later she says that during her young days in New York, there were so many "people who kissed me and did other things" that she is unable to remember their names (100), seemingly confirming her mother's dire predictions in *At the Bottom of the River* (95) and *Annie John*. In a *Salon* interview with Dwight Garner, Kincaid told him she went to a Halloween party as Josephine Baker, completely naked after removing her coat, with bananas around her waist. It is no exaggeration to say that often Kincaid (according to her writings) and the Kincaid characters (especially Lucy and Xuela) delight in acting the part of the "slut" as Kincaid always delighted in doing the opposite of what her mother desired—and shocking everyone. Lucy tauntingly writes her mother to inform her that she was enjoying her life in the United States "as a slut" (128).

Annie raised her children in the Ebenezer Methodist Church and sent them regularly to church activities, though at the time she was not herself an ardent churchgoer. She raised them to say grace before they ate and say prayers when they went to bed, not so much an indication, Kincaid suggests, of great religious devotion as an effort to *civilize* them. Kincaid does not often mention her mother quoting the Bible or calling down's God's wrath on them. However, her mother does tell her after she helped her brother recover from AIDS that God would bless her for bringing him the AZT from the United States (*MB* 72). In her later years, Annie became very active in the Beacon Light Church of the Nazarene, and her speech thereafter was more religious. In her letter to Sharon Chacko, written when she was almost seventy-nine years old, she twice wishes Chacko God's blessings, and she thanks God she can still move around. Joseph explained that his mother left the Ebenezer Methodist Church because at one event in 1979 her minister, Reverend Hodge, shook all the dignitaries' hands, but when he got to her, he passed her by: "She left the church at that moment and joined Beacon Light." The current minister of Beacon Light, Reverend Rosa Lee, recalled that when Mr. Drew died in 1975, Annie Drew was unable to get a minister to conduct his funeral because he was not a regular member of a church.[16] Reverend Lee's husband held the funeral at Beacon Light, and "then she started coming to the church. I don't remember when she started, but I know she became a member in 1980." The two accounts by Joseph Drew and Reverend Lee are not necessarily contradictory—one might assume that the slight by the minister of Ebenezer was the final straw that led her to actually join the other church that she had already started attending.

Kincaid attributes to her mother the lack of any feeling of racial inferiority. Kincaid insists that though she knew colonialism, though she knew the exclusive racist clubs in Antigua, such as the Mill Reid Club, where Mr. Potter worked, and though she knew American racism, she never even considered (much less embraced) the idea that she was inferior. She always knew, thanks to her mother, that people who behaved in a racist way were clearly the inferior ones. Despite this disclaimer, however, the fury with which Kincaid lashes out in *A Small Place* at some of the racist individuals and institutions in Antigua and elsewhere suggests that she is not untouched and unaffected by racism.

Annie helped to develop Kincaid into a confident person. Kincaid recalls that her mother used to tell her that she had Ma Chess's feet and hands—feet with a very high instep and long fingers, something she said was inherited from Ma Chess's mother and from the Carib people because they are mountain climbers.[17] Thus, thanks to her mother, Kincaid acknowledged, she grew up with a sense of being special.

Yet, as she was growing up, Jamaica was often teased by other children, who mockingly called her "Daddy Longlegs" (Paravisini-Gebert 4) and routinely beat her (*MB* 77). She told Ferguson that she often came home with her clothes torn and her face scratched up. Her mother would try to make her fight to protect herself, but Jamaica would only cry (Ferguson, "A Lot" 22). In one case, her classmates, annoyed that Jamaica was usually given the teacher's prize as the best student of the week, picked her up and tried to flush her down the toilet, "Feet first, thank God" (*Talk Stories* 222–23). Annie always fiercely defended her child, and when she once discovered a group of girls huddled over and flailing her daughter, she gave the girl punching her daughter a more severe whipping (*MB* 77).

Some of Kincaid's most vivid and pleasant memories of her interaction with her mother are of the sea; some of her most vivid and painful memories are also of the sea. While her mother was perfectly at home in the sea and relied on it not only for relaxation and pleasure but also for cures, Jamaica has, she told me, very recondite feelings about the sea (Kin/Dance). In "Antigua Crossings" the narrator confesses that despite her mother's efforts to teach her to swim between the ages of two and ten, she never learned because she was too fearful of the sea (48).

Kincaid writes several scenes of horrors in and of the sea. Madame LaBatte in *Autobiography* almost drowned when she went swimming and never went in the water again (75). Unlike his father, Nathaniel Potter, a fisherman who loved the sea, Mr. Potter feared and hated the sea, his mother having walked out into the sea and drowned (*MP* 12, 114) at Rat Island, where Kincaid's mother tried to teach her to swim (*MP* 75). In *The Autobiography of My Mother,* the house of Xuela's father, Alfred, had a view of the Dominica Sea, which is described as a black tomb (185). When Alfred was eight, his father drowned in the sea on his way back to Scotland (195). Xuela tells us that Alfred had no sense of the sea as beautiful, inspiring, and comforting, for, being mixed African and European, he was both the vanquished and the conqueror, and the sea reminded him of both—the conqueror, with his unending desire for more, and the vanquished, who experiences incessant pain and despair that can never be avenged or eradicated (191–92). Despite the echoes of colonialism in this passage of victors and losers, the powerful and the weak, European and African, there is no doubt here that through

Xuela Kincaid is reflecting her attitude toward her mother when she concludes her reflections: "Those who have lost are never hardened to their loss; they feel it deeply, always, into eternity" (193).

Though Kincaid has often said she is "terrified" of the water, the fact is, she explained to me, that she is not so much afraid of the water as she is of the feeling of having nothing under her feet: "As soon as it gets about my head, I panic. I love swimming in a pool that's no more than five feet deep." In his introduction to *Talk Stories,* Ian Frazier relates how Kincaid bravely followed him into a deep and fast river in Vermont (xiv), but in our conversation she pooh-poohed that as "just a little river with trout in it. It's not like a big sea." Nonetheless the height of fantasy occurs near the end of "At the Bottom," when the Jamaica character calmly enters the sea, which has no currents and is warm: "I moved through it as if I had always done so. . . . How good this water was. How good that I should know no fear" (79).

In one of the most moving episodes in *Annie John,* the Jamaica character writes an essay at school that is so impressive that her classmates are moved to tears, and her teacher makes it a part of their class library. It is a moving account of her mother's taking her to a remote part of Rat Island to swim naked in the sea as a means of strengthening her weak kidneys. Her mother, an expert swimmer fully at home in the sea, would swim around with her daughter lying on her back, her arms around her neck. She would sometimes sing a song to her, and at other times they were quiet, with the child placing her ear to her mother's neck, imagining that all the sounds of nature that she was hearing were coming from inside her mother. After their swim together the child would lie in a protected area on the beach and watch her mother dive and swim farther out in the sea.

One day the child was distracted by noisy passengers on three passing tourist ships, and when she then looked back for her mother, she could not find her. For a while the frantic child was terrified at the thought that her mother was lost. Then when she finally saw her calmly sitting on a rock, oblivious to her daughter's panic, the child was overwhelmed at her inability to get to her mother and embrace her, recognizing that only the mother could reunite them again. When the mother returned to the shore and saw that her child had been afraid and crying, she embraced her and assured her that she would never leave her. Later the child kept having nightmares that her mother was on that rock and never came back. Sometimes she dreamed that the father would join her, and the two of them would laugh together and amuse themselves on the rock. When the child told her mother about her dreams, according to the story the child wrote, her mother hugged and kissed her and offered her comforting assurances. However, the child admits that the ending assurances were made up and based on what used to happen in the old days—that in fact when she actually told her mother about her dreams, her mother simply warned her about eating unripe fruit before she went to bed (*AJ* 42–45).

This episode, like so many in Kincaid's work, recounts an actual event and illustrates the manner in which the author manipulates events and revises the reality (as she does the ending here) to serve her purposes. She confessed to Allan Vorda that from childhood, "I was a liar. I lied all the time. . . . I was incapable of just describing something as it really happened. . . . So that is essentially what my fiction is. It really happened, but the details became exaggerated" ("An Interview" 16–17). This episode also illustrates Jamaica's awe, dread, and fear of the sea, her inability to cope with the loss of the mother, and her jealousy at her mother's attentions to anyone else. This episode is one to which Kincaid returns time after time. In *Mr. Potter,* she notes that she still falls into nothingness when she recalls her fear when her mother dived and was lost to her sight at Rat Island and she feared she had died (*MP* 76; in the later version, the mother's disappearance is the result of a dive rather than the daughter's distraction by the ship).

It is interesting to note how *Annie John,* Kincaid's first clearly autobiographical novel, is a prototype of almost all of Kincaid's writing, focusing on the mother, the jealousy of others who have her attention, the anger at her distancing herself from Jamaica and not giving her her full attention, her fear of losing her mother, and the importance of the sea to her mother—the sea, which she has described as deep, mysterious, unpredictable, inviting, dangerous and beautiful—just like the women in her life (AC 48).

Another of Mrs. Drew's relatives also recalled Mrs. Drew's love of swimming. She was surprised to see her swim for the first time when she was in her seventies: "We went to the beach and this woman swam out—way, way out. She was a strong swimmer. I was shocked to see this woman swim so far and so strong" (January 20, 2009).

Kincaid recollected that her mother loved to swim fully dressed, noting that she seemed not be weighed down by her clothes, which created a big bubble. When I asked Kincaid what she considered her most wonderful memory of her mother, she replied, "A wonderful moment when I loved her most would be her swimming with me on her back [pause, smiling], and I could hear her heart beat."

Annie the gardener was as much an influence on her daughter as Annie the model, homemaker, teacher, guard, and defender. She was an informed and enthusiastic gardener, always planting flowers, vegetables, fruit vines, and trees at her home and exploring botanical gardens wherever she went. The busy mother treasured whatever time she could find to work in her gardens. She was, her daughter declares, "a sort of magical person. She could eat something and plant the seed and it would grow." It is quite certain that a young Jamaica was often with her in her garden, hearing her stories of the origins of some of her plants, perhaps being encouraged to drop a seed in the ground, pull up a weed, or water a flower. The family spent every Sunday in the Botanical Gardens near her home, and Kincaid frequently writes of the time that she and her father were happily sick together in that Edenic garden (*MG* 143–44). That both Jamaica and her brother Devon would grow up to be gardening aficionados and be so knowledgeable about plants was obviously attributable to Annie Drew's enthusiasm. Jamaica could even imagine Devon having written a book on gardening such as Russell Page's *The Education of a Gardener* (*MB* 11); and she acknowledges in *My Brother* that she knows she and Devon got their love of gardening from their mother (11). Oddly enough, however, she often fails to credit Annie Drew for her fascination, even obsession, with gardening. She opens *My Garden (Book):* by declaring that her attachment to gardening began when her husband gave her gardening tools and flower seeds for Mother's Day. Later in that book she says her mother is not a gardener—"My mother is someone who puts a few things here and there for her own use; the beauty or not-beauty of it, she decides" (138). Yet often she declares that she will never be the gardener that her mother is. The garden is another contradictory battleground in which both her love affair and her battle with her mother are recalled and continue to be waged.

Kincaid regularly works in her Vermont garden. She proudly displays it to visitors. When I visited her home in October 2008, she graciously walked me around her garden. It was fascinating seeing this garden I had read so much about. There were a few beautiful blooming plants, but most of the plants were no longer in bloom. Kincaid had just returned from a trip to Seattle, and she was terribly upset to see that deer had eaten several of her plants. She showed me one of the plants that she had grown from seeds gathered during her trip to the Himalayas. The garden also contained pots with flowers, fruits, and vegetables planted from seeds, and other plants at various stages of growth, all carefully marked. There was a beautiful big section of collards, fenced in to keep out the animals.

Kincaid's personality changes in her garden. It is amazing to see her passion as she rattles off the names and histories of plants. I was a little embarrassed that I know so little about plants. She enthusiastically told me about seasons when all around the several acres of the property certain plants are blooming. I expect it is a vision to behold in the summer![18]

She travels all over the world for seeds to plant in her garden and spends exorbitant amounts of money maintaining it. She writes books about it, and it influences her writing generally. She told Leigh Haber that she thinks of her garden when she writes and she thinks of her writing when she gardens: "I do a lot of writing by putting something in the ground." She even managed to get a word or two about her seeds, her plants, her blooms into brief e-mails we exchanged in our efforts to establish dates for my upcoming visit to see her ("The tomatoes won't ripen and it took my lovely pink hibiscus a whole week to open up to full bloom. Ah well!" [August 12, 2008]; "I am, at this very moment, trying to figure out if some seeds of a flower in my garden are viable" [August 7, 2008]).

It does not surprise when it occurs to Kincaid that her garden resembles a map of the Caribbean, and that her garden is a memory exercise taking her back to her past (*MG* 8). It is clear, too, that she is thinking of Ma Chess and certainly Annie as well when she writes, recalling some of the flowers her grandmother grew as Kincaid followed her around, that gardening is one of the primary benefits of childhood. She concludes that the memories of the smells of the flowers and of her grandmother's skirt will eternally inform and influence her own life (*MG* 218).

The garden inevitably stands as a symbol both of Kincaid's original Edenic relationship with her mother and of her loss of paradise. In *Among Flowers,* she writes: "Eden is never far from the gardener's mind. It is The Garden to which we all refer, whether we know it or not. *And it is forever out of reach*" (*AF* 188–89; emphasis mine). To study Kincaid's garden is to understand her writing, her memories, her conflicts with her mother, and her one goal—to recapture that paradise when she, and she alone, basked in the love of her mother.

However, the garden in Kincaid's work is ultimately much more than that. In MG she poses the question, "And what is the relationship of gardening to conquest?" (116). Throughout her works she not only reflects upon what Sarah Brophy describes as "the retrospective minimization of the ecological devastation and agricultural exploitation that characterized the European conquest of the Caribbean" (269), but she also recognizes the degree to which she is a part of that ruling class: "I have joined the conquering class: who else could afford this garden—a garden in which I grow things that it would be much cheaper to buy at the store" (*MG* 123).

According to Kincaid, mother and daughter didn't mind sneaking a plant through customs. When Annie Drew went back to Dominica shortly before Devon's illness, she saw a fern she liked and brought it back to Antigua, where she repotted it in a chamber pot. It thrived in the shady part of her yard. She also enjoyed a passion fruit that she had in Dominica so much that she pocketed the seeds and planted them when she returned to Antigua (*MB* 125). While Jamaica was visiting the Botanical Gardens with the recuperating Devon, they discovered a perfectly shaped fruit of a mahogany tree, which Jamaica brought back to Vermont and placed on her windowsill. Kincaid confesses that when she was in the Ukraine, she stole the seeds of some hollyhocks whose bloom she liked and hid them in a box of sanitary pads in order to bring them back to the United States (*MG* 83). At a flower show in Chelsea, she was fascinated with a mullein called Helen Johnson and spent days contriving ways to smuggle it home (*MG* 103).

While her mother exposed her to gardens and gardening and encouraged her to learn the Latin names of plants, Annie did not encourage her daughter to garden and did not, as Kincaid was to do with her daughter, give her a section of her garden for her own. (Of course, Annie had only a very tiny yard to share, whereas Kincaid had several acres.) Kincaid, who is a gardener of some repute, who has traveled all over the world to visit gardens and collect seeds, and who has written two books on her gardening, declares: "I never grew anything at home [in Antigua]. And I don't have her *skill* with it" (Kin/Dance).

Not only did Annie inspire Kincaid's love of gardening, but she no doubt led her to a philosophy of gardening that has permeated her literature, informed her worldview, and provided memorably symbolic metaphors. Frequent passages such as the following reinforce the manner in which the garden represents the lives, issues, and philosophies of Annie and Jamaica: "A garden, no matter how good it is, must never completely satisfy. The world as we know it, after all, began in a very good garden, a completely satisfying garden—Paradise—but after a while the owner and the occupants wanted more" (*MG* 220).

Kincaid memorializes throughout her canon the Edenic period with her mother and declares that that foundation of love made her strong enough to deal with the devastation of the change in their relationship. However, she sometimes charges that what she experienced as Annie's great love for her as a young child was really only a selfish act on her mother's part: the making of beautiful clothes, having her photograph taken, preparing special treats for her, etc., were really all about Annie; she wasn't enjoying her little girl, Kincaid told me: "she was enjoying herself."

From the beginning, in fact, there were threats to the idyllic relationship that Jamaica enjoyed with Annie in their Garden of Eden. Annie had to wrestle with some behavioral problems that Jamaica manifested early on. She bit a lady who reached to kiss her when she was almost two ("Biography" 94–95). She sometimes bit other children with whom she was playing, something her mother gently referred to as Jamaica's biting phase (*AJ* 22). She was very jealous of anyone whom she saw as vying with her for her mother's attention. She lied and stole things. She often disobeyed or challenged Annie. On one occasion when her mother was ironing, with her four irons kept hot by a fire in their coal pot, Jamaica kept dancing around the pot, ignoring her mother's warnings that if she kept dancing around the pot, she might fall into the fire. Jamaica fell and still carries the scars of the burns around her elbows (*MG* 46; *AJ* 22). Jamaica was forbidden to touch some treasured china teacups that commemorated the coronation of a British monarch and caused a big argument when Annie found her taking some of them out of the cabinet in which they were kept (*MG* 42). Kincaid has recorded in her works innumerable instances of the conflicts she had with her mother when she was growing up. They are really quite commonplace except that they left such an unrelentingly devastating imprint on her.

When Jamaica was quite young, Nalda, a neighbor's daughter, took ill, and Annie held the child as they rushed to get her to the hospital. The child sighed, went limp, and died in her arms. Nalda's mother was so distraught that Annie had to bathe and dress the corpse for burial. When she returned home, she smelled of bay rum. Jamaica was so upset by the personal tasks that her mother had performed for this dead child that she would not allow her mother to touch her, fix her food, or help her with her bath. The very sight of her mother's hand was unbearable to her, and the scent of bay rum nauseated her. Obviously this reaction was partially attributable to Jamaica's ongoing fear of death, but it also was a result of her jealousy that her mother, whose attention she desired only for herself, had tended to someone else.[19] It only aggravated the child's resentment that shortly after Nalda's death, Miss Charlotte, a neighbor across the street, died in her mother's arms as Mrs. Drew tried to comfort her as she suffered the pains of a heart attack (*MB* 5).

None of the prior aggravations was as perturbing as the day the Jamaica character in *Annie John* returns home from Sunday school and walks in on her parents having sex. She blanks out everything that she sees in this primal scene except her mother's hand caressing her father's back, and, as with Nalda's death, she feels a quiet fury toward that hand that used to lovingly caress her: she vowed that she would never again let those hands touch her, nor would she allow her father to hold her hand during their walks (*AJ* 31–32).

She is frequently upset by her mother's attention to her husband, especially when she sees it as the cause of her ignoring her daughter. After one bad day at school, she is upset that her mother does not note her miserable state and comfort her but goes on talking to her father and laughing with him, apparently unaware of how angry it makes her daughter to see how much she loves the father (*AJ* 83).

When the Jamaica character is sick and presumably delirious, she decides that some of the photographs in her room are dirty, and she washes away everything that made her uncomfortable: a photo of her father holding a cricket bat with one hand and his other hand around her mother's waist is washed away from the waist down (*AJ* 118–19); in a photo of her at her confirmation, she leaves only the shoes that she had insisted upon even though her mother did not consider them appropriate for her confirmation (*AJ* 119–20).

Annie Drew was ever the patient mother in the face of her daughter's misbehavior, enforcing mild punishments but always being very loving. When the young Jamaica character fell into the fire and burned herself, the mother cried; and later when she told her daughter about burning herself, she kissed her scars (*AJ* 22); and when Jamaica destroyed the family's photographs, the parents simply decided that they could not leave their sick daughter alone anymore (*AJ* 120). When Jamaica did something bad, Annie sometimes banished her from the table and made her eat outside under their soursop tree, causing Kincaid to dislike soursop fruit until this day (*MG* 42).

Jamaica was a bed wetter until she was fifteen, if we can accept *Annie John* as accurate on this point (112). Kincaid told Goldfarb she wet her bed until she was thirteen and having her period: in the morning her sheets would be "filled with my bloody pee" (98). Annie seemed to have been the most patient of mothers regarding this annoying problem, recounting to her sister the many cures she had tried: "sour sop heart, turtle berry baths, tonics and even some rigamarole exercises" (AC 49). In "In the Night" (*AT*), the mother gently wakes her daughter in the middle of the night to clean her up—there are no reprimands, just a gentle reminder that it is still night and the bed needs to be changed; the sleepy child comments that her mother can change everything (8). In *Annie John*, the fifteen-year-old wakes up to find herself sitting on her father's lap and wearing a different nightie while her mother changed her sheets. When the daughter asks what happened, her father explained that she was wet (112); when the mother finished changing the bed, she lifted the fifteen-year-old who was already taller than she off her father's lap and tenderly put her back in her bed.

There are no accounts in Kincaid's fiction of Annie physically abusing her child. However, Dan Cryer quotes Kincaid as making the following accusation when she spoke to a group of students at East Harlem's Union Settlement Community Center: "I don't want to use the word 'abused,' but there was a great deal of cruelty directed at me when I was a child. . . . I met a woman the other day [in Antigua] who told me that when she gives her children a good beating and they complain, she always says to them, 'It's not as bad as what Miss Annie used to do to Elaine'" (Cryer B4).

In her interview with Allan Vorda, she said that when she lied during her childhood, "they tried to beat the truth out of me, sometimes literally, by giving me a spanking—no a beating! (There is great cruelty to children in the West Indies)" (17). However, she does not define the "they," which could refer to her mother, her parents, other relatives, other children, or her teachers. Given how often she points to specific acts of cruelty to her by her mother, this reference is probably not to her mother. Given the common references to brutal beatings in the schools in the Caribbean, the "they" might more likely refer to teachers and principals.

However, J. Brooks Bouson points to the Cryer interview as a confession by Kincaid of actual physical abuse (12) and asserts that Kincaid was reluctant "to describe in her fiction the very real hurts inflicted on her in her girlhood by her mother." She argues that Kincaid's "hatred and anger toward her mother points to a hidden drama in her early stories and novels" (12), which she suggests was actual beatings. Bouson insists that the Jamaica character's remarks in *Annie John* about dead people, "especially dead children, reveal that she lives in an emotionally unpredictable—and potentially dangerous—family environment" (44). She continues: "The fact that Annie associates her mother's caring hands . . . with the death of a child reveals even as it conceals the family secret that haunts the narrative: the secret of maternal abuse" (44–45). Bouson even describes as "hostile" the mother's statement in *Annie John* when her child in the womb kicked and caused her stitches to be flawed: "You see, even then you were hard to manage" (Bouson 45, quoting *AJ* 22).

For her there is a hidden "shadow story" in *Annie John,* which is ultimately a description of "the potentially lethal impact of the mother's abuse and scorn" (63).

Rabinowitz, too, suggested in our interview that Annie abused Kincaid. She said that at her first meeting with Annie: "I said there's something I really want to know, and this was just dreadful, but it's so typical of me—I guess that's why she became sort of fond of me, but I said, 'I have to know. Did she really play marbles under the house?'[20] [laughter] It just was incongruous in the story to me, and she said [soft voice], 'Did she write that I beat her?' And I said, 'No.'"

When I asked Kincaid about abuse, she vehemently denied any physical or sexual abuse in her household. She had her share of spankings, but they were not extreme or abusive. "I count as part of my literary strength the truth," she insisted. "And I would have been able to understand if I had been physically abused. In fact my mother was very protective of anything that happened to me." The abuse, she declared bitterly, was being taken out of school: "I think the interruption of my education was massive abuse!"

I raised the question about whether or not Mrs. Drew beat her children with Dr. Ermina Osoba, an Antiguan anthropologist, and Jocelyn Reid, who grew up in the neighborhood, who was the source of Kincaid's "Red Girl," who was one of Kincaid's best friends growing up, who remains close to Kincaid, and who was also Mrs. Drew's best friend later in life.[21] Both women laughed, with Reid declaring, "Yes, she beat them," and Dr. Ermina Osoba adding, "Everybody was beaten. I got some good blows myself." Throughout Caribbean literature, accounts of the beatings, strappings, and licks that children got at home and at school—ranging from mild spankings to vicious floggings—are commonplace. Clearly Jocelyn Reid did not witness anything that she would call abusive, and she also recalled the previously cited instances when Mrs. Drew would pretend to beat Jamaica without really hitting her.

Whether or not Kincaid suffered abuse as a child, it is clear that Kincaid and the Kincaid characters frequently enjoyed abusing others. The Kincaid character hurts others not just because she is focused on and protecting herself, but sometimes for the sheer pleasure of inflicting pain upon others. The narrator in "Wingless" vows that she will grow up to be a beautiful woman who will amuse herself by causing others great pain (*AT* 22). Later the narrator speaks of her disappointments, pain, and tears and concludes that she will exaggerate her disappointments and seek vengeance for them (23). Frequently the Kincaid character as a child inflicts pain on her playmates. The mother in “Blackness,” who like Annie Drew chewed the food for her child, tells us that her child is cruel to her hunchback playmate, smiling a cruel smile while she pulls at the hairs on his back (*AT* 50). The behavior here is precisely like that of the Kincaid character in *Annie John,* who torments a “dunce” named Sonia, pulling the hair on her limbs until she screamed (7).

Like fellow Caribbean novelist V. S. Naipaul, Kincaid and the Kincaid characters sometimes seem to delight in being unlikable, taking the opposing side, shocking people, making people feel uncomfortable, causing them pain. The Naipaul biographer Patrick French wrote that Naipaul “says outrageous things very decisively” (419); “when he was being rude or provocative . . . Naipaul was full of glee. Creating tension, insulting his friends, family or whole communities left him in excellent spirits” (xi). Kincaid, too, seems to delight in storming through life, shocking, offending, and insulting. As Kincaid herself admits, there is something of the author in the *Scabiosa ochroleuca,* which reminds her of herself in its inclination to expand everywhere that is susceptible to it (*MG* 27). In “Jamaica Kincaid’s New York,” she wrote that when she was nineteen, she went to parties and tried to behave so badly that she would not be invited back; she also recounts some conversations at parties where she was as abrasive and insulting as possible (73). In an interview with Donna Perry in 1990, she said she “no longer wanted to be a civilized person”—that she now rejects *At the Bottom of the River* because it is “very unangry, decent, civilized” (498–99). She continues to emulate “the little savage” she aspired to be as a child (*Talk Stories* 28). Now, she declared, she’s “interested in writing about sex and smells. I’m interested in being not a decent person” (Perry 498–99; see also *Lucy* 83). In *Lucy,* the Kincaid character asserts that she wanted to have a repulsive odor and she didn’t care if others were offended (27). When her mother explains that she named her after Satan, shortening Lucifer’s name to Lucy, she is happy and embraces her name, commenting that she regarded her mother as godlike and that the children of gods were devils; she only wished that her mother had named her Lucifer instead of Lucy (152–53). Kincaid told Vorda that she identified with Lucifer from *Paradise Lost* and that she only later realized “how much I was rooting for the devil” (“An Interview” 18).

It is not surprising then that this same contrariness extends to Kincaid’s attitude toward critics. She declared to Vorda: “The criticism I most value comes from people who do not like my writing. There’s almost nothing to make you feel more superior, as the people who don’t like you” (24).

Unlike Annie, who had a ready laugh and was given to teasing, Jamaica pictures herself as a child with no sense of humor when it came to her mother. Despite the fact that Annie would smile and reassure her child when she teased her, Jamaica never forgot some of the "cruel" things her mother said to her. For example, when Annie Victoria told the Jamaica character, Mignonette, that she was excited about leaving Dominica so that she would never have to carry a hand of plantains on her head, Mignonette is appalled that her mother laughingly adds that she might have thought twice about that if she had known then that she would have to carry her (AC 50). The child in "Antigua Crossings" is appalled that her mother can laugh at her grandfather, declaring that she is confounded by a woman who laughs at her own father (50), and adding that laughter is something alien to her (AC 50). In "Wingless," the mother warns the daughter not to eat the strings on bananas because they will kill her; the alarmed daughter inquires if that is true. The mother admits it is not and laughs at her daughter's efforts to remove the strings (*AT* 24). In that same story, the child again tells the mother that she frightened her, and the mother again laughs at how funny she looks when she is afraid (*AT* 26). In *Annie John,* after her daughter has eaten all of a dish disguised to look like rice, the mother laughs as she tells her that she has just eaten breadfruit, infuriating her daughter so much that Annie looked to her daughter as if she had changed into a crocodile (84). Annie Drew often found humor in situations that failed to amuse her daughter; Kincaid appears to be like Xuela, who could not be amused and had no time in her life for laughing (*Auto* 125).

Despite the conflicts between mother and daughter, despite the cruel things they sometimes said to each other, Jamaica's love for her mother was always absolute until her brothers were born. The beautiful Eden that was their lives alone together is described and yearned for throughout Kincaid's writing. In "In the Night," she dreams of marrying a woman, who is obviously Annie, and living with her near the sea in a hut with two of everything. They would be alone together, eating together, doing everything together, running off anyone who threatens their privacy. The girl would sing to the woman, and the woman would never make her cry. They would be completely happy as the woman told the girl beautiful stories every night (*AT* 12).

4

AFTER EDEN

> I did not like my mother's other children.
> —Jamaica Kincaid, *My Brother*

Jamaica's dream of complete happiness was shattered by the birth of a brother . . . and then another brother . . . and then yet another. Joseph Alexander was born on March 5, 1958;[1] Dalma Alfred on November 24, 1960; and Devon Anthony on May 4, 1962.[2]

Her first brother's birth marked for Jamaica the loss of her idyllic existence with her mother. Of Joseph's birth, she lamented: "I thought I was the only thing my mother truly loved in the world, and when it dawned on me that it wasn't so, I was devastated" (Listfield 82). In *My Brother,* she describes her happiness in her childhood home, and then adds that her unhappiness in that house was concurrent with the births of her brothers (111).

Kincaid told me that her parents felt a certain romance about their first child born when they were properly married,[3] and they regarded this firstborn legitimate son as a very special child who had to go to a great school from the beginning and had to have the best of everything. Thus when one day this special child almost choked to death after swallowing a plum that he picked up under the tree in their yard, men from the prison in black-and-white jail uniforms came to her yard to cut down the plum tree: "You could see a kind of imperialism about it. You know, as if they were the king and queen of the land—[what follows is a booming issuing of a decree]—*'All plum trees would have to be cut down!'* because he had encountered a plum tree. It didn't mean that he would never encounter another plum tree. It had something mythic about it." Joseph was sent to Miss Walter's School, a private infants' school (George interview), reinforcing the parents' determination to provide the best for their firstborn.

In *Lucy,* the Kincaid character recounts how with the birth of each son her parents would dream of him going off to England to become a doctor or lawyer. She could forgive her father, but not her mother: Lucy felt as if a sword were thrust through her heart when her mother proudly anticipated a bright future for her sons but seemed to have no similar dreams for her female child.[4] Bitterly, Lucy began to dub her mother Mrs. Judas and to plan a life without her, knowing even then that she would never completely break the ties that bound them (*Lucy* 130–31). She couldn't understand why her mother never even considered the possibility that she could have been a doctor. Even as an adult, Kincaid tells us that sometimes she views her mother as her mother only; at others times she is her brothers' mother; and then again she is the mother of all of them (*MB* 114–15).

Certain events of the birth of each brother are etched in her memory in sharp detail. She vividly recalls the blue of the evening sky when she went to summon the midwife for the delivery of her first brother, the white chemise her mother sewed for her second brother, and the red ants that attacked her last brother. She also painfully recollects the blue of her first brother's sailor suit when he went off to a cricket match with his father, and the lack of lipstick on her mother's mouth after all of the brothers' arrivals (*Lucy* 131).

Kincaid was in Dominica when her second brother was born: "I came back from Dominica and had *two* brothers."

She recalls that she was old enough to understand what was going on when her mother became pregnant with Devon and attempted to abort this last child. Many years later, when he was ill with AIDS, Devon, who had read one of Kincaid's accounts of her mother's efforts to abort an unwanted child, asked her, "Ah me de trow'way pickney?" and she laughed and told him no, that what he had read was fiction (*MB* 174).[5]

If one wishes to provide a charitable account of Devon's birth, it might be described as the event that disrupted the family's routine: Jamaica had to go to notify the midwife, the children had to go to neighbors' houses, and Mr. Drew couldn't take his evening walk; but in fact Kincaid's description of his birth in *My Brother* makes it clear that this fourth child was an added burden on a family already suffering economic hardship. The chemise that Annie had made for Devon was plain, unlike those that she had elaborately embroidered for her other children. Annie had to deliver him at home rather than in the hospital. The hand-me-down crib that had been refurbished for the arrival of each child did not receive much attention for Devon's birth (*MB* 174). His birth it was that ultimately pushed the family over the brink, Kincaid concludes (*MB* 174). As soon as Devon was born and wrapped in his chemise, he was placed in his tired mother's arms and they both fell asleep, but not before a small piece of his afterbirth was dried and pinned to the inside of his clothing to protect him from evil spirits (*MB* 5).

The day after his birth, Devon was sleeping with his mother when he was attacked by red ants from an okra tree that Annie had planted, an event that Annie claimed not to remember but that Kincaid frequently recounts. In "Antigua Crossings," she has Victoria write to tell her sister that Devon was almost killed by ants that came from the okra trees (49); in "At Last," the baby is almost eaten up, eyes first (*AT* 14).[6]

While there are numerous indications in several works that Jamaica's conflicts with her mother began with the birth of the first son, it appears that with each son there was some further deterioration. She asserts in *My Brother* that with the birth of the second brother the mother became cruel and bitter (78). She declares that the birth of the third son, Devon, increased the bitterness and led to constant quarrels between her and her mother (*MB* 71). Jamaica insists that her mother even lost her beauty with Devon's birth (*MB* 71). It was certainly Devon whom Jamaica blamed for ending her education and for what she considers one of her mother's most egregious and unforgivable actions: burning her books. When Devon was two, his mother left him in Jamaica's care while she went to run errands or perhaps to work, but a rebellious Jamaica chose to read rather than look after him (*MB* 129). When she finished her book, she rushed to do the few chores she knew her mother expected her to do. Annie was infuriated when she returned and saw her baby with hardened stool that caused his diapers to sag. She gathered up all of her negligent daughter's books, some of which she had in a special hiding place under the house, doused them with kerosene, and set fire to them.[7] This is one of Kincaid's most painful childhood memories. She described it as an attack on her very being, a brutal scar on her memory.

It is interesting that Kincaid, along with most of her critics, sees only herself as the victim in this incident. Her critics can only reflect on how the horrific destruction of her books might have thwarted the genius whose writing has brought them such pleasure. In fact, as Kincaid always relates, this incident, as painful as it might have been to her, motivated her to write. Annie obviously considered the true victim to be the helpless and neglected toddler, left not only to walk around all day with a load in his diaper but to get into any danger or trouble to which an unsupervised toddler is prone. Annie no doubt wondered if Jamaica paid Devon enough attention to give him a sip of water or a bite of food.

Jamaica's recollections of her brothers suggest that she viewed them only as nuisances who destroyed the paradise that was her life before, took her mother's love away from her, destroyed the financial stability of her family, and disrupted any plans for her education and her future. Almost nothing she writes suggests any bonding with or love for these brothers. She told me that during her childhood she never hugged them, kissed them, told them stories, read to them, or acted as a protective big sister: "I didn't think of them as my brothers at all. When they were little, I just thought ahhhhhhh [gesture of disgust and exasperation]." In *My Brother,* she complains that she always had to give up her leisure activities and then her schooling to care for her mother's other children. As a thirteen-/fourteen-/fifteen-year-old, she did not like having to make these sacrifices; she did not like these children (128). Even as late as 2006, she would declare her friend Sandy Frazier her "true, true brother, the only brother I have ever needed" (foreword, *Gone to New York* xi).

If accounts of Jamaica's youth, such as those in *Annie John,* are indeed autobiographical, Mrs. Drew was not neglectful of her daughter after the birth of her sons. Though the boys do not appear in *Annie John,* the novel treats years in the Kincaid character's life long after their births.

As previously noted, the ever-observant mother figure in *Annie John* obviously made a considered decision to respect and acknowledge her daughter's budding maturity and stop treating her like the needy little toddler. Thus when mother and twelve-year-old daughter went to shop for material to make new dresses, the mother, as usual, let her daughter select the cloth for her dress but announced that she would no longer make her own dress out of the same fabric; the daughter would no longer go around looking like a smaller copy of her mother (*AJ* 26). This was traumatic for the daughter, causing her to feel that the earth had been swept away from under her (*AJ* 26). The Jamaica character bitterly recalled that her mother did not even ease the pain of this perceived separation with a kiss. On another occasion, the mother showed her daughter how to fold sheets and commented that she would have her own house one day. That her mother could envision them living apart was a painful reality that the Jamaica character was not prepared to accept (*AJ* 28–29). Perhaps the mother did not anticipate or ever fully appreciate the ongoing stress her daughter would suffer from these events, believing, as any parent would, that at twelve, her daughter's own individuality needed to be emphasized and her burgeoning adulthood encouraged. However, the daughter in the Kincaid canon frequently portrays the ideal world as one in which she is one with her mother, often picturing herself in the fetal position, or as the cuddled baby, as in "My Mother," where the daughter fits perfectly in her mother's arms, on her back, in the hollow of her stomach. They eat and drink from the same utensils, they sleep on the same pillow, they merge (*AT* 60). What transformed the loving Eden of the mother and daughter into a battleground was not, as Simone A. James Alexander insisted, "the mother's need to control" (45), but rather the mother's efforts to grant her daughter some independence.

This oneness with her mother is something Jamaica Kincaid first savored, then craved, then rebelled against, and later in life was forced to acknowledge, often painfully declaring, "I am my mother." At the time, though, the budding teenager, seeing all of her mother's actions to prepare her for adulthood as cruel rejections, resolved that a war had begun. Her beloved mother was now her enemy, and the daughter was prepared to call upon an arsenal of weapons to attack her. For one thing, she would find a replacement, someone else to love, a continuing quest, beginning with girls with whom she went to school, young boys she met, young men she courted, a husband, and then her own children. Occasionally she would forget her determination and once again enjoy her mother's bathing her back and fixing her favorite dishes, and be appeased by her mother's concerns about her health and her well-being; but for the most part, she regarded her mother as a threatening and hypocritical enemy against whom she must always be on guard. She was constantly torn between love and hate, a dilemma that would haunt her long after her mother's death, a death that from this point on she both desired and feared, for she believed she knew that her mother would kill her if she got a chance and that she would kill her mother if she had the courage (*AJ* 89).

Although she constantly playing a false role with her mother, always devising ways that she might defeat her, she was never truly able to feel victorious over Annie: as she notes in "My Mother," when her mother makes a pacifying gesture toward her, "I let out a horrible roar, then a self-pitying whine. I had grown big, but my mother was bigger, and that would always be so" (*AT* 56). At one and the same time that she dreamed of just the two of them living somewhere together, she wished to see her mother lying withered in a coffin (*AJ* 106).

She also focused on her dreams of escaping her mother and Antigua. When she was around nine, just as "back chat" to her mother, she declared, "When I am 19 I am going to be living in New York. Just wait and see. I am going to be living in New York" (NY 73). When Lucy was twelve, she told her mother that she would be living at home when she turned nineteen only if she (Lucy) dropped dead. This was, Lucy declared, her first expression of hatred and anger toward her parents (112).

Jamaica's behavior at this period in her life was enough to challenge the most patient of mothers, but Annie was very, very patient. Kincaid has Lucy declare that when she was ten, she was very two-faced, always projecting a false self (18). Jamaica (or the Jamaica character) would talk back, lie, steal, disobey, refuse to come directly home from school, intentionally commit acts that her mother had forbidden, and do whatever she could to cause her mother pain. When she was late coming home from school and forgot to stop to pick up fish from Mr. Earl for dinner as she had been directed to do, she lied to her mother, insisting that he didn't have any fish that day in the market because the sea had been too rough to fish, whereupon her mother uncovered the fish that Mr. Earl had brought by when he got tired of waiting for her. Her mother made her eat her dinner outside that night and threatened not to kiss her goodnight, but she relented and kissed her later when she went to bed.

The Jamaica character also befriended and idolized the "Red Girl," a girl who represented everything her mother raised her not to be, who wore dirty and ragged clothing, who walked about in her bare feet, whose uncombed hair was matted and tangled, who was so dirty she stank, who climbed trees and played marbles with the boys from the juvenile reform school, and whose mother neglected her completely. Needless to say, the Jamaica character "worshipped the ground [the Red Girl's] unwashed feet walked on" (*AJ* 59), and she began to steal money from her mother to buy gifts for her new friend. It was necessary, of course, to lie to her mother about her whereabouts as she snuck off to meet this forbidden love in prohibited places such as the top of the lighthouse (a structure at the end of Nelson [now Charlesworth Ross] Street and just behind Dr. Ramsey's office).

Sometimes the Jamaica character's offense was something as small as putting the spread on the bed so that the bowl overflowing with flowers that her mother had embroidered on it was not centered in the middle (*AJ* 29); and sometimes it was more egregious, like throwing stones when she was twelve at the same lady she had bitten when she was two ("Biography" 95), or singing benna[8] in Sunday School, of all places, or being what the Jamaica character in *Annie John* declares herself to be: one of the "worst-behaved" students in her class (73). She recounts several such instances in *Annie John*. She would walk home with Ruth, the British daughter of a minister, and sing obscene songs to her just to make her turn red from embarrassment (73). She was the ringleader of a group of girls discovered by their teacher, Miss Nelson, in the graveyard sitting on the tombstones of the colonial masters and singing obscene songs, using profanity, and displaying forbidden parts of their bodies.

The Jamaica character, who at this time was determined to do whatever was contrary to her mother's teaching (*AJ* 61), was very much like Xuela, who declared that she loved whatever she was taught to hate (*Auto* 32). No wonder, then, that the Jamaica character in *Annie John* became enthralled with the unladylike and forbidden game of playing marbles, hiding them as she did her other contraband under the house. One day her mother discovered her coming from under the house with a couple of marbles and confronted her about playing marbles, an accusation that the child vehemently denied. Another war had begun, with the mother determined to find the marbles and the daughter determined to deny her guilt. The mother fruitlessly searched under the house, often actually touching some of the containers in which the child had stashed them. The mother told the father about the daughter's bad behavior. The mother watched the daughter constantly. She sometimes sweetly appealed to her daughter to confess. Then she told her daughter a story about having to carry, as a young child, a heavy bunch of figs on her head all the way from the fields to her house in Dominica. In moving dialogue she detailed the pain that she felt in her head, her neck, her shoulders, the base of her spine as this oppressive load became more and more onerous. Soon she could hardly walk, and she plodded along, falling behind everyone else. Then the fear of being alone caused her to imagine all kinds of fearful confrontations in the woods. Finally when the frightened and exhausted child came to her house and took the load off her head, a long black snake crawled away. So enraptured was the Jamaica character in empathizing with the suffering of the beautiful young girl who would become her mother that she felt moved to confess and hand over her marbles;[9] but then her mother, perhaps recognizing the power of her story, demanded to know where the marbles were, reanimating the sense of warfare that now governed their relationship. Her daughter insisted she didn't play marbles (*AJ* 64–70).

The Jamaica character's efforts in *Annie John* to find happiness through perverse behavior do not really bring her happiness. The pleasure of her revenge is short-lived, and she is finally like that ultimate rebel Lucifer in the painting *The Young Lucifer,* whose smile after he has been cast out of heaven is only a front to cover the fact that he is indeed unhappy and lonely (*AJ* 94–95). Such is the case when the mother tells thirteen-year-old Lucy that every Christmas Eve she and her husband went to see a Bing Crosby film that they had seen when they first started dating, and the daughter sarcastically replies that that must have been a spiritual experience: immediately contrite, Lucy cannot bear to look at the hurt expression on her mother's face (*Lucy* 22).

The Jamaica character's description of her teachers in *Annie John* suggests that she held as much enmity toward them as toward her mother—and, in fact, toward any adult authority: Miss Moore looked like a prune and sounded like an owl; Miss Nelson had ironed hair (39); Miss Edward was a roaring dragon (78) with bulging eyes (81) and steatopygous hips (82); Mr. Slacks has dingy teeth (73). Even without the denigrative modifiers, their names are chosen as negative signifiers: some are named after British kings (Miss George, Miss Edward); British admirals (Horatio Nelson); and prisons (Newgate); the name Mr. Slacks speaks for itself.

She often talks of hating to sing "Rule Britania" (*sic*), a popular song often confused with the British national anthem: "I am not a big fan of the English. They made me sing too many 'Rule Britania' [*sic*] in the hot sun, and the thing about that song is that it has a line in it that goes, 'Britons never, never shall be slaves.' But we were not Britons and most of our ancestors were slaves" (NY 73).

Jamaica also annoyed her mother and others in her family with her tendency to put on airs and pretend she was something she was not. The Jamaica character looked forward to attending a new school in *Annie John* for the opportunity to do just that (29). When she went back to school at the age of fifteen after her long illness, she assumed a strange accent and acted in such a self-centered and superior way that she provoked resentment, which made her very happy (129).

By her own accounts, Jamaica was a blatant liar and thief as a child. She justifies that behavior in "Antigua Crossings," explaining that when she was nine she started talking very fast and her mother said she had better watch her because fast talkers were liars. This caused her to start to lie, and when her mother noted her outrageous lies, she said she would have to watch her because liars would steal, thus provoking her to start to steal (49). Jamaica must also have tortured her mother with her ability to project a false front at the same time that she had no intent to attend to what her mother was saying. In "Antigua Crossings," she says that she said yes to all of her mother's cautions as she prepared for her trip to Dominica, though she paid no attention to her mother's words (50).

Jamaica was sent to Dominica on occasion to spend time with her grandmother. She no doubt regarded these first trips away from Antigua and her family as a kind of exile or banishment for her rebellious behavior. In "Antigua Crossings," the Jamaica character said she was sent five times because she caused a lot of trouble as a child and they thought that was caused by her father's outside women working Obeah on her (49). It is not unlikely that her first trip at nine was really occasioned by an event she recounts in *My Garden* (44) and Cook's *Generations:* she dropped her baby brother on his head and found herself immediately on a ship bound for Dominica, the first time she had ever been away from her mother (Cook 9).[10] In *My Brother,* however, she suggests she was first sent because the mother of a girl Annie had beaten for beating Jamaica threatened to set evil spirits on Jamaica, and it was known that evil spirits could not cross water (77) and that Dominica Obeah was superior to Antigua Obeah (77–78). In the "Antigua Crossings" account of her first trip to Dominica in June, when she had just turned nine (50), the stern mother is so pained at her child's leaving that she doesn't think she can go to the boat to send her off; similarly the rebellious child is moved to apologize for all of her infractions and beg to stay with her family that she loves. However, neither of these adversaries will express to the other her true feelings (50). In Kincaid's account of this trip in *Best American Travel Writing,* she does have her mother take her to the ship (xv), whereas it is the father who takes her in "Antigua Crossings" (50). Annie was constantly fearful of embarrassment by her incorrigible daughter's behavior. When she sent her off to Dominica, she repeatedly reminded her not to behave in such a way as to bring shame to her family (AC 50).

When in Dominica, Jamaica longed for her mother, "the person in whose body I had lain curled up" (Cook 10), and for Antigua: "It *rained* all the time in Dominica. I never saw so much rain. The terrain was different. There were mountains. There were so many trees. It was so *dark*. There was a long walk to and from school. *Oh, my God*! There were so many things I missed. [I missed] my home so much!" (Kin/Dance; similar sentiments are expressed in *The Best American Travel Writing* xvi, and Cook 9–10). So she started to write letters to her mother falsely complaining that her Aunt Mary beat her and treated her badly. She didn't mail the letters but hid them under a stone. When her aunt, who loved Jamaica very much and treated her kindly, discovered the letters, she promptly put her on the *M. V. P. Rippon* and sent her back to Antigua. This incident was an early indication for Jamaica of the power of writing, and it provided the basis for a similar incident in *The Autobiography of My Mother,* where an unhappy Xuela, sent to be raised by Ma Eunice, the woman who did her father's laundry, addressed letters to her father, but actually meant them for her dead mother, in which she complained that Eunice and everyone treated her cruelly. The letters were discovered and sent to her father, who "rescued" her and took her to live with him and his new wife. Xuela concludes that through her writing she had perhaps saved her life (22).

Jamaica's first voyage was a replay of her mother's. She, too, was seen off by a worried parent fearful of her behavior; she, too, was placed in the hands of a captain who was asked to look out for her; she, too, suffered seasickness; she, too, never forgave her parent.

W'en ya no se mumma, ya seek granny.

These trips to Dominica were not all bad for Jamaica, who loved her grandmother and her wonderful cooking and enjoyed being the sole center of attention in a household mercifully devoid of the despised brothers. She fondly recalled her morning routines with Ma Chess, with whom she slept in a separate dwelling from Pa Chess. Ma Chess would roast coffee beans, grind them, and make coffee, which she and Jamaica would drink as they sat huddled around the fire that they made from wood the two of them had brought on a donkey from up in the mountains (Cook 11). She also grated a coconut, squeezed out the milk, and made Jamaica a drink out of unripe bananas, which they ate with flying fish. Jamaica fondly recalls following her grandmother around like a little shadow as she gathered things like castor oil beans from which she made castor oil. Indeed, she found herself becoming one with her grandmother and being in complete union with her (*AT* 59–60). Kincaid frequently comments on the "amazing female smell" of this woman who did not bathe very often (Kin/Dance; see also Cook 10). She also notes in *Annie John* that one of her three favorite foods was the chocolate that Ma Chess made from the beans that she grew and sent to them in Antigua (114).

Jamaica also spent time with her Aunt Mary Elizabeth, who was injured in an accident after she had slipped off to meet the man she later married, a man of whom her father never approved. The accident left her with a mangled eye and a limp and provides part of the plot of *The Autobiography of My Mother.*

Many of Jamaica's experiences with her grandparents in Dominica find their way into her work. Sometimes while there, she writes in *My Brother,* she would be looking at the full moon shining over the large mountains and be mesmerized by what she considered the most amazing and enchanting thing in the universe. Then she would be frightened by a light moving around, which she knew was a Jablesse (38). The Jablesse, or Diablesse, is an often attractive and enticing demonic woman in Caribbean folklore.[11] Allusions to the Jablesse appear occasionally in other Kincaid works, including "In the Night" and "The Letter from Home" (*AT*) and *The Autobiography of My Mother.*

In *My Garden (Book):*, Jamaica tells of being sent to her mother's friend in the country—she doesn't say why—perhaps another expulsion for rebellious behavior. This woman had guinea hens, pigs, and chickens. She also grew cotton. At harvest time when Jamaica was out of school, she occasionally was asked to help pick and gather it. She hated her time in the country with her mother's friend because she hated being away from her family, she did not like the animals, and she hated separating the cotton from the seed, which hurt her hands (150–51). Recalling this period, she told me, "It was the most awful thing!" It is important to note that she was *occasionally asked* to help; it does not appear that she was forced to spend all of her time there enduring such drudgery.

For Kincaid the most traumatic event in her life was being forced to stop school when she was fourteen or fifteen to care for her brothers. Jamaica was an outstanding student whom everyone expected would go on to ace her qualifying exams and get a scholarship to the University of the West Indies. Throughout the twentieth century, winning a scholarship was the magic ticket out of poverty for many bright West Indian students, and their parents prepared them for the scholarship's qualifying exams with everything they could command (the best food, the best supplies, tutoring, release from household duties). V. S. Naipaul and scores of other West Indian intellectuals from poor families acknowledge that they would have been doomed without that scholarship. Thus, had Jamaica won a scholarship to a British university or to the University of the West Indies, she would likely, she told me, have prepared for a profession that was traditional for women, one that would have made her a person of distinction in Antigua, very likely a teacher and a scholar. The idea of being a writer did not occur to her because "I didn't think people *wrote any more.* I thought all people did was *read.* And since all people did was read, I would have been a scholar like you. That would have been the natural thing for me to do . . . be . . . a scholar and a teacher." She was so shocked when she was told that she could no longer go to school that she plunged into a depression; she declared, "If I had known you could kill yourself, I might have. I didn't know people killed themselves."

It was a period in her life that Kincaid finds it difficult to remember and to talk about. In addition to her experiencing what felt to her like a sort of end to her life, Mr. Drew seemed about to die, and several acquaintances were dying. Jamaica did not resist when she was taken out of school; the crushed child believed there was nothing she could do about her dilemma—everything was falling apart in the family, and she felt she had a responsibility to them. Thus, while her mother went out to work, cooking and cleaning for people, she stayed home to care for her brothers and help with the household tasks. During this dark period, her only release was reading, but things got even worse after her mother burned her books, an event that is rehashed ad infinitum in her works and interviews.

Jocelyn Reid declared that "the worst thing Ms. Annie did was to take Jamaica out of school to care for her brothers." Jane King also comments on this issue: "I do not understand why she was pulled out of school just before her chance to win an Island Scholarship" (887). This subject occasioned much discussion among Reid, Dr. Osoba, and myself, all of us recognizing that taking her daughter out of school was very much out of character for a woman who had made every sacrifice to provide the best possible education for her. We all agreed that it must have been dictated by the most dire of circumstances and that the distraught mother had had no other option. Reid pointed out that Annie did enroll Jamaica in typing class during those two years, so obviously she was still seeking ways to prepare her daughter for some career.

Annie was very strict with Jamaica and did not allow her to "jump up" in Carnival.[12] Kincaid recalls that her greatest desires at one time were to jump up in Carnival and get American shoes. There was a big argument when Jamaica was fourteen and wanted to dress as a worker bee and march in a band. Her mother refused, but then compromised and let her get some sneakers from America, which fell apart as soon as they got wet, as her mother had forecast (*Talk Stories* 16). The mother also did not like her daughter to go to the movies.[13] Jamaica's one pleasure during the last years she lived in Antigua was lying on her bed with her feet in her windowsill reading books, a sight that infuriated her mother, who viewed such behavior as portending a life of idleness (*MB* 44).

And then suddenly plans were made for Jamaica to leave Antigua! This separation was without a doubt fated to be the most traumatic event in the relationship of mother and daughter, changing forever the course of their lives and producing results that neither could ever have imagined. Forever after there was to be Jamaica in the United States (or England, or the Himalayas, or wherever) agonizing over her mother's imagined response to every event in her life ("for the rest of my life [she might be a] shadow standing between me and the rest of the world" [*AJ* 107]); and there was to be Annie Drew in Antigua, agonizing over every action (actual or imagined) of her daughter in America. And on the few occasions they met, it was to be like the confrontations between mother and daughter in *Annie John*: "We looked at each other, and I could see the frightening black thing leave her to meet the frightening black that had left me" (101). Tragically their "two black things" were destined always to get "the better of" them (106).

All of Kincaid's accounts of leaving Antigua indicate that she went directly to the United States, but Joseph Drew, Jocelyn Reid, and another of Mrs. Drew's friends all told me that she went first to Puerto Rico with a doctor and his family. Jocelyn recalled the specific date that Jamaica left (June 5, 1965) because it was the same time she started working at Barreto's on High Street. When I asked Connie Rabinowitz if Kincaid had gone first to Puerto Rico, she responded, "That may well be. I don't know." That so close a friend and such a longtime Kincaid fan showed no surprise at this "information" only served to confirm its accuracy in my mind.

There are widely varying accounts of her age and the year she left in sundry sources, including Kincaid's accounts. The year of her departure is variously listed as 1965, 1966, or 1967. Her age at the time of departure is given as sixteen (Covi 97; Dilger; *MB* 20; Cook 20, Kincaid, introduction, *Talk Stories* 10; Snodgrass 125); sixteen and a half (NY); just before her seventeenth birthday (Ferguson, "A Lot"); seventeen (Covi 31 [Covi lists seventeen on p. 31 and sixteen on p. 97 of the same book]; Cryer B4; Lee; Garis, 42; Gilmore, "Endless Autobiography?" 213 and *The Limits of Autobiography* 99; Vorda, "An Interview" 15; *AJ* 131, 132; Ferguson, "A Small Place," 117); and nineteen (*Lucy* 134). One expects these variations are the results of what Jamaica told the interviewers or what a fictional account dictated. Sixteen fits in very well in terms of the parallel journey that her mother took at the age of sixteen (and the mother's age also varies in some sources). Much evidence from reliable sources points to the accuracy of the information she gave me in our interview: she arrived in the United States in December 1965, at the age of sixteen—five months before her seventeenth birthday. If this is indeed accurate and if Jocelyn Reid's recollection of the date Jamaica left Antigua is correct (and I feel quite confident that it was), then Kincaid stayed in Puerto Rico only six months.

Kincaid's departure from Antigua is variously interpreted by Kincaid, her mother, and numerous associates. Rabinowitz declared: "She [Annie] was as responsible for creating the antagonism as Jamaica, but in essence she had created it forever by what she did to Jamaica—sending her away to earn money for the use—or upbringing or whatever you want to call it—of her three legitimate brothers. She was *not* legitimate. She didn't meet her father for many years."[14] A friend of Mrs. Drew asserted:

> Kincaid has written a bunch of lies. Annie did not take her out of school. Bullshit! The mother met a woman to take her to work for her. This was the chance of a lifetime in her mother's view for her daughter to go to Puerto Rico as a servant. Given Annie Drew's education and her life, she did what she thought was best for her children. Opportunities in those days for education were hard to come by. It was normal in Antigua for people in Annie's position to pull children out of school to work. (January 21, 2009)

This assessment is borne out by the statistics. As late as 1970, only 4.5 percent of Antiguan children graduated from high school, according to Deborah Mistron (160).

This same Drew acquaintance also denounces the suggestion that she worked as an au pair as a fraud perpetuated by Tim Hector, a part of what he called "Tim Hector's rewriting of Kincaid." He insisted that au pairs are from wealthy families and take jobs working with their employers' children to learn a culture and a language: "They are not like Kincaid, someone who is poor and needs to earn a living. Kincaid was a servant, a maid, not any au pair. Hector tried to put an intellectual stamp on her. This au pair stuff is pure bullshit to the highest." In her interview with Deirdre Donahue, Kincaid acknowledges that she was not "the nanny" or the "au pair": "Someone of my complexion and class is the girl" (5D). Kincaid told Jane Mendelsohn that the real difference between Lucy and herself was that Lucy was an au pair while "my situation was that of a servant" (21); she told Buckner that her family sent her to America "as a servant girl" (465); and she told Cudjoe she was an au pair, but added that she was almost a servant (215). However, someone who knew Kincaid well at the time said that the Arlens hired her as an au pair (April 23, 2009).

What's in a name? That which we call a rose
By any other name would smell as sweet.

Though New York appears from these accounts not to have been her destination, Jamaica was probably at times as deliriously happy about leaving for Puerto Rico as she has portrayed herself as being about leaving for the United States and England in several writings and interviews; characteristically, however, her happiness was mixed with dread and anger that she was once more the rebel daughter being driven away from home.

In a sense, Annie Drew had spent a lifetime preparing Jamaica for her voyage abroad. Many West Indian parents desire the opportunity for their children to migrate to the United States, Britain, Canada—or at least to a larger and more prosperous Caribbean island. She had continuously insisted that her daughter be independent and understand the importance of being prepared to fend for herself in the event that her parents were not around to care for her (NY 72–73). Jamaica always imagined herself as a smartly dressed New Yorker strutting in her high heels, stockings, and hat. However, Annie persistently taught her that it was better to be smart than pretty, adding that pretty women were numerous, smart women were rare (NY 73).

All of Kincaid's accounts suggest that Annie was as meticulous in preparing her for this trip as she had been in preparing her for school. All necessary clothes were purchased or carefully washed and pressed. Jamaica's underwear and jewelry were taken to the Obeah woman for a special treatment to protect her from any misfortune. Her belongings were painstakingly packed in the new trunk her father had made for her. A red cotton handkerchief was placed in her purse for her to wave to them from the ship as it pulled away. A neighbor came to straighten and style her hair. Her mother prepared a special breakfast, where her parents were excitedly acclaiming the opportunities that awaited her. Jamaica reacted to all of this with suspicion, anger, and discomfort (for one thing, her new underwear was uncomfortable [*Lucy* 4]).

Clearly Annie's efforts were motivated by a need to prepare and protect her daughter, but the daughter in *Annie John* viewed the mother as a hypocrite who professed to love her child and not want to live without her at the same time that she was planning "separation after separation" (133), and treating her leaving as a holiday to celebrate (134). As the girl in *Annie John* prepares to leave home, she is torn between anger that her mother was sending her away and her purported joy in never again seeing her mother, her father, Antigua, or anything associated with them: "My heart swelled with a great gladness as the words 'I shall never see this again' spilled out inside me. But then, just as quickly, my heart shriveled up and the words 'I shall never see this again' stabbed at me. I don't know what stopped me from falling in a heap at my parents' feet" (*AJ* 145).

As usual, she did not share her angry and conflicting feelings with her mother but rather put on a false face so that Annie would have been shocked at her daughter's wrath and her perception of all of her mother's actions as false. The mother certainly empathized with what she knew was her daughter's pain at leaving home, and she held her hand, kissed her, hugged her, cried, reminded her to wave the red handkerchief she had given her for that purpose, and assured her, "It doesn't matter what you do or where you go, I'll always be your mother and this will always be your home" (*AJ* 147), words meant as consolation but interpreted as a threat, words that the daughter would always resist and futilely attempt to refute—but that she never, alas, forgot.

Though Antigua is only 14 miles long and 11 miles wide (or 12 miles by 9 miles, Kincaid usually reports), when Kincaid left for the United States, as she relates it, she had not seen much of the island. She considers it typically Antiguan not to be interested in exploring other places; a small street on which one grows up becomes one's world, she told Leslie Garis, "and you have no interest in anything else" (44).

On March 9, 1967, just a little more than a year and a half after Kincaid left Antigua, Annie Richardson and David Drew were married at the Ebenezer Methodist Church by Reverend J. Willingham.[15] David Alexander Drew's age is listed as sixty-one, his condition, "bachelor," and his profession, "carpenter." Annie Victoria Richardson's age is listed as forty-one, her condition, "spinster," and her profession, "home domestic." It is very likely that David Drew was actually sixty-six years old at this time as is suggested by his death certificate, which gives his year of birth as 1901. It is also likely that Annie was actually forty-seven at this time, given that all other records indicate she was born in 1919. The marriage certificate suggests he was twenty years older than she; other records indicate he was probably eighteen years older. As previously noted, Kincaid never mentions this late marriage and may have known nothing about it. She may not have known that all of Annie's children, and not just she, had, in fact, been born with a line through them.

But Joseph recalled it vividly, telling me exactly what grade and what school he was in at the time, and lamenting the fact that the ring that his mother always wore "disappeared" when she died. I wondered during this conversation (but said nothing about the possibility) if the ring he recalled was the one that Kincaid described to me as her grandmother's ring that Annie Drew gave to her before she died. Probably not! Kincaid suggested to me that her mother had stopped wearing the grandmother's ring; and thus the ring that Joseph suggested she always wore was probably her own wedding ring.

During the years after her daughter left Antigua, Annie Drew somehow found the time to become increasingly involved in political activity. To understand her involvement, it is necessary to go back to the formation of the Antigua Trades and Labour Union, of which Vere Cornwall Bird became president in 1943. Bird and other trade unionists then formed the Antigua Labour Party (ALP), which entered candidates in the 1946 elections and became the majority party in 1951, controlling the government for the next two decades. V. C. Bird became the first chief minister of Antigua in 1960 and the first premier in 1967, the year in which Antigua was granted self-rule with Sir Wilfred Jacobs appointed as governor, a man whom Annie Drew described as an "evil ass" (Snodgrass 12). Annie Drew had first been involved with the ALP and was an ardent Bird supporter in the 1960s. Finally Bird found himself criticized by former supporters, such as George Walter and a number of younger trade unionists and politicians, many of whom had been overseas and had trained in various professions. Bird, who, according to the Antiguan political activist Vincent "Tubby" Derrick, "was a ruthless kind of fellow [who] believed in instilling fear in people to [maintain] control," began to feel threatened by "those young people and started hounding them," even attempting to deport one "chap called Bobby [Robert] Margetson," a member of a prominent Antiguan family originally from Montserrat. About this time Annie Drew, too, had a big falling out with Bird, very likely, Derrick speculates, because of the dispute between her good friend George Walter and Bird. She would have none of Bird's attempts to "bring him [Walter] back in line ('manners him,' as we say here)" (Derrick e-mail, February 12, 2009). It was at this time that the Progressive Labour Movement (PLM), which was a coalition of several groups opposing Bird, was formed and Derrick became involved in government ("I thought it was so damn unfair for V. C. to be trying to pull that rank"). Around this time Annie Drew, too, joined ranks with the PLM. In 1971 the PLM contested the election, with Drew working in the St. John's City South constituency; and when they won they chose George Walter to lead them. Walter came from Tanner Street in the Ovals, the area where

Drew lived. Annie Drew was a close friend and a passionate defender of Premier George Walter. Reverend Lee declared: "She loved him quite a bit. She would always take up for him. If someone said some things about him, she would be very defensive." According to Vincent Derrick: "She really opposed anyone who, in her view, was opposing George Walter. She was a very strong person, very strong." Walter served as premier from 1971 to 1976. The PLM lost the next election in 1976. Derrick speculates on why they lost:

> At the time it looked like the Progressive Labour Movement was invincible and Bird could never get back in, but it didn't work out that way. The Progressive Labour Movement only lasted for one term. I suppose we were inexperienced politicians, so to speak, because George Walter still had a lot of respect and sympathy for V. C. Bird, so he didn't want to deal with him as any politician would really deal with the opposing forces. He was still sympathetic to Bird and treated him very well, but V. C. took advantage of that good will to deal with George.

Thus the ALP regained power, and Annie Drew was a bitter opponent of the controlling party for the rest of her life. When Antigua became an independent nation in 1981, Bird became the first prime minister and Sir Wilfred Jacobs was appointed as governor general. The ALP, the longest-serving government in the Caribbean, stayed in power for the next twenty-eight years, under the leadership of V. C. Bird and later his son Lester Bird, who became prime minister when his father resigned in 1993 and was then elected in 1994, serving until 2004. Lester Bird's was the regime so bitterly attacked in Kincaid's *A Small Place.* A similar view of the Bird years was provided to me by a taxi driver when during my January 2009 visit we passed campaign pictures of Lester Bird, who was running in the upcoming election; the driver started talking about the Bird government and all the things they did to enrich themselves during their tenure. He said the politicians always had high-sounding explanations for why they did things like prohibit the parking of ambulances on government-owned land and require that they be parked instead on the politicians' privately owned land, allowing the politicians to charge parking fees; he concluded, *"Big talk/shit walk."*

The 2004 election was won by the United Progressive Party UPP), and Baldwin Spencer became prime minister, an event that Annie did not live to witness but that brought much satisfaction to her family and a large number of other Antiguans. Derrick was the chairman of the UPP, which grew out of the PLM and was victorious in 2004.

Annie Drew was so active and so much admired for her work with the PLM that she was, her daughter insists, "considered at one point the most powerful woman in Antigua." Tim Hector declared that she was known from one end of the island to the other as a woman "who never failed to declare her views, in a society where people still fear to declare their views" (13). While Kincaid and others, including Rabinowitz, suggested that Annie Drew probably did some speaking, I couldn't find anyone who could recall an actual speech. Kincaid told me that her mother "would address *crowds!*" Rabinowitz told me, "I'm sure she did [make political speeches]. I never heard one." It certainly seems clear that when Annie chose to, she could speak very eloquently and convincingly and perhaps "cleverly" (the term Rabinowitz used to describe her speech); and even if she did not make political appeals from the stage, it is clear that she did a lot of effective political campaigning in her neighborhood. A close friend of hers who was also an activist told me: "She was not a speaker—she never appeared on the platform; she was active house to house. She worked like hell for the party and for her representative" (January 21, 2009). Derrick recalls that "she was a person who was out there carrying a message among her friends. . . . She was a force around town. She knew what was going on." Reverend Lee noted: "She would know how to get her message across. She did not speak at political rallies, but she would [talk to people one on one]." Dr. Osoba and some of the staff at the Miss Davis School[16] discussed Mrs. Drew's political activism, noting that she attended rallies, was vocal, heckled opponents, and cheered her candidates. One of the staff members concluded, "She was a community activist" (April 26, 2009).

Winston Derrick recalls: "Annie was some lady. She was a powerful lady. In the days of the mighty power of V. C. Bird, here was this woman being very vocal when local people were fearful of speaking out. She was all over the country at political meetings."

Mrs. Drew was also a member of a women's group, a part of the Antigua Workers Union, Reverend Lee recalled. They were a support group that campaigned, sponsored activities, and worked in whatever role they were needed during elections. They were not feminist activists at all.

There are several accounts of Annie Drew's courageous underground work for her political party, work that was so important that it has become almost legendary. Kincaid told me that in the 1970s after she left home, when there were a lot of bombings and other actions aimed at destabilizing the Walter government that her mother supported, she was the one who was able to study the evidence and discover who was responsible. Rabinowitz recalled

Tim Hector (the Pan-Africanist activist often acclaimed the "political intellectual" of Antigua [Buhle 3]) talking about Annie's heroism at her funeral:

> He [Hector] talked about Annie and some other woman [who] went out in the dark of night (I'm *serious* about this) and did some secret things (of course you know that he was very liberal—the Bird government called him communist to make him reduced in effect (it was a time, you know, it was a McCarthy time)—what he talked about her doing—which I cannot remember in *any* single detail—was something *terribly* courageous and important [to the political campaign and objectives]. That's what I remember. He was a *won-der-ful* speaker with a beautiful voice and everything.

Vincent Derrick said that a group of women, including Mrs. Drew, was finally, after working "quite a while," able to expose the so-called Antigua Freedom Fighters, who were really a cover for Bird's Antigua Labour Party and who covertly distributed posters and the like in the community. His account was verified by Conrad Luke: "She knew the people connected to the Antigua Labour Party who were printing illegal leaflets and she set out to find the connections, to find where the leaflets were dropped off, and as a result they were able to provide the information that exposed them." Paul Buhle provides greater detail of the situation and Annie's role. He explains that the former government attempted to destabilize the Walter government with a series of bombings and cane field fires:

> To hear of it on the Bird-owned radio station, the end of civilization was practically at hand. A mysterious "AFF" avowed, in anonymous leaflets, that the capital city of St. Johns would be destroyed by fire, on a certain date in September 1972. The police claimed that they could do nothing. None other than . . . Annie Drew, stepped in to lead a minimovement of Antiguan women to ferret out the bombers. (Buhle 177)

Drew and her female cohorts employed varied disguises and organized patrols; they went out early in the morning and late at night in their efforts to discover the "terrorists." At one point, Hector tells us, Annie Drew, disguised as a one-legged man, "hid under a culvert at dead of night" (20). Ultimately Annie and her female cohorts uncovered all the evidence to identify the culprits and handed it over to the police. Of her successful intervention, Hector writes: "All she did then was done without thought of reward or of honour. It was done because it had to be done. When history becomes truly history, . . . Annie Drew will get her just historical due" (21).

According to Jocelyn Reid, Mrs. Drew's political involvement wasn't always above board. She chuckled as she recalled her coming in one election day and laughing about how she had voted three times, going from one precinct to another. This brought to Reid's mind how "Ms. Annie" would often come and sit where we were sitting at the time on Reid's porch and chat and laugh with her. She sadly declared, "I really miss her."

Nothing could make Annie Drew compromise her political commitments and cooperate with the party in power—except, as we shall later see, when a fifteen-year-old Devon was arrested for robbery and murder. Even when she lost her government job cleaning for the Antigua Recreation Grounds that Vincent Derrick assumes George Walter had gotten for her when he was in power, Mrs. Drew would not recant her affiliation. Her minister, Reverend Lee, shared the following account with me:

> She was very political. She supported [the PLM]. Like now, when we're in the midst of an election. When I got close to her, it wasn't this government [UPP], but it was the Antigua Labour Party and usually when it was a *national* day, and we would put out a flag and we would sing the National Anthem, but because she was not supportive of that party that was in control, she would refuse to stand, and she got upset because I had to talk to her about it. She get upset because I had to talk to her. She wasn't abusive, but she let me know in so many words that she was displeased. She would talk like [yelling], "Nobody a tell me what fa do! Me a big woman. Nobody a tell me what fa do! I not stand up for Bird flag!" It would be an outburst like that. But then after a while, you would talk to her and she quieted down. You had to know how to speak with her.

She was much admired, according to Kincaid, by the late Tim Hector. She was also admired by many ordinary men on the street: Kincaid told me that whenever she walked down the street, someone would yell, "'Hey, Annie!' or, 'Mrs. Drew!' Young men would see her even as an old woman, and say, 'Oh, you gonna marry me?'"

According to some, Annie Drew moved in all circles. Hector tells us that few Antiguans were more socially mobile than she: "She moved among all strata, citizen and migrant alike, with such compelling ease and grace that she became a name and a figure in her own right" (17). And yet, despite her close friendship with many of the important figures in Antiguan politics, and her association with other prominent Antiguans as a result of her daughter's fame, the issue of class and status must have always haunted this woman who placed such a premium on proper behavior. Rabinowitz noted this several times in our interview. When I asked if Annie's snide comments and apparently deceptive behavior around her resulted from racial antagonism, she responded: "No, I didn't feel antagonism. I felt a real class difference. She was so—uncomfortable—you have to understand, she was working as a cleaner for Social Security. That is not a very classy job. And I think she was kind of intimidated and trying to be the lady." But even here, Annie was a complex character, and in response to my later question, "There was a certain amount of sophistication about her [Annie], wasn't there?," Rabinowitz responded, "Oh, yes, if she didn't choose to hide it," and went on to share with me an account of a big political march, including several local politicians, a *New York Times* reporter, and Jamaica Kincaid. When the leaders went up on the stage, Kincaid told Rabinowitz, "my mother was sitting up there like the Queen of anything." "And she was very sophisticated when she was doing any of these political things," Rabinowitz continued. "But as far as station in life . . ." Rabinowitz's failure to complete this thought was more eloquent and revealing than words.

Obviously Annie Drew was pleased to be associated with the political bigwigs and very sensitive to any slights that reflected on her class status, thus explaining her leaving the Ebenezer Church after the previously recounted incident in which the minister didn't shake her hand after shaking hands with the big shots. And yet she knew that social lines would continue to be drawn in her society. Vincent Derrick told me, "She *really* and *truly* was from the masses, if you know what I mean." Though he applauded the fact that the Progressive Labour Party included "people of *every* structure in the society," he admitted that she would not have interacted socially with the upper-class members, for there were many class distinctions: "You would find all sorts of prejudices in those days"—and this despite the fact that Vincent and Winston Derrick grew up on Rodney Street (now Lionel Hurst Street) in the same Ovals neighborhood in which Annie lived. That Annie was at times very thin-skinned was reinforced by Reverend Lee: "She was a very sensitive person. If she feel somebody looking at her for no reason, she would, 'What ya watch me fa?'"

Annie Drew's often dire economic situation only exacerbated her problems. Reverend Lee told me that after losing her government job, "she caught a little thing here and there and with what the daughter sent for her, and then what the boys would give her to cook for them." During the latter years of her life, probably through most of the 1990s, according to a few sources, she worked as a cook and cleaner for Dr. Albertine Mathurin, a psychiatrist, and her husband, Jurgenson Mathurin.

In addition to her work, her political involvement, and her efforts to raise her children, Annie Drew was also a force in her community. Winston Derrick declared that the neighborhood children all knew that she would not let them get away with anything wrong. At the same time, "she would stand up for you if you were in any way disadvantaged." Similar memories were shared by Splif, who knew her when he was a boy growing up in the neighborhood: "She was like an old friend of mine . . . She was like one of those old women who looked out for everyone who passed. She looked out for all the kids in the neighborhood."

Whenever Vincent Derrick returned to Antigua from abroad and saw Annie Drew, "She was always talking about the neighborhood, the changes, the people who were no longer there."

One expects her daughter was uppermost in her mind in these conversations.

5

IN AMERICA . . . FINALLY

> [When I was nine my prayers ended,] "And please, God, let me go to America."
> —Kincaid, "The Fourth," *Talk Stories*

Jamaica Kincaid's first three years away from home and mother are fused into one year in her autobiographical *Lucy,* where, she has declared, "I was writing about *my own experience*" (Perry 506–7; emphasis mine). She does, however, change her December arrival to the middle of January, assert that she came to the United States from her small island home rather than Puerto Rico, coalesce the two families for whom she worked into one, and make the just-arrived Lucy the age Jamaica probably was when she left the Arlens, the second family for whom she worked. She gives Lucy her own exact birth date and the name Potter (149), the last name of her biological father and the name that is on her own birth certificate;[1] but she never indicates the names of the cities in which "Lucy" lived in the Caribbean or the United States. Thus, while her destination is clearly in the United States, her vagueness about specific locations might be seen as a cover for her "layover" in Puerto Rico.

When the Kincaid character arrives in the United States in *Lucy,* she is picked up by her employers, the Masons, and has special sites pointed out to her on the ride from the airport. She is surprised at how ordinary these places looked. She has her first elevator ride going up to their apartment (*Lucy* 4). The next morning she is shocked to find that though the sun is shining, she is cold through and through. Already she finds herself longing for the home and family she despised so much she often wished them dead (5–6). She comforts herself by imagining that she is eating her favorite dish of mullet, figs, and coconut milk, cooked by her favorite person in all the world, her grandmother (*Lucy* 7). Here and elsewhere it is clear that almost everything she does in America is colored by her Caribbean childhood. It is interesting that at this point she remembers her grandmother, with whom she visited on her first journey from home. Most often, however, we are reminded that the specter of her mother hovers over her throughout every aspect of her

American sojourn: there is no escaping Annie Drew's promise that wherever Jamaica goes and whatever she does, she will always be her mother and Antigua will always be her home.

Though no location is specified in *Lucy,* Jamaica in fact lived and worked in Scarsdale upon her arrival. The one thing that she was most excited about was seeing New York City. According to "Jamaica Kincaid's New York," she asked her employers over and over again how far New York was. "Finally,"[2] in December 1965, they made a trip to New York, where Jamaica delighted in the tall buildings, the hectic pace of the people, their indifference to each other, the shoes she purchased, the chestnuts she greedily ate (even though she didn't like them), and the traffic. She was enthralled that finally what she had always prayed for (to see New York) had come to pass (72). She notes that this was the first time she had been so excited about something and had not shared it with her mother (72).

Kincaid's childhood friend Jocelyn Reid provided another version of her arrival in the United States; she told me that the doctor for whom she was working in Puerto Rico migrated to the United States, taking her with his family. Then one of the children in the family put a cat on Elaine, and she left them. One person who knew her well said he believed that before she came to live with the Arlens she had lived in Connecticut and that she probably left because the work was too hard and because she wanted to be in New York (April 23, 2009).

At any rate, it is clear that she left the family with whom she first lived in the United States and took a job she found through a newspaper ad as an au pair for the writer Michael Arlen, his wife, Ann Warner Arlen, and their four daughters in the Upper East Side of New York. The Arlens would appear thinly disguised in *Lucy* as Lewis and Mariah. In their home she lived in the maid's room, cared for their children, and went to school at night. The Jamaica character, Lucy, was thrilled to be in a family that did not say grace and did not punish the children for spilling their food or for not eating their food or for saying bad things. She vowed that if she ever had children she would assure that their first words would be bad words (*Lucy* 13).

In a telephone conversation with me, someone familiar with her at the time recalls her when she first came as "Elaine Richardson, . . . a tall and gangly, sweet, good-natured young girl who spoke well and had been brought up right" (April 23, 2009). (Annie would be so proud!) He also said she was good at her job as an au pair and had empathy with the Arlen children.

When she first came to the United States, Kincaid sent her paychecks home to her mother, but she soon stopped, finding it at sixteen "a great injustice" to have to send money home to her family. She later used her money to educate herself: "I became the parents I didn't have for myself" (Cook 20). Throughout Kincaid's writings and interviews, she treats her mother's expectation of support as a reprehensible affront, one which wins her much sympathy from many of her Western readers. However, we should keep in mind that when any member of a destitute Third World family was fortunate enough to manage to get to the United States, he/she was (and still is) generally expected to help the family, a point hilariously made by the comedienne Hazelle in "I Not Going to Stop til I Make It to de Top," where the Caribbean immigrant arrives in America determined to get to "de *top,* top, top" (11), but pauses to add, "But I must make it fast because my family is depending on me" (10). Coincidentally, a Jamaican acquaintance living in Richmond, Virginia, told me the day before I wrote this paragraph (March 2009) that her aunt in Jamaica had just died and added, "I've never forgotten her since I came to America; every month I sent her a little something." Checks from emigrants from all over the Third World are a major source for reducing poverty and provide a large percentage of the foreign exchange for numerous countries, including Antigua.

When Jamaica first arrived in the United States, she wrote reassuring notes to her mother, telling her that her life here was wonderful, except for the cold weather. In letters dated December 1965 and January 1966, she calls her mother dearest and frequently expresses her love for her and the family, signing off as her loving daughter (NY 71). She informs her mother in the January letter that she has bought some shoes exactly like a pair her mother had declared too extravagant for her to wear in Carnival, reminding us of Annie's choosing a dress to travel to Antigua that she knew would upset her father. Jamaica does reassure her mother that the shoes are acceptable in America. She assures her that she remembers everything her mother taught her (NY 71–72). In her comments on her letters, however, Kincaid makes it clear that she was not being truthful. In *Lucy,* she explains how much she exaggerated in the most flowery language how wonderful everything was in her life in the United States (10). It's very likely also that the letters that appear in Kincaid's accounts are not true copies of the letters she actually sent to her mother.

Her letters home became shorter and shorter.

Her mother's letters requested more information about her progress toward her goal of training to become a nurse. Finally she informed her mother that she did not want to pursue the life they planned for her. Her mother, thinking the change had been motivated by some man with whom she was having a relationship, wrote back with the usual warnings about men.

At one point the Jamaica character wrote to tell her mother about her first ride on a subway, and her mother wrote back to warn her of horrible things she had read about happening on subways, a letter that frightened her so much that she was afraid to go out (*Lucy* 20). Soon after that, she stopped opening the letters from her family and friends and walked around with the letters in her brassiere; she was filled with hatred for these people she had once loved (*Lucy* 20). The unopened letters piled up. She says at one point that she received ten—and later nineteen—letters from her mother that went unread and unanswered, admitting that if she read any of them she would be overcome with yearning for her (*Lucy* 91). Even a letter marked URGENT was consigned to Lucy's packet of unopened letters from home (*Lucy* 115). When Maude Quick, an acquaintance from her home island, hand-delivered a letter from her mother, Lucy finally opened it and found that her stepfather had died and left her mother a pauper (126). She prepared to send all the money she had been saving to her mother, and Mariah gave her double what she had to send as well. Lucy wrote her mother a cold letter, castigating her for marrying a man who died without leaving enough money for his funeral. She went on to declare that her upbringing had been a failure and that she was now enjoying her life as a slut. Her mother's response was that she loved her and the usual reminder that she would always be her mother and Lucy's home would always be with her. Furious, Lucy burned all of the letters from her mother (127–28). Soon thereafter Lucy wrote what she considered a last letter to her mother in which she told her she would be home soon, said that the family with whom she was living was moving, and gave her an address that she made up (139–40).[3]

Lucy was taken with the family to their vacation home, the house in which Mariah had grown up. From her room, she could see the lake, a comforting view for one who had always lived near the sea (35).

Mariah attempted to be kind to Lucy, but Lucy was full of resentment for *another* mother figure and often responded to her kindness with fury. When, for one example, Mariah took her to see some daffodils, Lucy was overcome with rage, recalling poems she had been forced to memorize about flowers she had never seen (29–30);[4] when Mariah expressed pride in her Indian blood, Lucy was offended at how someone who represented the victor could also maintain that she was the vanquished (41); she even disliked Mariah because she smelled pleasant, while Lucy preferred a powerful and offensive odor (27).[5] And yet, like *The Young Lucifer,*[6] her repudiation of Mariah brought her no more pleasure than similar actions against her mother: in one instance, Lucy admits: "The anguish on [Mariah's] face almost broke my heart, but I would not bend. It was hollow, my triumph, but I held on to it just the same" (41).

The Kincaid character's fury toward Mariah provides another example of the "tradition" the author felt obligated to keep up. Here, as with her mother, she always finds fault. Thus, while she acknowledges that though her situation with Mariah is fortunate, she brags that she is not the kind of person who acknowledges blessing; rather she is the sort of person who would never have enough blessings (*Lucy* 110). Kincaid says of herself: "I'm never satisfied. I'm always complaining. And I hope I stay that way" (Donahue 05D). This stubborn and obsessive drive to find fault with, defeat, annoy, and even injure others is often expressed by Kincaid and the deceitful Kincaid characters who delight in being contrary. In Kincaid's account of her travels with a group of fellow gardeners in China, for example, she wrote that one of the men had called her a bitch, though what he actually said was that she was always bitching; she admits that she intentionally misrepresented what he said in order to empower herself and bully him (*MG* 208).

While with the Arlens, Jamaica completed her secondary education at Westchester Community College and started taking college courses at night. She has said she studied to be a nurse (as her mother had intended), even though she could not stand the sight of blood, and whenever she saw anyone who was ill, she sympathetically developed the same symptoms. She knew she didn't want to be a nurse, but she continued her studies since her mother always cautioned against passing up any opportunity to better herself (NY 72). In the Cudjoe interview, however, she said that though she was *"supposed"* to study nursing, she never did. She studied photography at the New York School for Social Research in New York at night. There, she has noted, the White people found her charming, especially her speech, while the Black people hated her and found her and her speech ridiculous. She met and became particularly enthralled with Sally, whose clinging pants, bleached hair hanging over her eyes, continual smoking of Marlboro cigarettes, use of marijuana, casual picking up of strange men, and slang speech peppered with obscenities endeared this bad and tough American girl to Kincaid (NY 72). This attraction reminds us of Annie John's attraction to the Red Girl, whose upbringing and behavior contradicted everything of which her mother approved. Jamaica started hanging out with Sally, doing the things she did, frequently going to New York—behavior that she knew would upset her mother. Sometime later Sally moved to Newport Beach, California. In the summer of 1969, twenty-year-old Jamaica visited her for two weeks and discovered that Sally no longer held the same fascination for her (NY 72).

Jamaica decided to leave the Arlens. As she writes about this in *Lucy,* when Lucy told Mariah she was leaving, Mariah said she hadn't been with them the year as contracted (141). In reality, Jamaica stayed with the Arlens three years, so her employer's protest is obviously a fictional addition. Indeed, according to one source, she actually left them to go away to college for a year, and then returned to work for them again around the time that they were beginning the process of divorcing (April 23, 2009). Further, that source indicates that Kincaid returned from her year in college a different person, one "pranc[ing] around" for women's empowerment and caught up in the Black militant movement of the 1960s. Her relationship with the Arlens soon ended, leaving them with sour memories of her.

Finally, the nineteen-year-old Jamaica was on her own in New York as she had frequently prophesied. She has said she worked as a receptionist and took a secretarial job, but decided to go back to school. She won a scholarship to the now-defunct Franconia College in New Hampshire, where she started to write poems (Dilger 21), but then suddenly, as she tells it to Buckner, she declared one day that she wasn't doing what she wanted to do: she wanted to be a writer; and she packed her clothes and moved back to New York (Buckner 465; see also Dilger 21). She had attended college just a little more than a year (Cudjoe 216).

Kincaid often writes of her New York life. Though she was doing what she wanted to do, she was often miserable and poor. She had a variety of jobs to support herself: she worked with the magazine *Art Direction* (Cudjoe 216); she worked at a bicycle shop, as a receptionist, and as a model: "I made a living, modeling. Not nude, I don't think" (Buckner 466); she was a backup singer for a transvestite (Levintova). She even applied and was approved for unemployment, but she never received a check (Buckner 466). She said that sometimes her only meal was what she got at cocktail parties and other places where food was served, as a result of which she was very thin (Buckner 466). She lived with friends for a while, sleeping on different people's floors (Buckner 465). She lived in other people's apartments while they traveled. She finally got a small apartment for $225 a month (Buckner 466), but she couldn't afford to properly heat it or to purchase anything except a typewriter, desk, stereo, and lamp. She had no amenities, no bookshelves for her books and records, no nice cushions for her window seats. The kitchen was so small she couldn't turn around in it with outstretched hands (NY 73). She slept on the floor until a mouse ran over her, and then she managed to get a bed (Buckner 466).[7] Because of the problem with mice, in 1977 she had to move out for two weeks. Even after returning, she stood on a chair to dress and cook because of her fear of the mice who were no longer there (NY 73).

Yu made yu bed; now lie in it!

Annie Drew had no sympathy for her poor, hungry daughter shivering in a cold New York apartment. She had arranged for Jamaica to go first to Puerto Rico and later to the United States, live in a beautiful and comfortable house with a supportive family who fed her, clothed her, offered her opportunities for travel and education, and paid her enough money to allow her to send some support to her destitute family in Antigua. She could not help but think that her daughter's giving all of that up to follow what Mrs. Drew must have viewed as the foolish pipe dream of being an author was selfishness of the first degree. She was looking at three needy boys and a dying husband.[8] How could she sympathize with a young, healthy, self-indulgent daughter in the midst of all the opportunities that America offered?

Kincaid, who had grown up thinking that all writers were dead, maintains that *she* still found the idea of being a writer an oddity even after she moved to New York. She declares in "Jamaica Kincaid's New York" that she never knew a writer and that when she finally met a writer, a social columnist, she couldn't fathom that a grown man would consider that any way to make a living (73). It should, therefore, have been obvious to her that her mother would find it hard to envision her as a writer and writing as a desirable way to make a living. Jamaica knew her mother would like to brag to her friends that her once-troublemaking daughter now lives in America, where she has a prestigious job in industry and plies her with lovely gifts (NY 73). Kincaid says her mother does not respond to what she tells her about her desire to write, and views her daughter's New York life as a rebellion against her (NY 73).

One cannot miss the irony that Kincaid, who can never forgive her mother for not supporting her efforts to become a writer, could be just as judgmental of her own daughter's love of singing. In a *People* article, Kincaid insists that her own children "don't feel they *have* to be anything," and that she will support her children in whatever they do (Kaufman 114); however, the fact is that Kincaid's attitude toward her daughter's interest in music was much more cynical than her mother's attitude toward her efforts to write: She discouraged Annie Shawn's interest in a musical career, facetiously asking her husband if the world really needed another brown person singing (*MB* 44). One wonders if she ever told her daughter this and if her daughter were as pained at her lack of empathy as Jamaica was at Annie Drew's. At any rate, as a Caribbean parent, Kincaid was probably happy that Annie Shawn finished Harvard in 2007 as a pre-med student with a psychology major. Young Annie's interest in music clearly continued, however, as she also served as music director of the Harvard Opportunes, an a cappella vocal ensemble, from 2003 to 2008 and composed more than fifteen arrangements for performance (Annie Rosamond Shawn, résumé). In 2014 her vocation was listed in Wikipedia as singer/songwriter. Perhaps time explains Kincaid's different reaction to her son's musical career. She appears to be happy that he, now known as Harold Levelsoundz Shaw, is a producer and songwriter, and she is the president of the Levelsoundz Fan Club (Wikipedia, January 28, 2014).

Despite her anger at her mother's response to her living in New York and pursuing a career as a writer, Jamaica attributes her ability to make her own way in New York to her mother's insisting that she be independent and do for herself (NY 73). She also acknowledges how accurate her mother had been in her warnings that it would be rare to find more than one or two good men (NY 73).

In 1976, after eleven years in the United States, she celebrated the bicentennial as a resident New Yorker and declared that it was the first time that she considered herself an American (*Talk Stories* 59).

When Kincaid started writing, she chose a new name, partly so that no one in Antigua would know she was writing, partly so that she could anonymously write brutal things about herself and her family (Wachtel 63), partly so she wouldn't be ridiculed by her mother for her failure, partly because she always enjoyed creating new personas and taking on new identities, and partly because she "always hated my name" (Cudjoe 218); she told Allan Vorda that "the name Elaine always seemed stupid" ("An Interview" 15). When she discovered that her mother had named her after a Lebanese woman whom she despised, she disliked her name even more (Cudjoe 218). Kincaid's attitude toward her name is expressed through Lucy, who hated her name and would much have preferred names of her favorite authors: Emily, Charlotte, Jane, Enid (*Lucy* 149). Kincaid's most common explanation for changing her name is that she didn't want anyone she knew to know she was writing because they would laugh at her (Dilger 22; see also Buckner 467).

She told me that she chose her new name before she met anyone at the

New Yorker. At the time, 1973, her friends were in "a demi-world, very stylish people, gays, etc. I sat around with them and talked about changing my name." They seemed to like her choice. In an interview with Buckner, she makes it appear that the friends played a more active part, offering emotional support as they all discussed a variety of names for her (466); she also told him that everyone, except her mother, immediately accepted her name and never called her by her original name, and even her mother finally started calling her Jamaica.

She has given several explanations for her choice of the name Jamaica Kincaid. She told Cudjoe that, having become alienated from the Caribbean, she chose "Jamaica" as "symbolic of that place," and she chose Kincaid because it "just seemed to go with it" (220). Cryer asserts that the name "Kincaid" was inspired by a character in a play by George Bernard Shaw (B4). However, Kincaid insisted to Vorda that there was no logic to her choice of her name: "I was playing around with identities. . . . I had no idea anyone would one day be asking me how it all came to be or I would have made better sense of it at the time" ("An Interview" 14).

At any rate, we are forced to wrestle with the implications of this change of name when we recall Xuela Claudette Richardson's asking what a *real* name was and concluding that one's name reflects her history, how one judges oneself, and how one is judged by others (*Auto* 79). Everywhere in Kincaid, her personae, like the author herself, declare their names (often some version of their own or their families' names), and we are led to explore and weigh the meaning, significance, and *realness* of those names. The last chapter of *Annie John* opens, "My name is Annie John," and the last thing the narrator sees the night before she leaves home is her name written in big black letters on her trunk (130). *At the Bottom of the River* ends with the Kincaid character growing complete, "my name filling up my mouth" (82). Lucy hates her name and told her mother once that she wanted to change her name to Enid, provoking her mother so much that she turned blood red and was transformed into a furious monster (*Lucy* 150). Later Lucy understands her mother's fury when she discovers that the name of the woman who had tried to kill them through Obeah was Enid (150); thereafter when she saw her name she reached out to embrace it (153). The novel ends with Lucy writing her full name, Lucy Josephine Potter, and then crying so much that her tears transformed her words into a big blur (163–64). In *Mr. Potter,* Kincaid says she hated her name, Elaine, and planned every day of her life to change it; then having changed it she no longer hates it, she only hates her mother who gave the name to her

(163). The last words of *Mr. Potter* are "my father's name was Mr. Potter" (195). Ovando, who is both her enemy and herself, intones his name over and over, delighting in the sound of it while he caresses his body and masturbates until he finally falls into a blissful and deep sleep ("Ovando" 82).[9]

It is ironical then that the Kincaid personae are sometimes unnamed, as in "Biography of a Dress" and "Girl," and when named, rarely referred to by name by anyone else in her works. In *Annie John,* if Annie John is called anything, she is called "Little Miss." In *Lucy,* the only way Lucy is addressed by her employers is as "The Visitor" or "Poor Visitor." Only once does anyone refer to Mrs. Sweet as Jamaica in *See Now Then,* and that is before she becomes Mrs. Sweet (112). While Kincaid states that her family called her Jamaica after she changed her name, she rarely records in her books their addressing her as Jamaica. One of the rare instances is when the dying Devon calls her to look at his penis (*MB* 91). The only other time she is addressed by any name in *My Brother* other than the sarcastic "maiy deahre" (*MB* 56–57) when Devon is making fun of her speech, is when her husband addresses her as "Sweetie" as he prepares to tell her of Devon's death (99). In some autobiographical accounts and interviews, she indicates that other children called her "Daddy Longlegs" and that her husband called her "Sweetie."

It is also ironical that Kincaid never attributes her name change to her hatred of the colonial practice of renaming people and things, something she often argues is designed to assert their power and ownership over everything and everyone they dominated. "To name is to possess," Kincaid informs through a chapter title in *My Garden (Book):* (114). At the time Kincaid changed her name, Blacks throughout the African Diaspora were changing their "slave names" as a statement of rebellion against colonial oppression and possession and of renewal of ties with Africa. However, Kincaid did not think much of the Black revolutionaries of the time and certainly had no desire to assert any ties with Africa. "At the time I changed [my name]," she told Allan Vorda, "I didn't know there were African names, although I don't think I could have done that because by this time I have as much connection to Africa as you do. The connection I have to Africa is the color of my skin and that doesn't seem enough to have changed it to an African name" ("An Interview" 15).

Kincaid wrote her first published article, "When I Was 17," which was based on an interview with Gloria Steinem about what it was like when she was seventeen, for *Ingenue* in 1973. This was followed by other articles in *Ingenue* based upon interviews with other celebrities, as well as pieces in *Ms.* and *Village Voice.*

Kincaid's real breaks in her writing career stemmed, according to her accounts, from a series of chance—and highly unlikely—meetings with three men, and she has noted that she might not have become the writer she is if not for that series of meetings (introduction, *Talk Stories* 8). It started with her meeting, when she was twenty-three, with *National Lampoon* editor Michael O'Donoghue, who was taken by her bizarre appearance: at the time she had cut her hair and bleached it blond; she had shaved her eyebrows and painted in gold-colored lines where the eyebrows should have been; she dressed in vintage clothes; she wore white socks and old saddle shoes; she wore funny little hats. Her appearance at the time was such that all kinds of people would stare and laugh at her, and Black people, in particular, would say insulting things to her (introduction, *Talk Stories* 7).[10] In some accounts, the meeting with O'Donoghue took place in a subway; in others, in an elevator. O'Donoghue then introduced her to George W. S. Trow, who was fascinated by her personality, her accounts of her family, her interesting commentaries about her life and the events around her, and her various other anecdotes, and started writing stories about her in his "Talk of the Town" stories in the *New Yorker.* In her introduction to *Talk Stories,* Kincaid credits George Trow of the *New Yorker* with being the first person to give credence to her voice, to attend what she had to say, and to laugh with her (5). He was so fascinated by her tales and her sense of humor that he arranged in the spring of 1974 for her to meet William Shawn, the editor of the *New Yorker.* Shawn did not think she would make a "Talk" reporter, but he encouraged her to try to write some stories. Five months later she wrote her first *New Yorker* piece and gave it to him. He edited and shaped it and set her on her career as a writer, a career during which she continued to think of herself as writing for Mr. Shawn and to feel successful when he liked something she showed him (*MB* 196). Thus when she wrote *My Brother* after Shawn's death, the possible response of this "perfect reader" (*MB* 197) still governed her work, leading her to declare that she "wrote about the dead for the dead" (*MB* 197).[11] Ian Frazier, in his foreword to *Talk Stories,* declares Shawn "the greatest editor of his day" and notes how Shawn's editing was instrumental in Kincaid's development as a writer: "This collection, with its invisible plot of a unique new writer being allowed a freedom to emerge story by story, is evidence also of a great editor doing his job" (xix).[12] Kincaid often acknowledges this influence: "I don't think I would have become a writer if it wasn't for *The New Yorker.* . . . It was writing for them—for Mr. Shawn, really—that helped me learn how to write" (Perry 509). Her friendship with Ian (Sandy) Frazier developed during their years together at the *New Yorker,* and she continues to talk with him every day (introduction, *Talk Stories* 14). Kincaid's elaborate account of how her writing career was promoted by O'Donoghue, Trow, and Shawn deliberately writes out any possible influence of her mother or of Michael J. Arlen. One acquaintance declares that Kincaid would have met people at the *New Yorker* at parties at the Arlen house; and that Arlen's best friend, David Halberstam, a Pulitzer Prize–winning journalist and an author who was killed in a car accident in 2007, befriended Jamaica and made it possible for her to go to college (April 23, 2009). However, like her brothers in *Annie John,* Arlen and Halberstam are written out of Kincaid's accounts of the *New Yorker* influences. It is certainly hard to believe that Kincaid, who lived for at least three years with a staff writer and television critic for the *New Yorker,* could insist that she did not meet anyone associated with the magazine until after she left his house, that she could not believe when she moved out on her own in New York that anyone made a living writing, or that she could live three years with this active writer and not be influenced in any way.

On September 30, 1974, she published her first article with the *New Yorker* on which her new name appeared, "West Indian Weekend," an account of a West Indian Day parade in Brooklyn. There followed a series of short pieces for the magazine's "Talk of the Town" department, most of them anonymous. These first writings were nonfiction accounts of goings-on in New York, with only fleeting references to Antigua. However, on October 17, 1977, she provided a brief account of her life on a West Indian island, one that offers the seeds of what her focus would remain for most of the rest of her career, but she does not name herself or her family or her island (*Talk Stories* 87–93).

The first story she wrote, simply titled "Girl," was published in the *New Yorker* in June 1978 and became the first story in her first book, *At the Bottom of the River* (1983). It remains her most anthologized fiction. This short piece (little more than two pages) anticipated the canon that was to follow: the whole story is the voice of an increasingly frustrated mother dictating rules of behavior to her recalcitrant daughter.

The attempt to keep her writing from her family through the name change was immediately foiled, she told Buckner, when a Peace Corps worker in Antigua read one of the early anonymous *New Yorker* "Talk of the Town" pieces, recognized the street and her family, and went to them with the magazine (467). In fact, literary detectives were still putting the Jamaica Kincaid puzzle together in Antigua as late as 1983–85. After reading an article by Kincaid in the *New Yorker* in 1985, Hyacinth Veronica Dyde contacted Mrs. Drew, one

Antiguan informed me in an e-mail (March 6, 2009). As Connie Rabinowitz recalls, she gave Hyacinth Dyde a copy of the newly published *At the Bottom of the River,* and the two of them started looking for Mrs. Drew. Rabinowitz, having read earlier Kincaid stories with a reference to Post Road, deducted that Kincaid was Antiguan. One day Mrs. Drew walked into Dyde's map store and said [very authoritative voice], "I hear you're looking for me." Dyde made a date for Rabinowitz to go to her house, where they met (Rabinowitz interview). On Dyde and Rabinowitz's initial visit to Annie Drew's house, Rabinowitz shared with Mrs. Drew Kincaid's comments about her mother's writing her life for her. She interpreted Mrs. Drew's "quiet and docile" show of unawareness as "an act," and would later find other things she did "insincere." In fact, from that first meeting, the two women seem not to have hit it off: "Mrs. Drew called us 'Connie and Ronnie.' I mean she did a lot of—I can't tell you—it's things that were supposed to be appealing to us. They didn't work."[13]

Mrs. Drew must have been shocked to see her daughter in print. Clearly she knew that she could write and write well. However, the idea that her daughter would be/could be a writer was as alien to her as it had been to her daughter herself, who often declared that she had always believed that all the writers were dead and all the writing had been done.

Annie Drew would see herself portrayed in one degree or another in the works that followed during her lifetime: *Annie John* (1985), *A Small Place* (1988), *Annie, Gwen, Lilly, Pam and Tulip* (1989), *The Autobiography of My Mother* (1996), and *My Brother* (1997). The big question is, *Did she read them?* Dr. Catherine John told me that in her conversation with her, "I didn't get the impression that she had necessarily *read* it," but John acknowledged, "She may have." Carole Boyce Davies explained to me: "She seemed only minimally aware of her daughter's books and perhaps had not really read them. It seems she was aware of their contents based on what others had told her. There was no indication that she herself sat down with the books and read them." Pastor Lee explained, "I don't know if she knew about *all* of them." Annie Drew herself has told some people (including one of Kincaid's American friends who prefers to remain anonymous) that she read all of them (February 10, 2009), but at other times she has suggested that she didn't read them. Some people who have talked with her have said with certainty that she read *some* of them. Kincaid told Buckner that her family read her books but didn't admit it (467).

Both Kincaid and Annie Drew often perpetuated the lie that Mrs. Drew did not read her daughter's work. In an interview with Bonetti, Kincaid said that her mother is "the person I really write for, [but] I imagine she does not read what I write" (38). While it was painful for Kincaid to hear that her mother did not read her work, she told me that she found it useful to at least pretend she believed that "because it meant I was free to say what I was going to say, and she wouldn't have to read it."

It was probably even more painful for Annie Drew to read what Kincaid had written and every bit as much a protective device for her to claim she didn't read it. Obviously she knew that to ignore what Kincaid wrote was an affront to a daughter who, however she would attack her mother, really sought that mother's approval, indeed, wrote for her mother (Bonetti 38). Despite her claims at times not to read what her daughter had written, an avid reader such as she could not really have ignored her own daughter's highly publicized writing, and there is overwhelming evidence that she did read some, if not all, of it.

Clearly, she had to have been alarmed and upset by many of the things that were said about her or about characters who obviously reflected her. However, she could not have been surprised, because she had always been upset by the way her daughter remembered—she would say revised and altered—things. When Kincaid reminds her mother of the ants attacking the newborn Devon, for one example, her mother, who had apparently forgotten it—or perhaps repressed it—says, "What a memory you have!" and Jamaica comments that her memory was "perhaps the thing she most dislikes about me" (*MB* 6). There were times when she would reprimand her daughter about something she wrote: "I don't know why you have to go and say those things. I don't know why you have to do that!" (Kin/Dance). Her conversations with any number of people, including Reverend Lee, Jocelyn Reid, Dr. Ermina Osoba, and other close friends clearly reflected her knowledge of at least some of her daughter's works.

At times she would put on a tough front and joke with friends about what Kincaid wrote. Dr. Osoba and Jocelyn Reid insisted that Annie didn't take things to heart and would laugh about what Kincaid was writing. Dr. Osoba mimicked Mrs. Drew's comments when she gave her a ride to the hospital: "You hear about Elaine? You hear what she was writing? [laughter] Is she writing about me! Don't mind her. Leave her alone. Don't bother with she" [laughter]. Dr. Osoba declared of Annie's response to her daughter: "She wasn't the kind of person to grieve. If something upset her, she would utter a few choice curse words and then dismiss it. She didn't take things to heart."

At other times, Annie simply insisted that what Kincaid wrote was merely "fiction," but it is impossible that she could truly console herself that her daughter's work was anything other than a harsh critique of her. When Kincaid mentioned in a *New York Times* piece that she was writing *Mr. Potter,* a fictional biography about her natural father, Nathaniel Roderick Potter, she was told by someone (she doesn't recall whether it was a friend or a brother) that her mother angrily exclaimed, "Now she'll write about Potter. What did Potter ever do for her?" Clearly the mother who raised her, taught her to read, and in many ways made her a writer felt some jealousy that Potter would be memorialized in a literary work when she had not only *not* been the central figure in a literary work, but had oftentimes been the villain.

Nevertheless, Annie clearly took some pride in her daughter's writing. After laughing about Mrs. Drew's dismissal of what Kincaid wrote, Dr. Osoba concluded, "But she was proud of her." When Rabinowitz went to visit Annie for the first time, there was a copy of *Annie John* on the table by which she sat. When Jamaica Kincaid later autographed *Annie John* for Rabinowitz, Annie Drew also penned her autograph above Kincaid's. She told another individual with whom I spoke with the promise of anonymity, "I'm very proud of her. Praise God for her!" (February 10, 2009) This pride is suggested in her frequently informing people that she was Jamaica's mother. When she met Dr. Ramsey, "She asked me if I knew her daughter—who she was. I didn't know she was her daughter. I heard about Jamaica Kincaid before." An Antiguan with whom I spoke, who met Mrs. Drew only once (after seeing her walking from the hospital one night and offering her a ride), told me that in the course of their conversation she said she was Jamaica Kincaid's mother (January 17, 2009).

It is unfortunate that Annie Drew apparently never revealed to her daughter how proud she was of her. Indeed, she may not have been aware how hungry the widely lionized author still was for her mother's acclamation. Her mother's approval always transported Jamaica to that Edenic world she so missed. Even as an adult, she longed for praise such as the Jamaica character experienced in *Annie John:* there, after the five-year-old girl returns from her first trip alone to the store to purchase three items, she tells us that her mother was so proud that her eyes filled with tears as she lifted her in her arms and declared that she was wonderful; Kincaid writes that the mother would not have been as proud had she just conquered a great nation (139–40). In fact Jamaica is often transplanted to her Edenic world when she notes that she inspires others to admire her. After she reads her brilliant essay on Rat Island to her class, her classmates surrounded her, applauding her essay and fighting each other to offer individual congratulations. Their actions fill her with love for them and a desire to stay with them forever (*AJ* 45). However, when her Brownie leader compliments *all* of the girls in the troop, the Jamaica character is not pleased: she is accustomed to being the only one receiving special recognition (*AJ* 115).

Kincaid insists that her mother was never proud of her achievements as an author and mother, or even gardener, a fact that still causes her a lot of pain, though she claims that she doesn't mind. When Garis asked her if her mother were proud of her, she replied: "It's really painful because some people might actually be rather proud of me. But it doesn't enter my mother's mind" (70). Clearly the fifty-nine-year-old Kincaid whom I interviewed still sought to win again the approval of her mother. When I asked if her mother were impressed by her garden when she visited her in Vermont, she insisted that she is nowhere near the gardener that Annie or even Devon was. She said that her mother would not have enjoyed her garden in Bennington: "No, she would have said she could grow things better. And she could." Thus we are not surprised that the ultimate insult in their last conversation was her mother's telling her that her accomplishments did not amount to much: the best thing in the world, Kincaid says, would have been not to hear her mother say this ("The Estrangement" 40), but this addendum makes it clear that the "best thing in the world" would have been an expression of pride from her mother.

Whatever the many fronts Annie put on to different people, the fact of the matter, according to one of her close friends and Reverend Lee, was that she was devastated by the fact that she had a daughter who seemed compelled to reveal every sordid detail of their lives and their relationship. In a January 21, 2009, telephone interview, the friend declared:

> Annie was so hurt by Kincaid's treatment of her. She told her, "Look, to feed you when your father wouldn't feed you, I prostituted myself." She told me, "I did all I could for that girl." She washed clothes for people until her fingers were damaged. She worked like hell to put her children through school. Anyone who knew her would say (as we say here), "she work until her drawers twist." . . . That woman was badly bruised and maligned by her daughter. Life was not kind to her. She was helpful to people who needed her help. She was a Christian woman. That one of her children should turn around and stab her in the back . . . ! [uttered with passionate anger]

Reverend Lee, who found the books "deplorable," declared asserted:

> And I think those books—I might be wrong—but I think they *hastened* her death. I think she worried a lot about it. After that first book that she gave me to read, she was really upset, and she felt she "don't see how she can be writing those things about her mother." Some of them are true, you know—when I say true—like what I told you about getting angry and having outbursts—some of those things are true. But like the other side of it where her sexual life was concerned and so on, I wouldn't know about that. She was really upset about the book. I don't know if she knew about *all* of them, but she was really upset. She cried. She was really upset. She cried. That's why I think that contributed to her [death].

Reverend Lee understood that she was privy to a side of Annie that few people saw:

> She had a blunt appearance, and people feel that she's an austere and wicked person, you know what I mean, but when you get close to her, she has a heart of—underneath of that, she has a heart of love—and she gets hurt. And she's hurt and people don't realize she's *hurt* because you're not close enough to her to know she's hurt. And the reason I understand, you know, my husband was something like that. Yes, you know he had a loud mouth. When I say loud mouth, I mean, you know, he would preach and act like he doesn't care when people said things about him. And he would come home and cry, weep like a child. So because of him, I knew how to deal with her because she had the same kind of personality.

Whether or not her mother read her work, approved of her work, or disapproved of her work, "it didn't at all interfere with my writing," Kincaid declared. It was, after all, perhaps the one way that Kincaid could feel powerful and in control in her relationship with her mother. The mother was more than equal in the combat with her daughter in real life, but Annie Drew could not compete with the power of the pen, which was indeed so much mightier than the sword. Kincaid is very aware of this supremacy. As she told Dwight Garner: "I try not to corner my mother anymore. Because I have at my disposal a way of articulating things about her that she can't respond to." Similarly, in *Mr. Potter,* she delights in the fact that she alone has the power to give Mr. Potter the name by which he will be known forever, that she alone can provide the narrative that will be recognized as his life (87), that she has through this book become the central figure in his life (153), and that it is only because of her that he is no longer anonymous (189). Certainly she can make the same claim for Annie Drew's life as well.

On the other hand, Kincaid sometimes downplays the power of her writing, telling both Buckner and me that she doesn't expect people to be interested in what she writes, and thus when she writes, she is thinking that no one will read it, allowing her to write with more conviction and honesty than she would if she were thinking that it would be read (Buckner 468). While this might be an excuse that the author uses to allow herself the freedom to write whatever she wishes, the works themselves raise questions about the veracity of this declaration. Even with that first class essay that she shares in *Annie John,* she carefully edited it with a consideration of what people who read the essay would think of her: she couldn't bear to have her classmates see how unhappy her mother was with her (*AJ* 45).

Kincaid clearly recognizes and relishes her godlike power as a writer with the prerogative to determine who and what will be treated and how: "In the beginning was my word and my word became the world as I ordered it to be" (*Talk Stories* 11).

6

THE SILENT YEARS AND THE RECONNECTION

> Your mother is so sad you never answer her letters.
> —Family friend to Kincaid character (*Lucy*)

> I knew that if I read only one, I would die from longing for her.
> —Kincaid character alluding to nineteen unopened letters from her mother (*Lucy*)

As Jamaica Kincaid struggled to become a writer and found herself hungry and broke and living in whatever cold New York apartment she could find, even sleeping on apartment floors, she wrote to her mother, who retorted, "It serves you right." The mother went on to castigate her for always attempting more than she could achieve (*MB* 17). The coldness of this response and the mother's lack of sympathy for her plight are among Jamaica's most painful memories, a blow that she can never forget, another of the indications, according to her, that her mother is incapable of loving her children as "grown-up people—adults" (*MB* 17).

Kincaid resolved never to speak to her again.

For the rest of Annie Drew's life, she and her daughter would have protracted periods when they were not speaking to each other, neither ever knowing when they would start speaking again and then when they would once more stop speaking. Of these years, Kincaid told me: "We corresponded some in that time. But it had a kind of life of its own. It would stop. It would start again." Indeed, Annie Drew's casual comment during her first meeting with Connie Rabinowitz in 1983 or 1984, "I've got to call Lainy," clearly indicates that there was some communication. In 1977 Kincaid disclosed that she did not write to her family for two years after her mother's "serves you right" response (NY 73). Elsewhere there are many references to a silence of nineteen or twenty years. The fact is that there were intermittent, infrequent correspondences during this period, but Mrs. Drew and Kincaid did not see each other from the time Jamaica left Antigua on June 5, 1965, until she returned to Antigua for a visit in January 1986 (*MB* 111).

During these years of silence, the once fearful, angry, and impoverished emigrant whom people laughed at on the street became the revered and lionized international author whom people flocked into university halls to hear read. In 1979 she married Allen Shawn, a talented musician and a college professor who suffers from agoraphobia, the son of her revered *New Yorker* editor William Shawn and his wife, Cecille Lyon Shawn. Like her mother, the six-foot-tall Kincaid chose a man who was much shorter than she (he is five foot two, according to Joyce Wadler [1]), acknowledging that she was used to the idea of a man being shorter: "Listen, I am my mother [exasperatedly] Ahhhh! Aaahhh!!!" It looked better for a wife to be taller than her husband, the Kincaid character, Lucy, argued [47]).

Allen Shawn and Jamaica Kincaid clearly appeared an odd couple, he a short, shy, soft-spoken, fearful, Jewish geek; she a tall, outspoken, impulsive, Black Antiguan; but by all accounts it appeared to be a good marriage—at least for twenty-plus years. I recall that when she spent the night at my home in 1985 after a lecture at Virginia Commonwealth University, she called her husband as soon as we got back home and excitedly chatted with him for what seemed like an hour. I smiled as I reflected on such a loving couple, hating to be apart, sharing the details of their day, looking forward to her return home! Kincaid, given to extensive detailing of her private life, uncharacteristically provided few details of her marriage in her writings and interviews—until 2013. Earlier, she did tell Donna Perry that when she is writing, her husband reads what she is writing every night: "I really depend on him as a reader" (505). She often spoke briefly of her love for her husband and children and insisted in *My Garden (Book):* that though her rooming with Daniel (Dan) Hinkley on their Himalayan trip caused some disapproval from some, it was an ideal situation because they got along so well and they both had secure marriages that they would not compromise (192).

Neither Shawn nor Kincaid wrote about the cause of their 2002 divorce until Kincaid's fictional account of their marriage in 2013 (in the 2014 American Book Award novel *See Now Then: A Novel*), but Rabinowitz told me in 2009, "He left Jamaica for another woman." In *Wish I Could Be There: Notes from a Phobic Life* (2007), which is an autobiography focusing on his phobias, Shawn does mention frequently the young woman with whom he was then living (*he* doesn't emphasize her beauty, but Joyce Wadler does in her review, which begins, "The author's beautiful live-in girlfriend is asleep upstairs" [1]). He later married Yoshika Sato, with whom he has a son, Noa, both of whom he names in *Twin* (221). Allen Shawn never mentions Kincaid's name in either of his autobiographical works (*Wish* and *Twin: A Memoir*), and simply says in *Wish* that he divorced after "almost twenty-five years of marriage" (116),[1] and in *Twin* that he met, started dating, and married a woman he found "enthralling" (142). Several times in both volumes he mentions with pride his children by Kincaid, but he tells us very little about them beyond the fact that at fifteen his son was six feet tall (*Wish* 238). He does indicate in *Wish* that the women in his life have tried to put up with his phobias but that they know no more about them than that he tries to avoid certain situations. This seems consistent with Kincaid's disappointment that he never accompanied her to Antigua, not even for her mother's funeral: "[He] never went to Antigua. In fact perhaps one of those things that caused an estrangement in my life—that he didn't go to my mother's funeral, didn't go to my brother's funeral, and it was hard. It was an unpleasant . . ."[2]

Is it possible, as Shawn suggests, that she did not realize the extremity of his phobias? Might she have been less hurt by his actions had she understood? On the other hand, how did she reconcile his inability to travel to Antigua with his ability to travel to California, Atlanta, Paris, and Canada?

Reading the autobiographical accounts of Jamaica Kincaid and Allen Shawn, one is struck by the differences in their backgrounds and families—poor, uneducated, Black Antiguan working-class family versus well-to-do, highly educated, famous literary, wealthy White Jewish American family. However, one cannot help but note that despite the different appearances, Shawn's family, as he portrays it, was every bit as dysfunctional as Kincaid's: "No one in our family could have ever passed for 'normal'" (*Twin* 112). Shawn's description of his family as "like a ball of yarn in the center of which all its secrets were tightly bound" (*Wish* 216) reminds us of a similar simile that Kincaid used to describe her feelings about her conflict with her mother: a black ball wrapped up in cobwebs (*AJ* 85). Among other revelations in Shawn's books, he informs us that from the time he was two, his father had a relationship with another woman and sometimes ate several meals during one day in order to be present with both of his families.[3] William Shawn's lover, Lillian Ross, wrote of their forty-year affair in her 1998 *Here but Not Here: A Love Story.* Both of Allen Shawn's parents were, he says, under psychiatric care "virtually their entire adult lives," a fact that they concealed from their son, whom they cautioned not to reveal his own occasional psychiatric treatments (*Wish* 215–16). Allen Shawn's father, like his son, suffered from phobias that sometimes made it impossible for him to travel. The father travelled very little and did not drive. Allen Shawn, who sometimes found a simple drive down a country road to a friend's house so terrifying that he could not breathe and had to turn back, is also fearful, he tells us, of subways, elevators, planes, tunnels, heights, closed spaces, and open spaces—even, Wadler adds, "his [own] shadow" (1). After reading his description in *Wish* of his difficulty with expressing emotions such as anger and repressing them until they resulted in explosive violent outbursts such as shaking loose a banister, throwing plates, and pounding his fists into a wall, one can better appreciate his caution to his outspoken wife, "Dear, please! Mince words!" (Frazier xix).

After noting in Allen Shawn's memoirs the manner in which he and his parents maintained stony silences about emotional issues and evaded rather than faced their problems, one might even find the occasional outbursts and confrontations in the Drew family preferable. Further, Shawn's family, like Kincaid's, endured many years of silence during which a reconnection seemed unlikely. Clearly, what Shawn and Kincaid share is that their family dynamics left both with an identity crisis.

Shawn's twin, a schizophrenic and autistic savant, was institutionalized when she was eight, and the family visited her only once a year *or* had her brought to them once a year for lunch.[4] Shawn, even after his parents' death and his nearing sixty, initially had difficulties managing his annual lunchtime meeting with his twin. In 2005, during the last year of his ninety-nine-year-old mother's life, he tells us that he went to see Mary alone for the first time and began to be "more of a presence in her life" (*Twin* 172–73).[5] However, for almost fifty years of their lives there was so little contact with the sister that he writes in *Twin*, "Over the years Mary had almost seemed to become a fiction, as if her actual life was too painful to contemplate" (128). Throughout her life and these works, Mary is so removed from the family that she seems, Shawn writes, "transformed into a kind of mythologizing" (*Twin* 132). Mary is sometimes not mentioned in biographical pieces on the family; she is not mentioned in her father's will, though his lawyers did indicate that he had established a trust for her. Shawn admits that at times he led people to believe that he only had a brother: "Sometimes I lied by omission, cheerfully saying only that I had an older brother" (*Twin* 47–48).

As his mother was dying in 2005, fifty-seven-year-old Mary was allowed to visit her home for the first time since she had been removed. She was permitted to stay the usual two hours allotted for annual lunches with the family.

The whole time I read about the misunderstood and excluded sister, I couldn't help but imagine the kind of support and care Annie Drew would undoubtedly have provided her—in her tiny cottage. In both books Shawn frequently ponders what his sister's life would have been like had she been raised at home. In one instance he writes: "I often wonder what would have happened to her if she had been born into the—then rare—type of family that could have more resourcefully incorporated her into their routine" (*Wish* 100). A similar sentiment appears in *Twin:* "There were families that had the love, fortitude, and resourcefulness to incorporate such children into their world" (198).

Also interesting is the fact that the only sincere, effective, and natural (not guilt-ridden) attention the child seemed to get at home was from Bessie, a Black woman who took care of the children, cleaned the house, and cooked (*Wish* 102; she is one of the individuals to whom *Twin* is dedicated). In *Twin,* Shawn declares that Bessie "had an intuitive understanding of [Mary]" (58). It is interesting to note that Shawn doesn't tell us in *Wish,* the first book that treats Bessie, that she was Black; rather he tells us her father was a slave in Virginia. Is he consciously avoiding reinforcing the commonplace image in African American literature of the overworked Black domestic in the wealthy Jewish household? Indeed, though he does identify a couple of individuals as African American in *Twin,*[6] both books reflect what appears to be his occasional reluctance to speak fully, honestly, and directly. How does a man married for twenty-plus years to *Jamaica Kincaid* write two memoirs without ever mentioning her name or race or renown!

Kincaid's fear of becoming her mother is echoed in Shawn's terror of being his retarded and banished twin sister. Shawn, himself, makes many comparisons of his sister to himself (see *Wish,* 214–15, 218–19; and *Twin,* 9, 13, 21, 89, 99, 108–9, 139). The dread in both instances, of course, is exacerbated by the realization that their fears are to a large extent their realities. How like Kincaid's agonizing about her mother is Shawn's confession regarding his sister: "I have spent my fifty-seven years holding her at bay, while actually maintaining her inside me" (*Wish* 217). In fact, he tells us that when he was writing *Wish,* apparently at the age of fifty-seven, he "visit[ed] her alone for the first time ever" (241) and that his two visits since his parents' deaths were limited to two hours (217). In *Twin,* he continues to agonize about what Mary understands and thinks, what her life is like, what steps he can take to resume some of the closeness that he experienced during their infancy and forever thereafter craved. The fact remains that almost everything he knows about his twin comes from notes he discovered from her doctors and from the staff at her institutions (*Twin* 150, 151, 178–79, 193).

There are a number of references in his memoirs to his early sense of romance and sexuality being linked to this sister, the descriptions of which call to mind Kincaid's delight in physical contact with her mother, her focus on smells, and her own sexual hang-ups. Shawn writes: "My earliest memory is of sleeping next to Mary, and to this day the sight, smell and 'propinquity' of the female body gives me joy, actually more joy than any touch or affection or any athletic sexual grapplings can ever give" (*Wish* 219). Earlier he writes: "Mary was undeniably my first romantic object. . . . I don't recall the cuddling, the intimate play of infancy, yet something makes me blush when I even try to remember it. . . . I remember our rocking alongside each other with a vague discomfort" (*Wish* 100–101).

When he "found love" for the first time, he realizes that what he feels is connected to his feelings for Mary: "I didn't recognize that, having come into the world coupled to Mary, for me love was a return" (*Twin* 96). In his reflections upon the connection he had with Mary as a child, he cites Alessandra Piontelli's *Twins in the World:* "According to Piontelli, in cultures as different as Indonesia and Ghana, surprisingly, identical twins sometimes end up living together as socially condoned homosexual unions. In at least one culture, fraternal twins are even viewed as ideal mates and are supported in clandestine incestuous marriages" (*Twin* 167).

Shawn's family's evasion, if not outright denial of their Jewishness reminds of what some suggest is Kincaid's denial of her Blackness. He writes that "being Jewish was . . . a matter for some distant uneasiness," even "revulsion" on his father's part (*Wish* 112), and that Judaism and ancestral customs "meant nothing" to his parents (*Wish* 113); rather, his mother created myths of a Swedish heritage and his father changed their name to one that was Irish (*Wish* 112–14). His mother never objected that Mary was always referred to as Protestant at her schools (*Wish* 113). Indeed, Kincaid, who was raised as a Methodist and converted to Judaism in 1993 (Paravisini-Gebert 21), is probably more enthusiastic in her conversion to Judaism and her adherence to its rituals than her husband, whose family celebrated "a religiously deracinated Christmas and Easter" (*Wish* 114).

Both Shawn and Kincaid (or the Kincaid characters) are at times obsessed with imperfections in their bodies, especially their height—Shawn sometimes sees himself as too short; Kincaid or the Kincaid character sometimes sees herself as too tall. Facial features, hair, and color also affect Kincaid or the Kincaid character's sense of herself at points in her life.

It is interesting to note that, like many of Kincaid's works that repeat the same events, Shawn's *Twin* is a retelling of his first memoir, *Wish,* which treats his own agoraphobia. Though *Twin* focuses more on his efforts to understand his twin, his guilt about her situation, his fear that she was never able to realize her "untapped potential" (*Twin* 115), and the first occasion where he spent more than two hours with her, the same events are repeated in both books: his being discovered naked in his closet with a visiting girl when he was six years old; the death of his hamster, Sawdust, when he was seven; his pushing a man who revealed himself to a little girl with whom he (Shawn) was playing; his trips to France; his sister's problems (variously described as mental retardation, brain damage, autism, schizo-affective disorder); his fears that he may be susceptible to similar mental problems; his conflicting feelings about sex;[7] Mary's removal from their home; her two-hour annual visits from the family; his combining of Mary's camp and the Jewish concentration camps; his fears of death and especially of the loss of his parents; the family's difficulties with open communication; Mary's fascination with hands; her strange relationship to her arm (she chewed, bit, sniffed, kissed, and talked to her arm); the parents' psychological problems; the father's mistress; the family's love of music and their jam sessions, seemingly one of the few ways they connected (*Twin* 110); and his illnesses (agoraphobia; panic attacks; and flu).[8] His account of his suffering the flu is remarkably reminiscent of a comparable description of Kincaid's illness in "The Long Rain" (*AJ* 111–20): Shawn, in a confused state, also contemplates objects that seem farther away; his parents' voices linger and flit around the room; everything seems remote; he was oblivious to the external world (*Twin* 2–3).

Again like Kincaid, Shawn is sometimes aware that he may be "unknowingly reveal[ing]" himself (*Twin* 9, 13, 21); they both tell the same stories over and over, likely in the futile hope that they will find some relief and release. A reader might suspect s/he was reading Kincaid when Shawn writes in *Wish:* "No matter how old and jaded we have become, how long our parents have been dead, or how far we have traveled from their world, inside we are still waiting for our mother to come and kiss us good night, . . . or are hoping to be rewarded for eating our vegetables with a warm hug" (175).

In 1985 Jamaica Kincaid gave birth to a daughter, whom she said she named Annie Rosamond after her mother and Allen's twin sister. However, Connie Rabinowitz raises the possibility that she was named after Annie Thorne

Woodhull, Kincaid's good friend who is Annie Rosamond's godmother. Rabinowitz went on to add that Woodhull had "found [Kincaid] just the way I did—loved her writing." William Shawn's mother's name was also Annie (see Ross 82), so Annie could have been named after her great-grandmother as well. Kincaid's naming her daughter Annie offers much food for thought. The fact that in the most direct fictionalization of her life, she gives the Kincaid character the name Annie suggests she might have wished to have been named after her mother. By giving her daughter the name of her mother, she continues the name in the family line, recovers her lost mother, and can look forward to recapturing that Edenic love with an Annie over whom *she* can have control. Following Annie Rosamond's birth, the Shawns moved to Bennington, Vermont, where Allen joined the faculty of Bennington College.

It must have been difficult for Annie Drew, rarely hearing from her daughter during these years of her daughter's ascension and having to struggle to raise her sons during her husband's illness and death. Indeed, Mrs. Drew had had to go to work long before Mr. Drew died, and the jobs she had were domestic in nature. She cooked, cleaned, and washed clothes for people until near the end of her life. One close acquaintance declared that he was always there for his friend Annie, that he had a store in the neighborhood, and she knew that she could come to him for anything she needed from the store or for money. He concluded: "She was a person who goes to work every day and washes clothes for someone. She didn't go about begging. She was a good woman. I knew her for donkey years. I saw her every week. She visited me and I visited her every week" (January 18, 2009).

Annie Drew's son Joseph recalls that he helped with the care of his father during his illness: "I took care of him when he was sick, helped him, shaved him."

Mr. Drew died at Holberton Hospital on December 14, 1975, at the age of seventy-four. The cause of death is certified by Dr. R. Bak as C.V.A., a stroke. The funeral was handled by Noel Barnes, Undertaker. Mr. Drew's profession was simply listed as "retired."

Reverend Lee recalled how difficult it was for Mrs. Drew after her husband's death. Not only were there financial difficulties, but "she had struggles with the boys; they gave her a hard time." Reverend Lee was taken aback at the tiny one-room house in which she lived, with only one bed—Mrs. Drew told her that she slept on the bed and Devon slept on the floor. Despite her situation, Reverend Lee noted that the house was tidy and clean, always "nicely kept," and that Mrs. Drew was always the gracious hostess: "Whenever I would go she would tell me, 'You come and lie down,' because I would walk over—I like walking—and it was a good distance from here. And I would walk over there and she would tell me, 'Lie down.' She used to live over there in Ovals. She likes to give. She would rush to the market because she was not too far from the market, and she would get some provisions and whatever meat. Quickly she would cook that and bring some in for me to eat. It was really nice."

As previously noted, Kincaid was appalled when she learned that Mr. Drew had died leaving her mother a pauper without money for a funeral (*MB* 14).[9] She sent money to her mother. Then for a period before her marriage, Kincaid herself suffered financial deprivation and found herself philosophically opposed to providing support to her family. However, she did later resume some support to her family. It was a part of what she saw as growing up after she had children: "I felt I could do my duty and still not talk to her. I did not feel I could withhold from her because she was behaving badly." In Mrs. Drew's statement in Mariana Cook's *Generations of Women: Women in Their Own Words,* she said of Kincaid: "She's my support. . . . Jamaica looks after us and we love her" (20). Kincaid expressed some surprise at that acknowledgment because, she said, her mother often pled poverty despite her help. She told me that tourists who knew her work would often go to speak with Mrs. Drew and she would lead them to believe she had no money. Kincaid was at first embarrassed that her mother would ask those tourists for money, but she later simply ignored it.[10]

In 1980 Mrs. Drew joined the Beacon Light Church of the Nazarene and developed a warm relationship with her pastor's wife, Reverend Rosa Lee, who later became her pastor. Reverend Lee says Annie was more a follower than a leader in the church, but she was regular in attendance, she helped to clean the church, and

> she loved to pray. She was always at the altar praying because she realized that, you know, she had a background, and she was working hard on that. She had a lot of groundwork to do in her life because she realized that, you know. I don't really know what she was before she came to the church. In my opinion, dealing with people, you can tell when people trying to come from *way* down. It takes a daily walk. It doesn't happen all at once. She was always in and *plunging* because she realized that she had to get on a higher level.

This and other references to Mrs. Drew's "background" might allude to the fact that there may have been times she had to turn to prostitution, as one of her friends indicated (see p. 122), and as Kincaid may have intimated in her comments to me about the "shadowy figures" that she called uncle but now realizes were her mother's sexual partners. Pastor Lee seemed reluctant to refer explicitly to things sexual—she even avoided using the term "AIDS" when she discussed Devon Drew's illness.

Soon after Kincaid's first child, Annie Shawn, was born in 1985, the rebel exile decided that "I had to go and see her [Annie Drew]. It was important to end the rift"; and so when her daughter was a little over a year old, in January 1986 (*MB* 111), she and little Annie went to Antigua. Connie Rabinowitz, who would meet Kincaid on this trip and become a close friend, believes that Mrs. Drew somehow "got Jamaica to come back." She recalls that visit very well and provided details for me. Rabinowitz and Dyde joined Mrs. Drew and Joseph at the airport in the VIP lounge to await Kincaid's arrival. Annie Drew, who was "very properly dressed—she had on a hat," was obviously very nervous. She explained to Rabinowitz that she must have had fish poisoning, an excuse that Rabinowitz found implausible: "She no way could convince me, but I said [sarcastic tone], 'Oh, sure, I know—very bad here—fish poisoning. It can be terrible.' But that was in no way what upset her stomach. This was a *terrifying* moment for her—as well as a very satisfying moment—first time she had seen her grandchild—the first time she had seen Jamaica in twenty-two years."

The time here is open to question. According to my calculations and Kincaid's own recollections, the visit took place in January 1986. She had been away, by my count, twenty years and seven months. Some Kincaid scholars, such as Ferguson and Lee, say Kincaid had been away nineteen years.

This was a motley group, a poor Black mother and brother from Ovals who hadn't seen their daughter and sister for twenty years and two enthusiastic fans eager to meet the writer they adored, one a well-to-do Antiguan and the other a wealthy White American expatriate, obviously the ones who were responsible for the welcoming party being in the VIP Lounge.

And finally, there she was: "You know you can't miss Jamaica," Rabinowitz said. "I'd never seen her in my life. But you can't miss her. She had lots of luggage, and she had this babysitter—*White,* by the way."

Rabinowitz recalled that Annie Drew teared up when she saw her daughter and granddaughter, that she and Kincaid hugged each other and Mrs. Drew took her "roly-poly" and friendly granddaughter Annie in her arms. She didn't note any interaction between Kincaid and Joseph, but Joseph, according to Rabinowitz, is the "*out* brother—he doesn't talk to anybody in the family; nobody talks to Joseph." Rabinowitz continued: "We all guided [Jamaica] into the [VIP] lounge. I was so amazed at the whole thing."

They immediately became fast friends, with Rabinowitz seeing Kincaid almost every day of her visit and always noting the awkwardness that remained between mother and daughter.

Kincaid insists that Mrs. Drew was not very grandmotherly in her response to Annie, seemed not to be impressed that she was named after her, and really didn't like girls. Even though it is quite likely that Mrs. Drew embraced the common belief of the time that boys were the children who might become doctors or lawyers and do great things, there is much to contradict Kincaid's belief that Mrs. Drew did not like girls: her own pampering of Jamaica and the fact that she used to braid her first son's hair and put bows on it suggest that she probably delighted in raising girls; further, all accounts from the granddaughters, others who knew Mrs. Drew, and even Kincaid's works such as *My Brother* indicate that she had a warm and loving relationship with her granddaughters.

At any rate, the silence (or at least "a" silence) ended when a then-thirty-six-year-old Kincaid visited Antigua again after twenty years. There are suggestions that she was relaxed and comfortable with her family, lying on twenty-three-year-old Devon's bed in her favorite position—reading with her feet resting on the windowsill in the sun (her feet, she often informs, are always cold) (*MB* 43–44).[11] She told me that she just joined her family and did whatever they were doing. Her mother no longer insisted on such proper behavior as she had required during Kincaid's childhood: "She became like an old car—everything broke down." The boys were free to speak patois. There were no etiquette lessons.

On that 1986 visit Kincaid enjoyed her mother's cooking, even the foods she had hated as a child but longed for through the passing years (*MB* 115). Rabinowitz noted Kincaid's pleasure at once more enjoying her mother's cooking: "Well, she liked her mother's cooking all right. Very much. She may have told you. She thought her mother was a marvelous cook." And indeed Annie Drew was a legendary cook whose delicious cuisine was recalled by Dr. Ramsey, Reverend Lee, and many members of her family. A relative who lived with her for a few years liked her fried chicken best—"It was really good!" (January 16, 2009).

On one of Kincaid's later visits to Antigua, when she and her mother became alienated, one of Mrs. Drew's friends tried to get Jamaica and her mother on speaking terms, "but," he lamented, "it did not work out well. Annie blamed me for getting them back together, because Jamaica used the opportunity to turn her brothers against their mother" (January 21, 2009). He also said that she "came to Antigua and bribed her brothers to say what she wanted them to say—she flattered them and turned them against her mother" (January 21, 2009). The situation she created became so bad, he insisted, that "Mrs. Drew dreaded going home when Jamaica was visiting because she created such an atmosphere of dissention in the home."

Mrs. Drew clearly worried about her daughter's inability to be comfortable in Antigua or indeed to be comfortable with her identity as an Antiguan and her identity as a Black woman. In my telephone interview with Catherine John, she recalled that Mrs. Drew lamented her daughter's never being quite happy with her circumstances, always wanting to escape from her culture and heritage (February 20, 2009). Throughout her childhood, Kincaid's goal was to escape Antigua, ideally to go to the United States, especially to New York. After the long rain in *Annie John,* all the Jamaica character can think about is how she never wants to see anything in Antigua, and never wants to see her mother doing any of the things she used to love, such as cooking her food, caressing her, or talking to her (127). Later, as the Kincaid character prepares to go to England, she gives a long cataloguing of the things in Antigua that she never wants to see again, but it is clear that she is ambivalent about her desire to leave Antigua and her mother. Similarly, in *My Brother* she writes, "I love the people I am from and I do not love the people I am from" (149). Once Kincaid "escapes," she often lambasts her homeland and her fellow Antiguans, and especially her family and her mother. She told Leslie Garis that she didn't want to know another Antiguan and she wanted to "be something *other*" (Garis 44). She clearly feels that her life, like Devon's, would have been destroyed had she not escaped. In her introduction to *My Favorite Plant,* she writes, "I know where I came from, I carry it around with me all the time, and I know how lucky I was to escape" (x). She insists that she certainly could never have developed into a writer had she remained in Antigua living with her family (*MB* 162); these people did not love her and provide her the support she needed.

Conversely, Kincaid frequently expressed delight in her American family, friends, and house, perhaps too much.

Methinks the lady doth protest too much.

"I love the house in which I live," she gushes in *My Garden (Book):* (29); on another occasion, watching men working in her garden, she sits, basking in her comfortable life in a nation where she is a visitor in a position to judge others (*MG* 67), where she has the wealth to be a part of the conquering class and afford to spend lavishly on a garden, where she can, in effect, live in two worlds (*MG* 123).

Kincaid's delight in her home was obvious to me throughout my visit. When I showed up at her door for my 11:00 a.m. appointment with her on October 11, 2008, she was visibly disturbed because she had hoped to have her fireplace burning before I arrived. This was a final touch to the ambiance that she was determined to create, even though it was a 70-degree day. As she worked to ignite the fire, I surveyed my surroundings.

The room with the fireplace in which we talked the first day was something of an informal family room. The sofas and chairs were covered with throws as if to protect them from messy children, though there were no longer children in the house. There was a piano covered with family pictures, including a formal picture of her three brothers (I never saw a family picture that included her), her children's graduation pictures, and a photograph of Kincaid with Senator Barack Obama as both he and she were receiving honorary degrees. By the piano was a pot that Annie and other folks in Antigua cooked in when Jamaica was growing up. Some of the walls held overrunning book shelves; the others were covered with pictures of flowers, of birds, and of Caribbean scenes (most of the latter of ordinary folk and of small houses). A couple of masks were randomly placed on the walls as well. None of these seemed masterpieces of art but rather the kinds of crafts to be picked up in tourist marts or airplane gift shops in the Caribbean and/or Africa. There were flowers in the house, but not as many as I would have expected. Several pots of small African violets were lined up on a long table, perhaps awaiting planting outdoors in the spring. A large cat roamed around lazily, often pausing where I was seated on the sofa, making me wonder if I had usurped his favorite lounging area. This room led to a small sunroom off her kitchen where we sat at a table for our talks on my second visit, and from which we could look out into her garden. All in all, hers was a warm and comfortable abode, where the emphasis clearly was not so much on interior design as on books, art, flowers, and especially her expansive garden. A visitor can easily imagine the author happily at work in these surroundings.

However, despite her obvious pleasure in her Vermont home, the constant pull of the Caribbean (for which she often expresses hatred) is evident. For example, as soon as she writes at one moment that she would never want to live anywhere except in her Vermont home (*MG* 42), she declares that, having grown up in a family that cooked and ate outside, she really doesn't comprehend living in a house (*MG* 42). She recognizes, too, that despite the differences between her Vermont garden—with its stone walls and northern trees—and the yard of her Antiguan childhood, many of her activities in the Vermont garden approximate practices from her Caribbean home (*MG* 45). Her children even roast their marshmallows in the same kind of coal pot in which her family cooked, a pot that on a visit to Antigua she, like a tourist, shopped for and purchased (MG 45).

Me navel-string bury yah!

Like most Caribbean writers, Kincaid finds cold weather alien and disturbing, declaring that she hates snow, bare tree branches, everything associated with winter. She insists that everyone who lives in cold climates such as that in Vermont longs to go south where it is warm (*MG* 59). On one occasion on a very cold night in Bennington when she went out to dinner with a friend, she told her that she found the whole winter season, from beginning to end, overwhelming and desired only to spend the next day in a warm place, such as the West Indies (*MG* 76). She begins one chapter in *My Garden (Book):* by noting that she spent the afternoon one subzero day submerged in a bathtub of hot water, "trying to satisfy a craving for overchilled ginger ale and oranges" (86).

Despite all these longings to escape the intolerable and unending winter (*MG* 172), she notes that she can appreciate winter because it holds the promise of spring, her favorite season (*MG* 61). She writes of her excitement at spotting a robin in the yard, and the sense that imparts that all is well for her and her garden. She loves May, and if she could re-create the seasons, she says, she would make May last for ninety days while December, January, and February would only last ten hours each (*MG* 175).

Recognizing her ambivalence about home, Kincaid has acknowledged, "When I am in Vermont, home is Antigua; when I am in Antigua, home is Vermont" (Paravisini-Gebert 13). This is most poignantly expressed in *Lucy*, where the Kincaid character is surprised that she longs for her island home and for her despised family whom she had often wished dead (6). She told Donahue that Antigua was "the place I love most and it is the place I am most afraid of in the world," adding that she weeps and weeps whenever she leaves

Antigua, fearful that "it will swallow me up and never spit me out" (05D). For most of her years in the United States, Kincaid has been unable to fathom returning to live in Antigua. When Gerhard Dilger asked if she would ever return, she replied: "I can't live there and be myself so far. . . . I think I'm someone who needs contrary experience. I need to be in a place full of mountains so I can think about the sea" (Dilger 25).

But the possibility of return has become more and more a possibility. When I talked with Kincaid in 2008, she dismissed some of her earlier rejection of Antigua and Antiguans. She insisted that her comments to Garis that she didn't want to know another Antiguan and she wanted to be something other than Antiguan stemmed from her mother's telling her that she should not be with other Antiguans because they would be jealous and hold her back—"the kind of thing that oppressed people like to say about each other." She declared in 2008 that if she could afford it and if there were a university there where she could be employed, she would move to Antigua and build a house. She knows her children would love it: "They *love* Antigua. . . . It's really one of the things I've felt I've done well in my life is to give them a sense that that place belongs to them." Indeed, Kincaid now goes frequently to Antigua and attended Carnival there in 2008, where she enjoyed jumping up in Carnival, something her mother didn't allow her to do. She danced all through the night and then through the morning, and then "I thought, well maybe she [her mother] was right because I was so *tired.*"

But if Jamaica returns to Antigua, it is clear that she could never return to the Antigua that she knew as a child. After a lengthy description of her house and her yard and her living conditions when she grew up, she concludes that those standards of living are fine for those she left behind, but they are no longer acceptable for her (*MG* 45). Her Antigua now is in an exclusive mountain retreat where she socializes with her wealthy friends. But whether she returns to Antigua or not, it is clear, as she told Dilger, that Antigua is "the only thing I really want to write about" (Dilger 23).

Mrs. Drew visited her daughter in Vermont twice, first in early October 1987. One of Kincaid's favorite stories about that visit centers around her mother's eagerness to see snow, but Kincaid informed her that it was too early for snow: "I was actually, I think, kind of pleased to say, 'You'll *never* see snow!' [laughter]." However, there was an early snowstorm, one so big that it destroyed trees and knocked down wires. The delighted visitor walked out into the snow, picked some up, tasted it, and held it up to the heavens, declaring, "God wanted me to see snow!" Mrs. Drew was confident that it was a gift from God to her. Her daughter was appalled that she was delighting in a natural disaster that was wreaking such havoc in New England.

Mrs. Drew was very popular with Kincaid's friends in Bennington: "My friends adored her. She was *very charming, appealing, attractive, seductive,* very seductive, yeah, she was lovely." She moved in elite company. Mrs. Drew met and enjoyed socializing with Kincaid's in-laws, Mr. and Mrs. William Shawn, both of whom "adored her," and, according to Kincaid, "she *adored* them and would in fact just sort of push me out of the way and say how wonderful *she* was, and say [ostentatiously], 'Yes, I did a very good job!'" She hobnobbed with other wealthy Americans and distinguished writers. The noted writer Ian (Sandy) Frazier joined her on her trip to see the Statue of Liberty, invited her to his baby's christening, and even developed a correspondence with her. Kincaid went on to point out how everyone fell in love with Mrs. Drew: Kincaid's good friends and American family, even the au pair, the postman, and the butcher at a neighborhood market. However, Kincaid declares that if her mother discovered that she was particularly fond of a friend, she would say bad things to that friend about her and try to undermine her. Kincaid introduced her to one acquaintance who was "a treacherous friend," and her mother "of course liked that friend better than any of the others: At the time I said to Allen . . . 'She *would* like the person who was *most* destructive to *me.*'" Kincaid told me that her mother's duplicitous actions stemmed partly from jealousy, but that by this time, "I must have been so secure in my life that I wasn't upset with it at all—I just thought, well, yes, that's something Mother would do."

Though in Kincaid's account there is no hint that the successful and popular writer was in any way embarrassed by her mother, Jocelyn Reid laughingly recalled Mrs. Drew's account of a visit to the supermarket with her daughter when Mrs. Drew bought some "fish heads. It made Jamaica angry: 'Mom! You embarrassed me!'" Reverend Lee recalls indications of similar responses: "[Annie] was always neatly dressed. The only thing—sometimes when the daughter comes, she would stay at a hotel or something and she thought she should improve her appearance—the daughter would feel that she should be better presented, you know. It's not that she was walking dirty or anything like that, you know. She just liked to be what we call down to earth, you know, and the daughter wanted her to be a little more."

During her visit to Bennington, Mrs. Drew spoke Standard English to all of the people with whom she interacted, but occasionally when she and Jamaica were alone, she would lapse into patois. When she found that Jamaica no longer understood the patois, she would laugh at her and change again to proper English. She would also laugh at Jamaica's use of the Latin names for plants in her garden. Though she had encouraged her as a child to use the Latin names, she now regarded that as pretentious on the Vermonter's part, something that the mature Kincaid finds very disconcerting: "And I didn't think I was being anything but what I was told to do. And then by the time they didn't approve of it, I didn't know what else to do. . . . You know, they consider the way I talk, for instance, very pretentious. I use big words and so on. That was something I was told I should do, so I do it, and I don't know how to stop now."

De higher monkey clime, de more him show him behine.

Though Annie Drew had indeed insisted that Jamaica master and use Standard English as a child, as a part of a culture where even the most sophisticated could easily slip into the patois, she probably found it hard to believe her daughter's declaration to Dilger that she is no longer able to speak patois, and that Creole is limited to a spoken language that teachers cannot teach because books are not written in Creole. Furthermore, Kincaid insists, students have to learn "a language of the world" (Dilger 22). Despite such declarations, Kincaid often attacks the King's English as part of the imposition of a colonial power that delighted in destroying people by forcing their culture on them: "For isn't it odd that the only language I have in which to speak of this crime is the language of the criminal who committed the crime?" (*SP* 31).

During their interaction in *My Brother,* Devon parodies Jamaica's speech: he assumes a pretend English accent and calls her "maiy deahre" (*MB* 56–57). His satirizing of her speech suggests that he views it as a somewhat pretentious attempt at British English. Jane King chastises Kincaid for her vituperative attitude toward Antiguan Creole, insisting that she "is impoverished by her (surely willful) refusal to maintain a connection with her Creole roots" (891).

It was also during Mrs. Drew's visit to Bennington that Kincaid claims she remembered her mother's burning of her books, an incident that she says her mother did not recall (*MB* 134). As Kincaid recounts the incident, she was so traumatized by the burning of her books that she repressed the memory until she heard her mother tell one of her friends in the United States that her vigilance kept Jamaica from ending up with the proverbial ten children by ten different men; she insisted that Jamaica's friend Lindsay would pretend to want to borrow books as a ruse to come see Jamaica. This conversation presumably caused Jamaica to remember the book burning (*MB* 135–36).

However, there is a disconnect here. Kincaid has declared that the incident motivated her writing, that for the rest of her life she may have been attempting to restore the burned books by writing them over and over until they were flawless, unharmed by the fire (*MB* 197–98). If she didn't remember the event, then she certainly could not have been consciously motivated to try to restore them. And certainly she wasn't restoring the books that were burned. They were the British classics she read, very likely, she told me, "*Jane Eyre*, some Hardy, probably Dickens."[12] In fact, what Jamaica is writing over and over is her mother's stories.

When I asked Kincaid if her burning of her mother's letters were a kind of retribution for her mother's burning of her books, she reflected a long time and replied: "I hadn't thought of that at the time. At the time I burnt the letters, I didn't remember the book burning consciously. But of course. Of *course*. Of *course*! I hadn't thought of that. Thank you for that. I hadn't thought of it."

It was not unexpected that finally during her mother's visit, they had a bitter argument about their past relations (*MB* 27), and Kincaid demanded an apology for the pain that her mother had caused her. Annie Drew had no apologies to offer, declaring, as Kincaid recounts it, that she had the best of reasons for everything she did, that she was "never wrong" (*MB* 27). Surely Annie Drew recognized that Jamaica's pain stemmed from a number of events that she would never accept and understand no matter how much her mother apologized. Mrs. Drew would have to apologize for presumably trying to abort her; then she would have to apologize for giving birth to her illegitimate daughter. She would have to apologize for trying to help her develop a sense of independence; then she would have to apologize for continuing to treat her as a child. She would have to apologize for the tragedies she could not avert, and she would have to apologize for any attention that she showed to anyone else, including her husband and her sons. She would probably even have to apologize for being Black and poor. She wouldn't know where to begin, but Jamaica had offered some suggestions. In the interview with Kay Bonetti, she says: "When I first started [writing] among the things I wanted to do was to say [to my mother], 'Aren't you sorry that no greater effort was made over my education? Or over my Life?'" (141). Mrs. Drew knew that she could never appease a daughter who carefully recorded every infraction from the time of her conception and all too often appeared to forget (or at least overlook) every loving sacrifice. She was no doubt adamant that Jamaica was an ungrateful child who owed an apology—to her mother. Mrs. Drew was confident in the knowledge that if she hadn't trained her as she did, if she hadn't taught her as she did, if she hadn't encouraged her reading as she did, and if she hadn't protected her from being the "slut" she was bent on becoming (*AT* 4; *AJ* 102; *Lucy* 128), Jamaica would have ended up "with ten children by ten different men" (*MB* 28; Kin/Dance). Mrs. Drew no doubt remembered the "lies" her daughter told her to excuse the male visitors in the house, she remembered her daughter "flirting" on the street with boys and lying about where she was, she remembered her fears that her daughter was inclined to act like a "slut" and on the way to ending up like so many young girls in Antigua—or worse: it had not escaped her attention that the young man who apparently came to share books with Jamaica ended up as an AIDS patient on the ward with Devon (Kin/Dance). She knew that all the work she had done to get Jamaica's passage to America had been her passport to a new life. No, if any apologies were in line, they should come from Jamaica. "[Their] two black things" were once again hopelessly engaged.

Annie Drew's visit left her daughter sick for three months, suffering from the chicken pox and experiencing something akin to a nervous breakdown that required psychiatric consultation (*MB* 28). Kincaid blamed it all on her mother, but Annie Drew couldn't conceive that she bore any responsibility. Naturally, again, they were no longer speaking.

Despite the contention with her daughter, Mrs. Drew, according to her friends, enjoyed her trip to the United States, especially New York. Jocelyn Reid laughed as she recalled Annie Drew's accounts of her visits: "She liked the US. She liked Allen Shawn. But she and Jamaica argued all the time." On the front of the program for Mrs. Drew's memorial service is a picture of her smiling broadly with a New York cap on her head, possibly taken while she was in the United States and cherished as a memento of her trip.

Kincaid's 1986 visit to Antigua motivated *A Small Place* (1988), a scathing attack on just about every area of Antiguan life: *tourists* ("A tourist is an ugly human being [14], . . . an ugly, empty thing" [17] despised by Antiguans [18]); *colonials* ("human rubbish" [80]); *politicians* (corrupt, rotten); *businessmen* (thieves); and *ordinary Antiguans* (ignorant innocents [57]), a book in which she herself says, "I did nothing but cast blame and make denunciations" (*MB* 158).[13] And yet, the book ends with a poetic paean to the remarkable, indeed unreal, beauty of Antigua's land, sea, fauna, and flora.

A controversy with the *New Yorker* about the publication of *A Small Place* brought to a head some of the conflicts that Kincaid was having with its new editor, Tina Brown. She resigned from her position, blasting Brown as "stupid" (Langston; *MB* 101), a "totalitarian, a tyrant," who was destructive to creative writers. She declared that she would rather go to jail for life than allow the magazine to publish anything she wrote (Jacobs 57; see also Cryer). She told Joanne Kaufman: "I like Tina. I just don't think she should be an editor. She gives wonderful parties. I think she should be a hostess" (109).

Shortly after the appearance of Kincaid's devastating critique of Antigua, an enraged Mr. Potter, whose work at the Mill Reef Club depended upon tourism, went to complain to Mrs. Drew. Very likely the people with whom he had a contract for chauffeuring and taxiing tourists had warned the illiterate businessman about the impact of such an incendiary exposé of Antigua on their business. Potter warned Annie that she had better do something about the "shit" that "yu pickney" [your child] was writing.[14] Annie Drew had "some very bad words for him," Kincaid laughingly declared. Annie was obviously amused that her hated enemy who never willingly gave anything to help with raising their daughter was now feeling his prosperous business affected by the powerful revelations of this acclaimed writer. Years ago Annie probably would have been insulted at Potter's use of "*yu* pickney," but she could now take some pride that it was *her* daughter, and he had nothing to do with her talents. One can only imagine what this woman, noted for having quite a tongue, said to this man as she drove him from her door, undoubtedly laughing all the time.

As Annie Drew no doubt knew, Mr. Potter was not the only one upset by *A Small Place.* Kincaid told Dilger that after she wrote *A Small Place,* Antiguans would ask her mother why she would write that, even though it was true, revealing what Kincaid calls "a very typical statement of people where I'm from. They think you shouldn't mention the unpleasant truth, and maybe it will go away" (Dilger 24). The book was banned in Antigua, and though there was no formal banning of Kincaid herself, she said, "the government at the time being what it was, I thought I could be murdered!" (Kin/Dance). (She makes a similar avowal to Vorda ["I Come" 98–99].) Thus it was some time before she could safely and comfortably travel to Antigua. Finally things died down, and she was invited to do a reading at the museum in Antigua. She agreed to do it only if she could read from *A Small Place.* By this time, with the change of government, she received no flack for the book or her reading. In fact, she averred, people acknowledged how true the book was and thanked her for writing it.

However, many of the Antiguans I have met and whom Annie Drew knew are just as ambivalent in their reaction to Kincaid as she has been in her responses to them and their nation. Despite the enthusiasm of her good friend, the late Tim Hector, and an American expatriate such as Connie Rabinowitz, and despite the fact that a number of Antiguans are proud that one of their native daughters is an internationally known writer, many of the Antiguans with whom I spoke were remarkably lacking in enthusiasm for Kincaid. One of Mrs. Drew's friends declared, "The people who push her work are Guyanese teachers who come in—they don't know Antigua" (January 21, 2009). Vincent Derrick suggested that there was a small educated group of Antiguans who read her works:

> Her work hasn't been publicized in Antigua—not much talk about the work. There's talk about *her* but not really her work. People see her as an achiever. She came from very humble origins and I think people just lost touch with her. I'm not even sure how she got to the States. And she just sort of dropped out of the Antiguan scene. People didn't even remember her. And then when they heard of her again, it was *Jamaica Kincaid.* Well, who the hell is that? How did she become entirely some other thing? That has never been fully explained to the country.

Dame Tonge declared: "Jamaica isn't so popular here. Our people don't like this kind of thing. United States people like this kind of thing [a vague reference to Kincaid's lack of respect for Antigua]. Where did she get that name Jamaica? Couldn't she have given herself the name Antigua or something?" Another Antiguan with whom I spoke explained that many Antiguans see Kincaid's embrace by White Americans and her attacks on Antigua as evidence that she is not someone to whom Antiguans can relate (January 17, 2009). Even after Antigua finally honored her with an award, many Antiguans are still unable to embrace her or repress their suspicions of her. One Antiguan I met explained that she purchases Kincaid's books because she is "committed to reading Caribbean literature, especially Antiguan authors," but it was clear from our talk that she has issues with Kincaid, and it was not clear that she had read all the books (January 17, 2009). Dr. Ramsey, who has received gifts of all of the books and who has obviously read some, did not say that he had read all of them. Even one of Kincaid's relatives, a college senior, says she hasn't read her works, offering as an excuse that the only books she reads are those she is required to read (January 19, 2009).

The harshest assessment of Kincaid came from one of Annie Drew's devoted friends, who refused to talk with me at first, suspecting that my goal was to "whitewash" Kincaid: "I won't be a part of any whitewashing of Jamaica Kincaid. If I told you what I know about Jamaica Kincaid, you wouldn't be able to publish it. Jamaica is no good. Kincaid always degrades and pulls down Antigua. I would like to ask her, 'Why do you have this bitterness?'" (January 18, 2009).

Gordon George, a literature teacher at the Antigua State College, shared some of the same concerns, telling me that *A Small Place* has so many lies in it that he presented a conference paper dealing with the inaccuracies in that and other Kincaid works. He, too, affirmed that "Kincaid is not very popular here."

These and a few other Antiguans with whom I spoke certainly seemed to agree with the harsh parody of Kincaid as Unguentina Carribou in Gary Indiana's *Resentment: A Comedy:* "Unguentina Carribou married early into an incredibly prestigious white publishing family, securing for her slender, rage-inflected memoirs of an entirely invented Caribbean girlhood [an] inflated adulation" (156). It is certainly relevant to note here that Kincaid knew Gary Indiana as early as 1980, when she wrote a cynical piece on this "punk poet and pillar of lower Manhattan society," who after having his apartment robbed, decided to give himself a benefit, where his friends read their poems and stories. He raised four hundred dollars with which he planned to buy a new lock for his door and get some dental work done (*Talk Stories* 192).

Tit for tat,
You kill my dawg,
I kill yo cat.

Though I did not happen to speak with many Kincaid enthusiasts in Antigua except for Rabinowitz, it is clear that there are Antiguans, like the late Tim Hector, who ardently admire her work. Splif declared that everything boils down to politics: "Everything is political with Antiguans; those who supported the former government [the Bird regime that Kincaid criticized] still don't like her, and those who didn't like Bird like her."

This reluctance of some West Indians to embrace Kincaid extends beyond Antigua to other parts of the Caribbean. Two noted authors from other Caribbean nations with whom I have discussed Kincaid fervently questioned the great interest in Kincaid in the United States, suggesting that she was the "least Caribbean" of the Caribbean authors. This attitude was obvious at the first conference of Caribbean Women Writers and Critics at Wellesley College in 1988, where there were some heated exchanges regarding her work.

More recently, the St. Lucian critic Jane King, who begins "A Small Place Writes Back" by noting her similarities to Kincaid (homeland, age, names, etc.), analyzes Kincaid's harsh critique of Antigua in *A Small Place* and elsewhere, and proclaims: "Fine, so Kincaid does not like the Caribbean much . . . and would rather live in Vermont. There can really be no difficulty with that, but I do not see why Caribbean people should admire her for denigrating our small place in this destructively angry fashion" (899).

A few other critics also reflect this suspicion of the First World's embrace of Kincaid. Derik Smith and Cliff Beumel, for example, see the enthusiasm for her as a kind of "politically correct" effort on the part of postcolonial critics pleased to have her confirm the colonial view of the colony and the colonial subjects: "She is the trustworthy West Indian who exposes the mendacity of her people to a metropolitan audience ready to accept her word" (98).

However, it is also important to note that Kincaid is eagerly sought as a presenter at university programs and conferences throughout the Caribbean, that she has been honored in Antigua, and that she has been warmly embraced by some Caribbean writers, such as her fellow Farrar, Straus and Giroux author Derek Walcott.

One reason that some detractors have attacked Kincaid has to do with what they see as her lack of a Caribbean identity: A friend of Mrs. Drew berated Kincaid: "She is looking for an identity—bully for her! I wouldn't use my mother as a ladder on which to climb. Annie was a fantastic person, a wonderful person, and for her daughter to write all that bullshit! Many people in Antigua hate her" (January 21, 2009). One Antiguan with whom I spoke accused Kincaid of paying Hector to create a false image, of seeking to "create an image of aristocracy by hyphenating the name Potter-Richardson" (January 21, 2009). Gary Indiana levels similar criticisms in his parody of Kincaid: "Unguentina Carribou has the kind of menacing changeability associated with African military dictators. She is a surpassingly ugly woman with lumpy features and a wardrobe of frilly faded dresses worn to evoke the gentility and dignified oppression of her island forebears" (156). He later refers to her as "a classy gargoyle" (159). Perhaps indeed Kincaid embodies Foucault's assertion that "On écrit pour être autre que ce qu'on est" (One writes in order to become other than what one is) (qtd. in Halperin 144 and 228n31).

This whole matter of identity remains a critical issue throughout the Kincaid canon. It is clear that those like Xuela in *The Autobiography of My Mother* who think that they have found self-definition and who have given birth to themselves remain unhappy. Something of the dilemma of the self-named and self-made author is perhaps revealed in her interview with Moira Ferguson, where she declares in a statement that is perhaps more revelatory than she intended:

> I have come to . . . question whether such a thing as always claiming yourself isn't a great sense of insecurity because if you are not sure, you are always saying "I am." On the other hand, I do come from this tradition of possessing and claiming yourself, because if you don't possess and claim yourself, someone else will. You keep declaring that you are in full possession, which is to say that you are on guard. If you are not on guard, someone will come right in and take you. ("A Lot" 184)

Kincaid's identity issue may relate to race as well. One of Mrs. Drew's friends insisted that "Annie also thought that Jamaica didn't like being Black. She would have preferred not to be Black" (January 21, 2009). Kincaid often asserts that racial issues are something that she has risen above. She refuses to attribute most things to race, telling Cudjoe, "It's just too slight to cling to your skin color or your sex" (401). She insists that Mr. Sweet's constant allusions in *See* to the fact that Mrs. Sweet came to the United States on a banana boat is not racist but rather a result of her "foreignness" (Headlee). Discussing the fact that basically in history, Blacks are the losers and Whites the winners, she declares in her interview with Dilger that she is very pessimistic about the Third World, that she considers Africa a "disaster" and regards the word *diaspora* as weird (anyone who views himself as living in a diaspora should simply go home). She concludes by noting that the blood of many different nations flows through her veins, but she doesn't claim them. She is not African; she's not anything. They are all dead (24). It would seem that Xuela reflects her creator when she declares, "I refuse to belong to a race, I refuse to accept a nation" (*Auto* 226). Antonia MacDonald-Smyth explains: "Race is an issue which Kincaid chooses to ignore. The color of her skin is unimportant to her so comfortable is she in this castle of her skin, a comfort provided albeit by a loving mother who for a long time had made the child believe herself to be the center of the universe" (102).

Kincaid often speaks of Blacks in a disparaging way and relates more to the White world—or at least a world where she is not judged by color, something she insists was true in Antigua and in Bennington (Paravisini-Gebert 15). She maintains that she defines herself as a Black woman, but she feels no need to honor the people she came from. The only thing she is dedicated to is her writing and telling the truth: "When I'm writing, I am such a singular beast that I refuse to take in any worldly consideration for the people I'm from" (Buckner 464).

Kincaid, who seems to live in a predominantly White world and whose friends are mainly White, often stresses that she is accepted by Whites and ridiculed by Blacks. She sometimes makes a point of highlighting Blacks who ridicule and insult her for her odd behavior even at the same time that other people are responding in similar fashion (introduction, *Talk Stories* 7). She asserts that when she first went to school in the United States, the White people found her charming, especially her speech, while the Black people hated her and found her and her speech ridiculous. Naturally, she concludes, she chose as her friends the people who liked her (NY 72). In the Dilger interview, she complains that the most critical reviews of *Lucy* came from Black Americans, who obsess about the color of one's skin and write nonsense about who is and is not black, or really black, or part white (23). It is no surprise then that, in the words of Jane King, Kincaid lived "through the 1960s and 1970s in New York . . . but did not appear to notice the Black Power Movement, so she could manage to live at the hub of the movement through the period of second wave feminism without noticing it" (892).

Oftentimes it seems clear that Kincaid appears more likely to like and appreciate Whites than Blacks. She remains eternally grateful for the support she has received from White people like George Trow, Michael O'Donoghue, William Shawn, Ian (Sandy) Frazier, Connie Rabinowitz, and Annie Thorne Woodhull, and gushes over them for who they are and what they have done for her. O'Donoghue was "perfectly handsome and wonderful . . . and kind" (*Talk Stories* 4). Trow was the "first person to make me understand that what I said mattered" (*Talk Stories* 5). She would never have been a writer except for Mr. Shawn, "whom I think about each day with love" (dedication of *Talk Stories*). Her world became clear (introduction, *Talk Stories* 14) after she met Frazier, her "dearest friend in all the still sphere-shaped world" (foreword, *Gone to New York* ix). "Annie Woodhull is my daughter's godmother and she was the one who went with me to my mother's funeral. She's a very good friend of mine. Obviously a very good friend." When she goes to Antigua, "I stay with [Bud and Connie Rabinowitz] friends who are practically family. They are very dear friends." She loves all of Frazier's family—his parents and his siblings (foreword, *Gone to New York* xi). It might not be an exaggeration to conclude from her writings and her interviews that the only Black friends she has consistently admired and respected in anything approaching this degree are Tim Hector and Dr. Prince Ramsey. Annie no doubt had on many occasions felt the need to remind her daughter that *blud ticka dan water.*

Ironically, Kincaid has some strong words for V. S. Naipaul's love for the British and his self-hatred: "You see it in Naipaul's face—the inner loathing. I imagine him being the sort of person who, when he comes across his reflection, thinks that that cannot be what he looks like, because he must somehow think he looks like an Englishman" (Birbalsingh 139). Certainly her assessment of Naipaul is one that many would argue applies to her, though she insists that the difference between them is that she is not ashamed of the place she came from (140), an argument that seems inconsistent with her declaration that Antigua and the other colonies were "all better off under colonial rule than they are now" (Vorda, "An Interview" 11). Further, Jane King asks, "If Kincaid can see that Naipaul has been destructive, why can she not see that a book [*A Small Place*] which [shows] black people who are nothing but ugly is also damaging?" (900).

Kincaid says her mother suffers from an "innocence" of white racism (*SP* 29). One might say that she reflects the same malady in some instances. In her "Putting Myself Together," for one example, she wonders why she didn't get a job for which she applied at *Mademoiselle:* she is unable to understand a friend's surprise that she would apply for a job at a place that did not hire Blacks: "And I thought, But how was I to know that I was a black girl? I never pass myself in a corridor and say, I am a black girl. I never see myself coming round a bend and say, There is that black girl coming toward me. How was I really to know such a thing?" (100). She simply concludes, she tells us elsewhere, that the people who told her that the magazine wouldn't hire Black girls were stupid (introduction, *Talk Stories* 4).

Yet, despite these denials of the significance of race, she is not beyond implying that she has been the victim of racism. In the Buckner interview, she says she will not complain that she has been unjustly treated but insists that she would have had a different career if she had been White, and that her work does not get the same kind of response as lesser work by White men (464). She contended in several interviews after the publication of *See* that the negative criticism was a result of her race: "Race as a subject only comes about because of what I look like" (Alleyne); "People only say I'm angry because I'm black and I'm a woman. . . . I promise you, if I had blonde hair and blue eyes this wouldn't be an issue" (Loh).

Speaking of the writer and folklorist Walter Jekyll, a White British expatriate in Jamaica, Kincaid writes: "He did not like black people, so, naturally, he had to go and live among them. For some people, a fixed state of irritation is oxygen. I understand this all too well" ("This Other Eden" 73; *MG* 113).[15] One wonders if this is an unconscious reference to her own life, where she sometimes satirizes White racism and egotism, where she was married to a White man and generally living in a White world. Was this the "fixed state of irritation" that she understands "all too well"?

Might this also be something with which she, like Xuela in *the Autobiography of My Mother,* wrestled in her twenty-two-year marriage to a White upper-class man? In *Autobiography,* Xuela notes that the room she stays in at Philip's house was designed to house someone of higher status than she but of lower status than Philip (i.e., a nurse [150]). Xuela is constantly reminded of her low social standing. She writes of Philip's former White wife Moira, "she was a lady, I was a woman" (158). When Philip married Xuela, Philip's friends "abandoned him" and did not attend the wedding (206). However, Xuela's stepsister, who had always hated her and looked down on her, conceded her "the superior position" because of her marriage to a White doctor—"Philip was of the conquering class. She was in awe of this, my own conquest—this was how she viewed it" (211). Given Kincaid's insistence that everything she writes is autobiographical, one is led to ask whether or not she is dealing (even before *See Now Then*) with her own marriage and social situation.

Who de cap fit, mek 'im wear it.

It is ironical that in *My Garden (Book):* Kincaid pictures herself when she travels abroad as acting very much like the tourists she castigates in *A Small Place,* often despising the people among whom she travels, showing very little appreciation for their culture, expecting them to cater to her needs, and in every way feeling herself superior to them. At one point she describes her behavior toward the Chinese as "rude and truly insulting" (*MG* 200).

Kincaid, who continued to wrestle with identity issues, became a mother for the second time with the arrival of her son Harold Shawn in 1989. Annie Drew was delighted with her first grand*son.* Kincaid observed: "She *loved Harold.* She really seemed to love Harold." It's possible that Harold was named after William Shawn's brother Harold, his great-uncle.[16]

Three years later, on June 4, 1992, Mr. Potter died (*MP* 58). Mrs. Drew called Jamaica to tell her, "Potter dead, 'e dead you know," in the same kind of voice she might tell her about a natural disaster or some everyday occurrence (*MP* 185). Kincaid writes in *Mr. Potter* that his many relatives argued at the gravesite on the rainy day on which he was buried, their only sorrow seemingly that he had left all of his considerable fortune to a distant relative who had left Antigua (*MP* 185; Kincaid does not identify the heir). There is no indication that Annie Drew was fazed by his death or concerned about what he had made of his life. Hers was the victory—she had raised the daughter whom he rejected and who had turned out to be a great success (at least by the material standards of Antigua and the rest of the world); and even more importantly, she had outlived him.

Despite her 1991 declaration, "I am a citizen of Antigua. I will never become an American citizen" (Birbalsingh 143), Jamaica Kincaid became an American citizen in 1993. She also converted to Judaism in 1993. In 1994 she joined the Harvard University faculty.

Annie Drew was obviously aware of all of her daughter's phenomenal milestones, which she no doubt viewed with a mixture of pride and unease. But she was too busy trying to care for and manage her teenage and young adult sons during these twenty-plus years of silence to give much thought to Jamaica.

7

ANNIE DREW AND HER BOYS

Mumma won't nyam pickney, but pickney wi nyam mumma.
(A mother won't eat her children, but the children will eat the mother.)

Annie Drew's relationship with her sons was as complicated and as intense as her relationship with her daughter. Indeed, as they grew into teenagers and young adults, she often experienced an overwhelming loss of control. Kincaid asserts that Mrs. Drew had had to beat one son and threaten to beat another to get them to attend their father's funeral (*MB* 194–95). Tim Hector notes that Annie Drew had to develop a network of powerful "lawyers, politicians, merchants, teachers, doctors, psychiatrists, police, even badjohns, all designed to help her sons whenever and however the need arose" (17).

Her most painful challenge was her bright and talented last child, Devon, generally called Patches, but known as Sugarman later, when he fancied himself a dub musician (*MB* 45).[1] Splif recalled that "Devon was always a mischievous little guy." Devon was arrested for rape on one occasion and robbery and murder on another. According to Hector, Mrs. Drew asked him to stand bail for Devon when he was arrested for rape, but Hector balked because of the nature of the crime. Mrs. Drew, unperturbed, found another "important personage who immediately posted bail" (Hector 17). She then proceeded, according to Hector, to employ "her vast array of strategy and tactics and the alleged rape withered on the vine" (17). Imagine her fear and dismay when at the age of fifteen, in August 1977, Devon was arrested and imprisoned for participating in a robbery of a gas station in which someone was killed.

She used whatever money she could scrape together and called upon everyone she knew who could possibly help him. It is hard to imagine her sleepless nights, the trips she made to the prison to see him, to lawyers' offices to find someone to represent him, to the homes of powerful political friends to whom she could appeal. Finally, through some political connections that she had and Devon's agreeing to testify against the others who were involved, she was able to secure his release (*MB* 24–25, 175). Kincaid assumes that she "was able to bribe him out of jail" (Kin/Dance). As much as Annie Drew enjoyed telling her daughter stories about the past, this was an ordeal that she refused to talk about—even to Jamaica (*MB* 25). Reverend Lee, who was a trusted confidant, seemed to know nothing about this incident. There is no doubt that it must have been one of the most traumatic events in the life of this very powerful woman who often faced tragedy and death without blinking an eye. This was her lastborn, the son for whom she no doubt had cherished so much hope. She did what she had to do to get him out, and that may well have been too awful to ever mention.

One can imagine the lecture she must have given Devon when she finally went to the jailhouse to walk him home—the harangue about the need to go back to school, the threats about what would happen if he ever again associated with those hooligans who got him into trouble in the first place, the reminder of what his action had cost his family. As happy as Devon was to walk away from the prison, it's not likely that the obstinate and idealistic adolescent appreciated his mother's lecture. He very likely sought to escape her voice as quickly as he could and to get back out on the street among his friends. He certainly would not have shared with them his fears during those last long days in jail, but he would probably have bragged about how he and the other bad johns had pulled off that robbery and would have gotten away if . . . We don't know all the lies he might have told; we don't even know the accurate details of the event. We only know a mother's heart was broken and feeling untold fear that she might not be able to protect her vulnerable and foolhardy son. And we do know he continued to associate with what his mother considered a bad crowd, even bringing them to smoke marijuana in his mother's house. Mrs. Drew's complaints went unheeded (*MB* 41–42). Much of Devon's time was spent lying around "in a drug-induced daze" (*MB* 44), something that Kincaid declares her mother would not have allowed had he been a female (*MB* 44).

But, as far as we know, Devon did not again get involved in any robberies or crimes. And he did find some time to cultivate flowers, trees, vegetables. He was, like his mother, a gifted gardener. "He really could garden," Kincaid declared. "[He] had a garden growing in the back of his house. Oh, God, he had spinach growing on trellises! I used to take him seeds and things, and I'd go back and it would just be [raising her arms toward the sky]!"

For varied reasons some people maintain that Devon was Annie Drew's favorite child. Reverend Lee declared: "She loved Devon very much. She felt that he was the closest to her. He seemed to have been the one she loved best. I don't know why, [perhaps because] he looked like the father. Because he was darker than the others, dark like his father. So I don't know whether it was because he looked more like the father. But she always loved him very much."

If Mrs. Drew were like many "proper" Caribbean people of her time, she was not happy about her Devon becoming a Rastafarian, one of those rebel youths who rejected traditional Christianity, spoke their own "language," and insisted that ganja was a part of their religious rituals. Reverend Lee averred that Mrs. Drew didn't like it that Devon was a Rastafarian: "Now people are accepting it a little bit more, but back there whenever you hear Rasta, you thought that they were devils, going the wrong way. She just felt that it was a mark of rebellion." Kincaid believes that Devon's attraction to Rastafarianism was not so much religious as it was an affinity for the Rastas' modus vivendi: "I think the music, the weed, the lifestyle—I think he was a cultural Rastafarian, not a religious Rastafarian." Joseph Drew also discounted the fact that Devon was a true Rasta, noting that he did not wear the dreads, but he did take a Rasta name, "I-Jah-Man, which he used until his death. I never called him that. I called him Sugarman." Mrs. Drew did use his Rasta name, Joseph told me, but Kincaid never mentions it. One wonders if she knew it, especially since she does not include it when she details in *My Brother* the names the family called each other.

Much more of a problem to Mrs. Drew than the Rastafarian name was the inescapable fact that Devon was not only smoking the weed but was also using cocaine (*MB* 73) and God knows what else. If Kincaid saw fit to warn her brother about his lifestyle and the need for condoms when she finally returned to Antigua in January 1986, it was probably nothing compared to the constant warnings his mother gave him, knowing even more than his sister about his frequent sexual trysts, maybe even knowing (or at least suspecting) what Kincaid apparently never knew until Devon's death—that Devon also had homosexual liaisons. Given Kincaid's frustrations at Devon's casual retort to her warning about the dangers of AIDS, "Me no get dat chupidness, man" (*MB* 8), consider how such frivolous responses to Mrs. Drew's warnings must have perturbed the mother over the years. Clearly Devon had brushed his sister off as an oddball from America (Vermont, of all places—not even New York) who understood nothing about him and his culture; he was probably even more dismissive of his mother as an old lady who was always nagging him.

Mrs. Drew must have been upset that this talented child, who had taken third place in an island-wide exam to go to the Princess Margaret School (*MB*

24), had dropped out of school, and could not get or keep a job. Occasionally she must have become very hopeful, such as when he found employment in the Public Works Department. Knowing his temper and his "nasty tongue" (*MB* 13), she had probably lectured him about the proper conduct in a good job like that, which offered, in addition to a regular salary and some benefits, the opportunity to build some savings. How her heart must have broken when he soon reported that he had an argument with his supervisor, "cuss dem out," and was fired (*MB* 13). Oddly enough, his profession would later be listed on his death certificate as "Interior Decorator," but no one provided any indication that he was trained in or practiced that vocation.

Assessments of Devon's character vary considerably. One close family member said she was "close to Devon. Everyone liked him. He was everyone's favorite. He was jovial and had a great sense of humor" (January 20, 2009). Conversely, one of Mrs. Drew's close friends had nothing but the most bitter memories of him: "Devon was rude and awkward in his dealing with his mother. He was a little son of a bitch. He was a male prostitute" (January 21, 2009). Kincaid writes in *My Brother* that Devon "did unspeakable things." They were things she could not speak about and he could not speak about, she notes (93). She then goes on to write that he stole and lied, but then declares that these were things she, too, had done, posing the question again for the reader, "When I say he did unspeakable things, just what do I mean[?]" (93).

One wonders if these "unspeakable things," which she never really clarifies, might refer to the prostitution that one of Mrs. Drew's friends charged. It is indeed hard to imagine anything that Kincaid finds "unspeakable" about Antigua and her Antiguan family.

Annie Drew's relationship with her oldest son, Joseph, was as complex and as contradictory as her relationship with her firstborn. In our interview Joseph spoke passionately of his love for his mother and of her appreciation of the things he did for her. Reverend Lee suggested that Joseph "did a little better [than his brothers when it came to supporting Annie and helping out]," and added, "I don't know if he was *all* that she expected." And Jocelyn Reid confirmed that "Ms. Annie got along with Joe" (January 16, 2009).

But Joseph also talked of his mother's "hot temper" and her sometimes violent responses: "She don't play around," he declared. He insisted that his mother was hard on him—once even saying she disliked him and gave him "a rough time." He insisted that she didn't punish the other children as much as she punished him. She spanked him a lot when he was growing up. Once, he said, she intentionally burned him on the chest with an iron. (Jocelyn Reid also mentioned the burning incident but recalled that Mrs. Drew burnt Joseph on "the back of both legs [interview]). I tried to press for reasons for his mother's attacks on him. He insisted that he was always religious and never got into trouble or used drugs, and he declared—and Reverend Lee concurred—that he was the only one who sometimes attended church with his mother. When I asked about his father's reaction to her sometimes cruel treatment of him (Joseph), he said his father "didn't like it" and that he protested the fact that his mother used to braid Joseph's hair and put bows on it.

According to Kincaid, Joseph and his mother had an argument precipitated by his bringing a girlfriend into his house, which was so close to hers that she could hear everything they did. Mrs. Drew was so appalled by this "abomination" that she threw stones at him. He retaliated by flinging his mother to the ground and breaking her neck (*MB* 189). But Annie Drew, who survived to everyone's surprise, forgave Joseph and allowed him to continue to live on her property and eat at her table when he wished. Reverend Lee's description of this incident makes it seem less violent than Kincaid's: "she had some wrestling with one of her sons and she fell down." However, the severity of the injury is suggested when she adds, "She was in the hospital for quite a while" and when she later describes it as one of the factors that contributed to her death: "After she came around with that, she was never really herself, so to speak. She wasn't really down in bed, you know, but she wasn't as mobile as she used to be."

Despite Annie's conflicts with Joseph, Kincaid insists that Joseph was his parents' favorite child and received the best of everything, a claim corroborated by another close family member who told me, "Mrs. Drew spoiled Joseph" (January 20, 2009).

Joseph was recalled as sullen, uncommunicative, and unfriendly by almost everyone I talked to except his schoolmate Gordon George. Connie Rabinowitz told me: "But nobody talks to Joseph. And Joseph doesn't talk—or didn't talk—to anybody in the family. I don't know exactly why. He was the *out* brother—not outside child." Kincaid does not speak to him. She notes that she saw him at Carnival in 2008, but they don't speak: "I don't know what to *say* to him. I don't *know* him."[2] She wrote in *My Brothers*, "His [Joe's] story is another big chapter," but she declared in our interview in 2008, "Well, I certainly won't tell it. I've done with all that." Of his relationship with his sister, Joseph told me: "Her and I don't get on too good. I don't see her when she comes to Antigua." One family member, obviously reluctant to respond to my questions about Joseph, would only say of him, "We were not close" (January 20, 2009).

Silent ribba run deep.

My own meeting with Joseph contradicted the silent, sullen personality I had been led to expect. He was friendly in his reception, open in his discussion, and surprise of surprises, vocal and passionate in his recollections. Indeed, he is quite a storyteller, something he probably inherited from Annie, though he told me he did not recall hearing her tell stories as Kincaid and other family members shared. This may simply reflect the fact that he didn't think of his mother's memories as "stories." Indeed, if there were any problem in our communication it was in what appeared to be different interpretations of some words like *stories, ignorant,* and *homosexuality.* In fact, he did recount with great drama and laughter an account when a young Annie and her sister had a "cold pot" of food on the table in Dominica. When Annie got ready to sit down, her sister snatched her chair back causing her to fall. Annie jumped up, grabbed a mallet, and hit her sister on the head, injuring her so badly she had to get nine stitches. Joe summed up, "She had a temper. She didn't make jokes." He went on to tell me that she didn't like people to put their hands on anything she was cooking—if anyone touched any food she was preparing, he/she would be hit.

Joseph met me for a little over an hour on January 15, 2009, the night before he was scheduled for surgery. Then he kindly chatted with me on January 19, three days after his surgery, and on the telephone on January 22. Joseph had a remarkable recall of dates and provided me without a moment's hesitation the dates of births, marriages, and deaths.

Several accounts suggest that Mrs. Drew's relationship with her second son, Dalma, was also fiery. Once in a fit of anger, according to Jocelyn Reid, Mrs. Drew threw a knife at Dalma, stabbing him in his lower back near the side. According to Kincaid, Dalma, who lived in the house with his mother, rarely spoke to her in a civil tone, never responded to anything she said to him, and declared that he would not reply even if she pled with him to save her life (*MB* 194). He also, like all of his siblings at one time or another, according to Kincaid, stopped eating any food that his mother cooked (*MB* 116) and started calling her Mrs. Drew (*MB* 116). In his telephone conversations with Kincaid, he continually described his mother as evil (*MB* 54). According to

Snodgrass, Dalma's "apology for not siding with Kincaid's grievances against the fractious mother thaws by long distance some of the frozen wasteland between siblings" (219). Reverend Lee recalled that Mrs. Drew and Dalma "never pulled up too well as far as I know. . . . I think she felt that he was not—that's my opinion from the way she would talk—he wasn't, you know, very supportive, helping out at the house."

Despite all of the conflicts between Annie Drew and Dalma and despite the fight she had had with Joseph for bringing home women with whom he was having sexual relations, in 1986 Mrs. Drew seems to have welcomed Dalma's pregnant girlfriend into her home. Though the girlfriend's parents were disappointed that she was pregnant, Reverend Lee noted that they had not put their daughter out as Annie Drew told her they had:

> But I knew the parents, so when Annie Drew spoke to me and told me they had put this girl out, I said, "No, they didn't put her out." Because I knew the true story. I told her: "If you were in the parents' place, you would have behaved the same way. You send this person to school, you're expecting better from them. You're Christian—it was a Christian home, and that's not what you were looking for." And she got upset because I spoke. And Annie Drew took her in thinking that she had been mistreated, and since it was her son's child . . .

Very likely the girlfriend left home because she didn't want to be daily faced with her parents' disapproval of and disappointment in her situation. She had two children by Dalma when she was living with Mrs. Drew, both of whom were enrolled in college in 2009. Kincaid, who declares that her mother did not like girls, told me that when her brother Dalma's daughter was born, Mrs. Drew visited the girlfriend in the hospital and said, "Why did you have to go and have a girl? You know we don't like girls in this family!" Another family member did not deny this incident and concurred that Mrs. Drew "did express a preference for boys," yet, she told me, Mrs. Drew pampered her granddaughter and never did anything to let her know that she preferred boys (January 20, 2009). Dalma's girlfriend and their two children lived with Mrs. Drew until the first child was two; after that they moved to the house next door, but the children continued to go frequently to their grandmother's house after school. By all accounts, Mrs. Drew spoiled her grandchildren, and if their mother hit one of them, Mrs. Drew would reprimand, "What you hit my child for!" (January 20, 2009). Annie Drew, who loved to cook and to eat, particularly enjoyed cooking for her grandchildren.

A close family member described Mrs. Drew as "sweet" and fondly recalled her telling "old-time stories about Dominica" (January 16, 2009). She shared with me Annie's accounts of her swimming in Dominica and young Dominican students having to take their desks to the river to wash them. She also said that Mrs. Drew told her that if anyone bothered her in school, she would wait until after school, pick a fight, and take something from the culprit.

During Annie's lifetime, none of her sons achieved the education and prominence that the parents had anticipated. In 1975 Mrs. Drew sent Joseph to college, and he became a licensed electrician. Dalma finished school and held a respectable job in Antigua working in the Social Security Department; he also had a store near his mother's home; but then in his early forties, in 2001 (after Mrs. Drew's death), according to Kincaid, he decided to make a new life for himself, migrated to America, and was working on a master's degree in accounting in 2009. When I visited Antigua in 2008, his family was still living in Annie Drew's former home.

Annie Drew's relationship with all of her sons was often strained, especially as it is pictured in *My Brother.* In 1995 Kincaid recalls that all of Annie Drew's children had suffered the "famous tongue-lashings" from a mother who insisted that she "reserves her right to verbally humiliate her children" (*MB* 53). However, we might empathize with Mrs. Drew when we reflect that at the time of Kincaid's rebuke, these were grown men in their thirties who still lived with her and behaved in ways that certainly seemed to justify her lectures. Dalma, the second son, lived in her house with her, but according to Kincaid, spoke to her only when forced to and then did so with a voice of hatred, and told Kincaid every time they spoke on the telephone that Mrs. Drew was evil (*MB* 54). Joseph, the oldest son, lived in a shack behind her house that Kincaid described as "pieces of galvanize all nailed together with one opening" (*MB* 55), and quarreled with his mother all the time (*MB* 53). Devon, the youngest son, had a somewhat better shack beside his mother's house, but he would move back into his mother's house after he became ill in 1993. Before his illness, Kincaid reports that Devon no longer ate food cooked by his mother and stole from his mother and brothers to support his drug habit.

As pictured by Kincaid, the sons' behavior toward their mother was nothing less than abusive, and none of the family seemed to get along. To discourage Devon from stealing his valuable electrician's tools to maintain his drug habit, Kincaid writes, Joseph ran a live wire around his house. Luckily for Devon, a puppy ran into it and was electrocuted. Mrs. Drew generously insisted that Joseph had not really meant to kill Devon (*MB* 56). Devon begged from his sister so much that she knew that whenever he tried to speak to her alone, it was to ask for something, sometimes the clothes she was wearing. He lied to everyone, even himself. Kincaid found their relationships so disturbing that she resented the minister's promise at Devon's funeral that they would all be reunited at a later date, declaring that she did not want to be with *any* of her family in eternity (*MB* 193–94).

The brothers, however, do not seem to feel such antagonism toward her. Though Joseph acknowledged that he and his sister didn't get along well, he had no negative comments to make about his sister, whom he described as decent and respectable; he also seemed pleased with her success. Dalma, who was told by his mother that he was Jamaica's favorite brother, got along well with her growing up and, as an adult, frequently spoke with her on the phone. Devon always welcomed his sister warmly and enjoyed her visits. For her part, Kincaid has said that she tended to regard Joseph, Dalma, and Devon as her mother's children rather than her brothers (*MB* 20–21). However, she did dedicate *A Small Place* to her brothers "with love."

Despite all of the indications of frequent and sometimes violent quarrels between the members of this family that remained in Antigua, there certainly were some better times that Kincaid didn't know about or that she didn't choose to relate, times when the boys frolicked together and times when Annie Drew enjoyed the company, protection, and even love of her handsome sons. For one example, in my interview with Joseph, he relished memories of the three brothers being close when they were growing up and enjoying playing cricket with tins of milk in the lot across the street from his house, one of the few vacant lots on the street, one on which he never remembered any structure. Another family member recalled that the three brothers enjoyed playing cricket and other games and playing in the lighthouse, the latter of which was a problem for Mrs. Drew, who often chased them out of the lighthouse "with some strong words" (March 5, 2009). The same family member told me that one of the main problems among the brothers dealt with "who had to do the most difficult chores at home. Devon got off easily most times because he was the youngest" (March 5, 2009). Further, there is a touching scene in *My Brother* when Jamaica, stranded on the shore, describes her mother and Devon swimming together: "They looked so beautiful, the water parted for them in ripplets [*sic*], forming fat diagonal lines on either side of them, the two of them, one black, one gold, glistening, buoyant, happy" (*MB* 70).

This scene brings to mind a younger Kincaid, also stranded on the shore, crying while she watches her mother swimming on one occasion and her mother and stepfather laughing together on a distant rock far out in the sea in a dream (*AJ* 44). Might the envious author, often a sad outsider, conveniently fail to relate many of the scenes of family harmony that she observed, thereby leaving readers to be stranded on the shore and only wondering what transpires with Annie Drew when she swims away from those who have neither the courage nor the ability to venture beyond the shores?

There is no doubt that the complex relationships in this family challenge any judgment by those who knew and related to them. Kincaid's close friend Connie Rabinowitz declares:

> Every family, I guess is dysfunctional, but they *really* were—all the way. I think they're a whole *brilliant* lot. Just Joseph may not be because he doesn't talk, because he used to be overlooking the room where Devon was fading away. He wasn't *in* the room—he had this little place next door. Devon loved Jamaica very much—and she loved him. She told me at one point [laughter]—such a silly thing but it was very important to her when he was in this weakened condition—that when he was junior high age he had the *highest* math score in the *whole* island!—And why was that so *important* to her? That's a kind of snobbism too. They all *had* it! All of them.

She concludes that they are/were all liars: "I think everybody in that family *lied,* but I think Jamaica did fiction. That's very different. She never would lie to a *person,* I don't *think.*"

A number of acquaintances pointed to positive aspects of the Drew brothers. Rabinowitz declared: "Devon was the most brilliant. Dalma was the most acceptable—most *like* everybody else, OK. [laughter] They were all very good-looking—to me anyway." Splif concurred, "The brothers were all good-looking."

In 1993 the problems in the family at home became even worse: Devon became very ill and was in and out of the hospital. It was then that Reverend Lee got to know him. She started visiting him in the hospital:

> I found out that something was wrong other than what he was saying. And I was at his bed and two doctors came in and some nurses. And when they

come you give them some space. And I went out and I notice they were consulting like something *serious.* So after they left, I went back in there. So I said, "What did the doctor say?" They say he have *pneumonia.* I said, "Does your mother know that?" I left the same time and went out to her house and told her, "If I were you. I would go to the doctors and find out exactly what's wrong with him." From what I saw there, it was like a serious case and they were consulting. So she left, and she went out, and she called me on the phone, and she was thanking me because she found out it was really serious.

8

A BROTHER'S DEATH / A SISTER'S FEAR AND FURY

> Devon symbolizes . . . a parallel self, a self that Kincaid literally and figuratively left behind when she arrived in New York.
>
> —Louise Bernard, "Countermemory and Return"

During one of the periods when Jamaica Kincaid and her mother were not speaking, she received a call from an Antiguan acquaintance who insisted that she needed to call her mother about her brother. This news was exceedingly disruptive, taking her away, she has said, from her "absor[ption]" with her own children and her husband (*MB* 7); a new book she was enjoying (*MB* 10); and her writing ("I think I was writing in my room there" [Kin/Dance]). Clearly, whichever of the above memories is correct, she was annoyed to be snatched away from something she enjoyed. The caller, Jocelyn Reid, then her mother's best friend, had ironically been despised by Annie Drew when she was the Jamaica character's unkempt childhood friend, her source for the Red Girl in *Annie John:*

> She said, "I have something to tell you—your mother wants me to tell you this."
>
> And I said to her, "What?"
>
> And she said, "It's about Devon. He's in the hospital."
>
> And I said, "What's wrong with him?"
>
> And she said, "I *can't* tell you."
>
> And I said, "He has AIDS?"
>
> And she said, "yes."
>
> I knew it. I knew it. I thought if *anybody* would get that disease it would be him. I didn't know the way he would get it, but I knew. (Kin/Dance; see also *MB* 6–7)

Kincaid immediately fell into a depressed state, recognizing that she feared he would die before she saw him again and shocked to discover that she loved this person whom she really did not know (*MB* 20).

She quickly made plans to travel to Antigua.

When Kincaid saw her brother, he was near death. He had turned very black, his entire mouth and tongue were coated with thrush; he had large ulcers from his throat all the way down his esophagus; he could hardly swallow any solid food, he could barely sit up or walk; he ran a constant temperature; he had lost weight; he was in a "terrible" hospital that had no medications (the Holberton Hospital, in which Annie had given birth to her other children) (*MB* 11–15).

Devon was as foolhardy on the brink of death from AIDS as he had been throughout his life. Kincaid was shocked that her emaciated brother was still flirting with women. In the hospital when he saw a woman wearing tight-fitting pants, he stared at her crotch and made sexually suggestive comments. Kincaid was appalled that a dying man who already looked like a corpse would have the audacity to try to seduce a woman (*MB* 43).

Mrs. Drew's complicated life was now even more so. She got up each morning and cooked special food for Devon, packed it, walked a mile to the hospital (a walk that involved climbing a steep hill), bathed her son, massaged his legs, combed his hair, dressed him in clean pajamas, changed his sheets, offered him encouragements as she helped him eat his food ("Come on, man, yam up you food" [*MB* 16]), cleaned his room, emptied his pan of urine, gathered his dirty clothes and bath towel, took them home to launder (*MB* 15–16), and prepared to come back in the evening to care for him again. After detailing her mother's attention to Devon, Kincaid, who sat outdoors with him and walked through the yard with him, but, she tells us in *My Brother* (115–16), never provided any personal care and gives no indication that she even touched him.[1] complained that her mother loves her children when they are "weak and helpless and need her," and that such love "served her better than it served us" (16). Given Devon's helplessness at this time, the nature of the hospital care he was getting, and the difficulty he had eating, I imagine Annie Drew would be shocked to find that she was being accused of "serv[ing] herself better than [her children]" (*MB* 16). I expect, too, that it took some real control to do all the things she had to do for Devon without reminding him that had he listened to her, he wouldn't be dying of AIDS. And even when he broke down one day and apologized for not listening to her, she did not rub it in. She simply consoled him and told him it was no use crying over spilt milk (*MB* 29).

De good me do, a de tenky me get.[2]

Mercifully, Jamaica was able to get the medicine AZT for her dying brother from the United States. Within the week that Jamaica remained in Antigua and Devon was taking the medicine, he gained a pound, his temperature went down, and there was every indication of a miraculous recovery. Later her mother gleefully informed her that he had requested and heartily eaten a dinner of fried chicken from Kentucky Fried Chicken. When Devon was released from the hospital, he had to move into his mother's house and sleep in the bed with her because Joseph, assuming he would die, had taken his shack (*MB* 54–55).

Kincaid often acknowledges the unlimited love and attention that Annie Drew gave to her children and her unique understanding of them: she was the best mother possible when they were small and needed her care; she understood them completely when they suffered the usual adolescent issues; when as adults they fell apart, she cared for them in jail or in hospital ("The Estrangement" 40). And yet, for Kincaid this becomes a negative and Annie a mother who would not allow her children to grow up: she declares that no mother ever loved her children more than Annie when they were children, but she is unable to love them when they are attempting to be independent adults (*MB* 17). The mother's taking her sick son home to care for him is, for Kincaid, "another example of the extraordinary ability of her love for her children to turn into a weapon for their destruction" (*MB* 53)—but there was nowhere else for Devon to go. Kincaid herself was shocked and indignant at the suggestion that she take Devon to her home in the United States and disrupt her life with the people she loved: "I wouldn't have made that kind of demand on my family [or] myself. . . . I am not a martyr" (Goldfarb 97).

Ironically, although Kincaid criticizes her mother for being best able to love Devon (and her other children) when they are weak and helpless, her own attention to Devon begins when he is dying, and she frequently reminds the readers of *My Brother* what a sacrifice she was making for him in terms of time away from her family and things she would rather be doing and in terms of the financial strain his illness was causing her (the travel and the medications had put her in debt [68]); in her interview with Brad Goldfarb, she details the expenses for medicines, doctors, flights to see him, telephone calls, Federal Express shipments [98]). Speaking of Kincaid's "love" for her brother when he was dying, Derik Smith and Cliff Beumel write: "This love ensures the dominion of its projector. It is a manifestation of inequality and is its abettor; it is colonial" (111).

Annie Drew, likely unaware of the vehement objections to her support for her son but unable to ignore her daughter's customary enmity, went about her usual task of doing whatever needed to be done to protect and care for her children. She built a room next to her bedroom so that her sick son would have his own bed, despite the fact that she couldn't afford it (*MB* 78–79, 81–82).

Oddly enough, Kincaid condemns her mother for cutting down a lemon tree Devon had planted in order to build that addition. She is infuriated that she would have removed one of the few "things left of his life" (*MB* 13). Annie Drew, of course, more practical than her sentimental daughter, was taking the necessary steps to make comfortable the last few days left of Devon's life. She chose a room for him to stay in over a lemon tree that he certainly had no concern with at that point.[3] At this time Kincaid recalls and also castigates her mother for cutting down an okra tree in which red ants had bred that attacked Devon when he was an infant. It is not unusual for Kincaid to prioritize trees: when she invited a landscaper to dinner at her home in Bennington and he suggested she cut down some trees, she vowed she would never have him to her home again and "went around and apologized to the trees" (*MG* 34). Kincaid expresses no remorse, however, for losing the one tape Devon gave her of him singing a reggae song (*MB* 45–46), something that he would likely have found a more important memorial of his life than a lemon tree.

Despite all of Kincaid's detailing of the problems with her brothers and all of the complaints about the mother that the siblings shared with each other and that she shared with her readers worldwide, she berates her mother for saying anything about one of them to the other. After Devon recovered from his near-death experience with AIDS, he, Jamaica, and Mrs. Drew were at the beach sitting on the sand, and Mrs. Drew laughed about Devon taking some unusual fern that she had brought from Dominica and replanted in Antigua and selling it to buy cocaine. She laughed and rubbed his head, an action for which Kincaid forcefully castigates her for embarrassing Devon and for telling her (Kincaid) about it: "I should not have been told about his selling the fern" (*MB* 73)—an odd dictum from a writer who is in the same book telling the world in the most vivid manner every detail of Devon's sex life, his illness, and his deteriorating body with the yellow stream of pus constantly flowing from his anus and the white thrush in his mouth and on his lips (*MB* 138), and who, in an interview with Goldfarb, insisted, "I almost feel that one's sources of humiliation should be immediately put on public display so they lose their power" (98).

Here and elsewhere in *My Brother* (as well as throughout her canon), Kincaid's nonpareil rage is directed toward her mother. Witnessing in her dying brother her parallel self, she strikes out at Mrs. Drew. It is interesting that the very things that connect Devon, Mrs. Drew, and Kincaid, such as their love of gardening, can be construed so that Annie's behavior is viewed as abhorrent by her daughter. Kincaid and her mother often steal plants and sneak them into their home countries. In *My Brother,* her mother enjoys a passion fruit so much that she pockets the seeds and plants them when she returns to Antigua, and it grows so vigorously that it leaps into the soursop tree and weakens it, causing it to attract parasitic insects, which finally infest the house. Unable to get rid of them, the mother burns the soursop tree and the passion-fruit vine, an action that infuriates the daughter and calls to mind all sorts of demonic implications, the mother's impulse, according to Kincaid, to do away with *any* annoyance (*MB* 126). Jamaica was not there to witness the burning of the tree, but she is distraught as she envisions a raging inferno destroying the tree and the insects; she breathes a sigh of relief that that the powerful mother did not destroy anyone or anything else (*MB* 126).

Perhaps more understandable is Kincaid's anger at the tourist trade and the political corruption in Antigua in *A Small Place* and her rage at her colonial history, something that she has written leaves her "filled with rage, . . . nothing can erase my rage" (*SP* 32). In "On Seeing England for the First Time," she writes that she "wanted to take it into my hands and tear it into little pieces and then crumble it up as if it were clay, child's clay" (16).

Several scholars have noted Kincaid's anger. Her dear friend Ian Frazier described her as "warlike" (qtd. in Paravisini-Gebert 18). Gary Indiana describes her work as "rage-inflected" (156). Leigh Gilmore notes that her work is marked by "a persistent, even signatory anger" ("Endless Autobiography?" 216). Jane King insists that "it is anger and insult and little else which Kincaid offers her native Caribbean" (907). Bob Gottlieb refused to publish *A Small Place* because it "was very angry. Not badly written. Angry" (qtd. in Bouson 93). Lillian Ross relates only one comment by William Shawn about Kincaid, which she describes as a response to an essay she wrote about growing up in Antigua: "'It's a poem of rage. . . . It's a remarkable and powerful piece of writing,' he said, shaking his head and repeating, 'an unbelievable poem of rage'" (228).[4]

Kincaid has occasionally pridefully commented on her own anger and rage. She told Perry that she considered anger "a badge of honor" (497), and went on to say, "I've really come to love anger" (498). She told Jane Mendelsohn: "Apparently, I'm a very angry person. I hope I never lose it. I hope to be an eternally angry person" (21). She often insists that the anger she expresses in her writing is therapeutic. She also maintains that it is a natural reaction since "there is so much to be angry about" (Larry Mantle, "Airtalk," 1996; qtd. in Paravisini-Gebert 15). At other times, she insists that it is not anger but truth that she expresses (Alleyne).

Ultimately, however, her anger at others never approaches her persistent fury at her mother, and her frequent visits to Antigua during Devon's illness provide situation after situation in which this rage and bitterness are manifested. Those visits also force her to face and wrestle with another of her consuming fears: the dread of becoming her mother.

On her second visit to see her brother, Kincaid brought her own children, who reveled in their grandmother's company, wanting her to spend time with them, to swim with them, to eat with them. They loved her cooking, eating everything she offered. Obviously Annie Drew delighted in her grandchildren's love for her and her food, especially as her daughter no longer ate at her table. Kincaid, forced again into the role of outsider to a family that now included her own children, was jealous of her children's love for her mother, much as she had been jealous of her mother's love for her brothers and her father and their neighbors—for anyone else.

Mrs. Drew loved Annie Shawn and Harold Shawn very much and was proud of the bright, loving, sensitive, and independent children Jamaica and Allen Shawn had raised. She undoubtedly had some sense of the issues Kincaid had with her own children, her jealousy of their love of their grandmother, and her fear that they might feel some of the contradictions and resentments and anger and even hatred for her that she felt for her own mother (*MB* 63). In Kincaid's introduction to Mariana Cook's *Generations of Women,* she recalls how her mother (Annie) first loved her mother (Ma Chess) and then hated her and how she (Jamaica) loved her mother (Annie) and then hated her (9). She is as desperate not to have that repeat itself with her children as she was determined not to have a line drawn through her children where the father's name should be. She was determined that her children would be born into a legitimate marriage and that they love her. Though she does not often detail her day-to-day interaction with her children.[5] it is very likely that she attempted to be the loving and caring mother that Annie Drew was to her and that she had used as her model for her work as an au pair. For example, when Miriam (the child for whom the Jamaica-character was au pair) won't eat her plums and yogurt, the Jamaica-character tells her that it wasn't really plums and yogurt but a special food sought after by fairies that would make her see what other people can't see, the kind of tale that Annie would often tell the young Kincaid to get her to eat something (*Lucy* 44). Kincaid insists that as a result of her own childhood, she will always apologize to her children for pain that she causes them: "I'll always plead guilty and ask forgiveness" (Mendelsohn 21). Elsewhere she has declared that she spends much of her time on her knees apologizing to her children (*MB* 27). Despite her efforts, she has constantly been alarmed at interactions with her children that threatened to be a reenactment of her own troubled relationship with her mother. After telling me of her efforts not to be the hard and unyielding mother that Annie Drew was, she laughed and said, "Annie, my daughter, might say I am hard and unyielding anyway." Connie Rabinowitz says Annie Shawn has a sharp tongue and that she and her mother have issues though they love each other dearly. "*They* are very close," she told me. And they have a lot of conflicts."

In a moving passage in *My Brother,* Kincaid movingly expresses her fears that her son may view her as she viewed her mother, as a strong, overbearing, larger-than-life creature whom he loves and hates, even often wishes dead. She hopes that he will not ultimately regard her with the eternal bitterness that she feels for Annie (*MB* 62). In "The Estrangement," where she focuses upon her estrangement from her own mother, she discusses her relationship with her children and her desire that they really love her: "Nothing has gone wrong, as far as I can see, but tears have been shed over my not being completely enthusiastic about going to a final basketball game in a snowstorm, or saying something I should have kept in my mind's mouth" (43). She goes on to speak of their considering "unforgivable" a book's dedication in which she noted her "confused love" for them and their (accurate) belief that her gardening keeps her from being the perfect attentive mother to them. She dedicates *My Garden (Book):* "With blind, instinctive, and confused love, for Annie & for Harold who from time to time are furiously certain that the only thing standing between them and a perfect union with their mother is the garden, and from time to time, they are correct." Later in *My Garden* she indicates that her children worry that her extravagant expenditures for her garden might deprive them of necessities. The real problem seems to be that her time in the garden denies them her "absolute attention" (186–87). She admits in "The Estrangement" that she is perpetually thinking of her mother, and that her every action is absolutely a result of Annie's influence (43).

She must often feel some guilt that she is not the ever-present, always attentive mother to her children that Annie was to her. Her account of making a Halloween costume for her daughter in "Putting Myself Together" reminds us of the meticulous work her mother did in making outfits for her, but it is clear that this outfit is the exception rather than the rule and that Kincaid does not often spend days creating special outfits for her children.[6] As one who often negatively portrays mothers who discard, neglect, or abandon their children, leaving them to be raised by others, Kincaid portrays herself as often feeling guilty about her mothering. In *See,* Persephone and Heracles resent the Kincaid-character's constant writing "about her goddamn mother . . . and the stupid father . . . and the fucking stupid little island" (*See* 129), her frequent trips to give readings, and her failure to be there on time to pick them up from the bus stop.

Kincaid's guilt is apparent at several points during her trip to Nepal to find Himalayan plants that will grow in her garden. Her thirteen-year-old son had not wanted her to go, had cried when she left, and had asked others to keep her from going and causing him to suffer (*AF* 9). Many things on the trip remind the remorseful mother of her son: "We ate a supper of noodles, the exact concoction that my son, Harold, likes to eat all the time" (*AF* 172). She is very attentive to a young porter who is about the age of her son and gives him an enormous tip (108), a symbolic peace offering to her abandoned son. Reflecting on the trip on her way home, she writes: "I remembered how practically every step I had taken was fraught with the memory of my past, the immediate one of my son, Harold, all alone in Vermont, and my love for him and my fear of losing him" (188).[7] The "memory of my past" undoubtedly refers to her alienation from her own mother, and her description of Harold as "all alone" is obviously an exaggeration resulting from her guilty conscience, since the boy was with his father, sister, and housekeeper. Constantly throughout this journey, she reminds us of the dangers of the ever-present Maoist guerrillas all around them, of the terrain she navigates, and of a host of other perils that made that journey a hazardous and foolhardy one for a woman with young children. During a similar trip to China recounted in *My Garden,* she keeps talking about leaving her children behind and wondering if they are OK (*MG* 191, 197).

She painfully acknowledges that no matter how good a mother she is, her children will probably spend the rest of their lives loving and hating her and sometimes wishing her dead, but she hopes they will not feel the awful bitterness that she feels for her mother (*MB* 62). She ends "The Estrangement" wondering if her children will want to be with her in eternity: "For in eternity is she [Annie Drew] in me, and are even my children speaking to her? I do not know, I do not know" (43). There is no doubt that the shadow of Annie Drew hangs over all of Kincaid's mothering, a fact that was reinforced time after time during her reflections on family, mothering, relationships, and love when she was in Antigua with her dying brother.

Thanks to his sister's intervention, Devon's health improved to the point that he declared he had never felt better. However, his behavior indicated he had not learned much from his brush with death. His doctor suspected he was on drugs again; he denied that he had AIDS; he started having unprotected sex with women; he boasted about his sexual needs and prowess, declaring to his doctor, who also produced worked with calypso singers, "When me sing, gahl a tak ahff she clothes" (*MB* 68), and showing Jamaica a pavilion at the public recreational grounds where, he proclaimed, "Mahn, me used to bang up some girls under there" (*MB* 81). Dr. Ramsey recalls one incident when his sister lost all patience with Devon:

> Well, when Devon had his mobility, she was concerned about his behavior [promiscuity]. I remember one time [laughing] Kincaid said to him [angry tone], "If I had my way, I'd put a scarlet ribbon around your head and march you down High Street and put, 'I have AIDS!'"
>
> He said to her one day he's not taking any more chances—he's wearing *three* condoms. I explained that two condoms worse than one and three worse than two. The more you put on, the more likely they are to burst, you know. Kincaid was very upset that he should make a statement like that because he was already infected. He say he's not taking any chances. He wear *three* condoms! Oh, Kincaid was *mad,* she was upset, she was upset! She couldn't believe him. I'll never forget that—said she would put a scarlet badge around his forehead and march him down High Street.

Dr. Ramsey continued: "I was there [in Annie Drew's house]. I couldn't laugh. At the time I didn't think it was funny either. In retrospect, you can take a laugh. After a while it's just become a joke, but the seriousness of that time, you know. Here it is, we trying our best to get this man out of the hole, and he's talking about going with woman. He felt better after a while and he feel he could go back out there, you know. He's a good-looking guy, you know. The girls like him, you know."

Rabinowitz also reflected on Devon's behavior: "I think that until the point where Devon said to Jamaica (this is all secondhand) that yes, he was having sex with his girlfriend but he didn't tell her he had AIDS, which made him a murderer at that point. He would lie. I think that's what drives Jamaica crazy [laughter]. She has never said this to me." Mary Ellen Snodgrass reinforces Rabinowitz's point when she suggests that Kincaid must have experienced some guilt that by extending her brother's life, she "allow[ed] him to infect more unsuspecting women with HIV" (157).

Kincaid's discussion with Devon during her visit to Antigua raised the question of whether her brothers read her books. Though Kincaid insisted in our interview in 2008 that her brothers even now have no interest in reading her books, during that visit Devon refers to one of her novels in which the mother attempts to abort her third male child: "Ah me de trow'way pickney" (*MB* 174; with no question mark, perhaps because Devon's comment was more a statement than a question). Kincaid laughingly denied it, insisting that the novel was fictitious, but noting that Devon did not say he knew she was lying and she didn't tell him she was lying (174). In fact, all of the brothers' comments give the lie to her belief that they have no interest in reading her works. Dalma has said that he read all of her books. Joseph was very hesitant when I asked about whether he read his sister's work. There was a long, "Well," and then he went on to tell me that he has always read his Bible every morning and besides that "most I read electrical books." When I followed up on this question later, he said he read her first two books—and he named them. He later said he had also read *A Small Place*. When I named the other books, he seemed to know nothing about them, and when I mentioned *My Brother* and told him it was about Devon's death, he seemed really shocked, exclaiming, "She wrote about his death!" He also noted that he had read that Kincaid said Mrs. Drew made her drop out of school "to take care of us," but he neither confirmed nor denied that claim. Though Joseph did not seem particularly proud of Kincaid's achievements, he did note the surprised reaction he sometimes gets when people find out he is her brother.

According to Rabinowitz, Kincaid made six trips to Antigua during Devon's illness, lugging each time "two suitcases full of retroviral drugs that you couldn't get here," drugs that she was always (inexplicably) able to get through customs. Clearly one of Mrs. Drew's friends did not share Kincaid's and Rabinowitz's assessment of the value of her help to Devon: "Kincaid talks about how she came back with AZT to help retard the progress of his AIDS. Retroviral nonsense! Once you have AIDS, unless you're rich like Magic Johnson, you're dead" (January 21, 2009). He also avowed: "Annie said that all she did was to come and write a book. Jamaica came back and wrote about it, but she had been away, and she did not know the local nitty-gritty."

After spending her days with Devon during these trips to Antigua, Kincaid, who had decided not to eat any food that her mother cooked (*MB* 116), went to stay with friends. According to Rabinowitz: "She always stayed with us, as a matter of fact, after the first time [when she stayed in the Crosbys' guest house]. She never stayed with her mother when she came. *Never!*" One wonders how this affected little Annie Shawn, who wanted to be with her grandmother all the time that she was in Antigua (*MB* 63).

Annie Drew told a friend that she was upset that Jamaica did not stay with her, and she and Jamaica almost quarreled about it (*MB* 27). But Jamaica continued to stay in the Rabinowitzes' palatial home in Cedar Valley, Antigua, high up on the top of a mountain, overlooking the whole island. Her daughter had joined the wealthy and privileged community of White American expatriates who, some said, looked down in a real and symbolic way on everyone else in Antigua. Annie Drew must have wondered if Jamaica now considered herself too high-class to stay in her childhood home. She must have wondered if Lainy had forgotten all the good times they had enjoyed together, doing the chores, preparing the meals, eating special Antiguan dishes, going through her/their trunk, reliving the past, telling stories of her/their lives. She had to wonder if Lainy had forgotten all the sacrifices she had made to make her more comfortable and happy. She probably thought about how much like the old times it could be now—just the two of them stretched out on the bed with Lainy's feet in the windowsill and her head nestled in her mother's neck, remembering the good times, laughing and maybe even crying together! But it was not to be. Lainy no longer existed, and the famous Jamaica Kincaid did not stay in Annie's little Antiguan shack or eat at her mother's table.

Annie Drew probably thought a few of these painful thoughts as she walked home from the hospital, but she was not the kind of personality to spend too much time agonizing over her daughter's behavior. She had plants that needed weeding and a book that she hadn't had time to read in weeks. Further, she had clothes to wash for Devon, and food to start cooking for his breakfast in the morning. She knew that if he should by some miracle get better, he probably wouldn't appreciate what she had done either, but these were her children and she was their mother. She did what she had to do.

Rabinowitz understands that Annie was hurt and perhaps did not like her very much because of this situation: "She was *upset* with Jamaica for *not* staying with her. I don't blame Annie Drew for being upset with me." Though she recognized the impact of this situation on Annie, she empathized with Kincaid, whom she declared "needed to be near people whom she loved and who loved her." Reverend Lee agreed that it was probably best that Kincaid did not stay with Annie: "I don't think the daughter and the boys did too well, either. For that reason, I don't think it would matter that she didn't stay there."

Annie Drew took care of Devon at home during the latter stage of his illness. It was not easy. Rabinowitz sarcastically notes: "When [Devon] came home she played supermom, really." Dr. Ramsey recalls Annie Drew's devotion to her son:

> Ramsey: Oh, yes, she loved Devon to death. Oh, yes.
>
> Dance: Did she love him more than the others?
>
> Ramsey: I'm not sure. I don't really know, because they come in only sometimes. It was usually just the three of us there. I might pass there after work when they [the other brothers] were not home. Sometimes I was coming to work, and I just pass in there, and the boys were not home, so I did not see much interaction between them. Or I would walk there during the lunch break. They call me up. So I don't see much interaction between her and them. But I know how she felt about him. That was her last one, right? You know how it is with the last one [laughs]. They had a *good* relationship, you know. She did care about him, and she made sure that he was clean when he was sick, and she gave him everything that he wanted.

When Jamaica went to Antigua to see Devon two months before his death, she was not speaking to her mother (*MB* 89). She was shocked at a "funny smell" when she entered her mother's house (*MB* 90), something that she wouldn't have considered possible in Annie Drew's immaculate home. It was a smell that Kincaid, like Ernest Hemingway's Robert Jordan, could not describe. It was, Annie Drew (like Hemingway's Pilar) could have told her, the smell of death.[8]

Even a meticulous housekeeper like Annie could not avoid the odors inevitable in the chamber of the dying, especially one in a tiny and cramped Antiguan cottage. Despite the horrible odors, Annie kept him clean: Kincaid notes that she might occasionally express concern about the odor, but then she would immediately proceed to clean him up and change his clothes and bed (*MB* 150).

Everyone reinforces the care that Annie provided her son, Reverend Lee declaring: "She took *real* good care of him. If it was for care, he wouldn't be dead. She really took care of him." A friend of Annie's asserted: "The poor mother had hell taking care of him when he was ill and was almost willing to go into the coffin with him" (January 21, 2009).

When Jamaica went into Devon's room, he held up his penis and ordered Jamaica to look at it—at that penis that had defined his manhood, had made girls take off their clothes, had banged schoolgirls under the pavilion, and was now like a broken flower covered with sores (*MB* 91).[9] One wonders if, now that his mother was braving the smell of death and the loathsomeness of his body to bathe, clean, change, feed, and comfort him, there might have been some gratitude for this faithful mother. I suspect not. Jamaica has asserted that when Devon died he was a monster who would have taken them all with him if he could have (Goldfarb 98).

Throughout Devon's illness, he was attended by Dr. Prince Ramsey, now Sir Dr. Prince Ramsey, a highly acclaimed and honored charismatic physician who is every bit as dedicated and effective as a doctor and teacher and social crusader as he is popular for his work in Antigua. He stands out as the only Black Antiguan who is praised in Kincaid's work—indeed, he is lionized by her.[10] Rabinowitz, too, extolled Dr. Ramsey: "He [Devon] was lasting quite a long while. She [Mrs. Drew] kept him alive. And so did Prince Ramsey! The *only* doctor who would go *near* him. Can you believe that! He was put in a private room. His name was put on everything he touched. Prince was marvelous."

Dr. Ramsey was a longtime acquaintance of Annie Drew's. He had first met her in 1973, when he returned to Antigua as a medical student to do a rotation in pediatrics. He was housed in a home provided by the government on Factory Road, where Mrs. Drew worked as a maid. She was a memorable personality, he told me, "very talkative to me, a very pleasant woman, very helpful, very friendly, and easygoing, quite sincere." He fondly recalled that the meals she cooked for him were true treats for a young Antiguan who had missed native cuisine during several years in college in England and then in medical school in Jamaica. Later Dr. Ramsey would establish his practice in the Ramco Building, within sight of her house. He would often see her walking past: "Sometimes I see her pass here and I shout to her through the window. I call her up, you know." At the time they met, she asked him if he knew her daughter. He had heard about Jamaica Kincaid but had not made the connection. He had seen some of her work that Tim Hector had published in the newspaper. However, he was initially "turned off" by some things she had said about her mother, something he told Kincaid when they met. Kincaid had explained, "I have to write what I see and I have to be honest," and, he said, "I respected that." Indeed, they became close friends and she has brought to him autographed copies of all of her books. When she comes to Antigua, he joins her at the Rabinowitzes for supper at least one evening.

Devon died on January 19, 1996, at the age of thirty-three. Kincaid was on her way back to Bennington at the time. As Devon was dying, he called out over and over the names of his brothers and his mother, the familial names, not Mrs. Drew as Kincaid claims they had all taken to calling her, but Muds; not Joseph, but Styles; and Dalma, the only name by which he ever addressed the brother closest to him in age.

He did not call Jamaica by any name. He knew her birth name, Elaine; he knew their mother's pet name for her, Lainy; and he knew the name she had assumed, Jamaica; but she was not a part of this final roll call. She recognized that it was "so natural, so perfect, . . . so right" that she would be omitted: "I had never been a part of the tapestry [of this family]" (*MB* 175).[11] The account of Devon's death was provided Jamaica by her mother. It is very likely accurate, though given the manner in which these two remembered events, the antagonism between them, and the revisions they both made to achieve certain goals, it is possible that Mrs. Drew would find it signified much to have Jamaica omitted from Devon's roll call. Had she intentionally failed to include the possible mention of Jamaica to punish Jamaica for her alienation from their family, her goal was achieved.

The book jacket of *My Brother* notes that Devon "died painfully and alone in his mother's house," but that seems far from the truth of the accounts the family and friends have provided. Though there may have been pain, he was not alone. His mother was his constant companion and caregiver. Reverend Lee and Annie Drew's other friends visited. Kincaid visited frequently and had just left. Dr. Ramsey regularly attended him. The other brothers were nearby, according to Joseph, and were summoned by their mother when Devon expired. When Kincaid went to her brother's funeral, she took her children with her. Her husband, who suffers from agoraphobia and fears flying, had never been to Antigua and did not accompany them.

Kincaid finds much to criticize about her mother's response to Devon's death. In Cook's *Generations of Women,* she sarcastically observes that her mother, who was never bothered by disappointments or sorrow, showed no grief, while she would have found the loss of either of her children unimaginable (10). Given Annie Drew's constant witnessing of her son's pain and suffering, one can only assume that as a Christian, she was probably grateful that God had taken him and that his agony was over. Kincaid herself certainly was relieved at his death; indeed, during his illness, she had often looked forward to his demise: she didn't like being involved in his illness and having to leave her family to visit him; she had at times thought it would be nice if he would just die and be buried quickly and end it all (*MB* 90; see also *MB* 87). By the time Kincaid saw him alive for the last time, she writes, "I was sick of him and wanted him to go away" (*MB* 108). Furthermore, the bereaved mother had certainly let his suffering matter enough to give her life over to providing care for him during his long illness, and there is no doubting her heartfelt declaration following his death: "Me miss he, you know, me miss he" (*MB* 151). Indeed, Reverend Lee's recollection is that she grieved intensely and never got over his death.

Rabinowitz shared another incident regarding Devon's death that struck her: "[Whispered tone] And then she [Mrs. Drew] did some really strange things. Jamaica had a beautiful bracelet. It was kind of tortoise and white. White abalone or maybe mother-of-pearl—I think white abalone. And Devon liked it, and she gave it to him. Her mother took it off before they buried Devon so that she could have it. Is that a complex psychological scene? Jamaica told me about it; I didn't see it."

Clearly Kincaid's trips to be with Devon during his illness had helped her to form a closer relationship with him than she had had with any of her brothers before this time. Throughout *My Brother,* she wrestles with determining whether or not she loves him, noting at one point that she loved him (20) and at another that she did not love him (106). It is clear that at many points during his illness she continues to have very contradictory and complicated feelings about her youngest brother, who disrupted her life with his birth and with his death: "I don't want to say it's 'perfect symmetry,' but it happened that way—it was his arrival in the world that plunged—changed the course of my life, and, it was the first three years of his life and the last three years of his life. It was because of him that my mother burned my books. It still remains a scar on my memory."[12]

Except for the romanticized childhood when her mother, "the only true love in my whole life" (*Lucy* 132), spends all of her time with her, the Kincaid-character is never confident of her love for anyone other than her children or of their love for her. Kincaid often asserted in very general terms her love for her husband, but he is never treated in any of her works until *See,* where the Kincaid figure's "love" for her husband is as complicated and as problematic as her love for her mother. Indeed, throughout her works, Kincaid is always questioning whether or not the Jamaica-character loved someone, or she was always demanding too much of love, or she is lamenting the absence of love. Xuela's confusion perhaps reflects the author's own:

Xuela declares her father incapable of loving her (though he believed he loved her [*Auto* 113]) and insists that he loved her mother (his wife [80]) and his son (111), but both of them died. She declares that while she never liked her father, she may have loved him, but she was unable to force herself to admit it (185). In fact, Xuela says, "I grew to love not loving my father" (211). After his death, she declares that it was only when he died that was she able to love him (214). While Xuela constantly reminds us that she does not love her husband, Philip, though he loves her, she continually declares her love for Roland, with whom she had a brief affair. The reader has little confidence in this "love," however, because it is so instantaneous: "I love you" are the first words she says to him after she sees him for the first time and is instantly sexually attracted to him (167); because it is purely sexual; because it is inspired by his unavailability; and because a part of his attraction is that he is the opposite of Philip—Black and working-class (a stevedore). In fact, at one point Xuela insists that she could live best without love (29). From beginning to end of *My Brother,* Kincaid wrestles with whether or not she loves her brother Devon. Throughout her works, Kincaid portrays characters who are unable to love and be loved, or even to understand what love is. Kincaid writes in *My Garden,* "Love itself must be had in such a large amount that it eventually causes you to be sick of it" (78). Xuela says, "To this day, I have tried to tell the difference between [love and hate], and I cannot, because often they wear so much the same face" (*Auto* 22). In *See,* the Kincaid character declares that "love is accompanied by hatred and contempt" (122).

Interestingly enough, Kincaid seems at times to relish her contradictory feelings of love and hatred for others. In "Jamaica Kincaid's New York," written in 1977, Kincaid says she has never seen a psychiatrist because she doesn't want to know why she both loves and hates her mother so much, but, she concludes, despite the fact that her mother really loves her, "I have a sort of tradition to keep up" (73), as if this contest between mother and daughter that she details throughout her oeuvre is a challenge to be continued rather than resolved. At one point she noted that her mother was in her thoughts from the moment she awoke in the morning until she went to sleep at night, and that those thoughts were replete with bitter hatred (*MB* 154).

Perhaps Kincaid's difficulties with deciding whether she loves others may reflect that she is able to love only herself. She seems to be a person who, like Xuela, is full of self-love and who never considers the possibility that she might be like Xuela's sister, not herself a person deserving of love (*Auto* 119). She expresses conviction that her success in life is a direct result of the fact that she didn't allow herself to be concerned about her Antiguan family and acted with only her own welfare in mind (*MB* 69). Xuela speaks of her love for herself, her mouth, her thick lips, her half-flat nose: she is so pleased with herself that she actually worshipped herself (100). Later, however, she notes that self-love is what led Philip's wife, Moira, and other White British to transgress against other people (156). Always contradictions!

After Devon's death, Kincaid finished the book she had begun during his illness, *My Brother* (1997). That I was deeply touched by the book is clear in the closing of a review that I wrote soon after its publication:

> For many readers the blunt baring of Kincaid's angst in *My Brother* has been played just one time too many, but rare is the reader who is not again captivated by her lyrical phrasing, her deceptively simple imagery, and the mesmerizing effect of her ritualistic repetitions. And even as one shudders at the bitterness and anger and unforgiving vindictiveness in the face of her brother's suffering and death, one also recognizes that Kincaid is truthful if nothing else as she all so casually exposes those bitter truths most of us would never admit even to ourselves. We would perhaps agree with her own observation that many of her memories are "something only a mind like mine would think about" (6); and certainly there are painful revelations here that only a Jamaica Kincaid would give voice to. Recalling an interview immediately after her brother's death, she declares, "Whatever questions she asked me about anything, it was easy to be without mercy and to answer truthfully" (101). Throughout this book, Kincaid is indeed without mercy and truthful, whether she is describing the gruesome attack of AIDS on the human body, her brother's wasted life, her mother's "villainy," or her own selfish and self-centered life. And we as a society, a nation, a sister or brother, and a daughter or son are not simply viewers of this flawed and tragic family facing the worst epidemic of our times; we are implicated in it. (Dance, Review of *My Brother,* 62)

Oddly enough, the book that is about Devon's death and dying ends with an emotional paean to Kincaid's then-deceased father-in-law and editor William Shawn, whom she celebrates as "the perfect reader" (*MB* 198) whose response to her work was the most important thing in the world to her (*MB* 196); and thus the book closes not with some reflection on Devon, but with the determination that though her perfect reader is dead, she will and must continue to write for him: "The perfect reader has died, but I cannot see any reason not to write for him anyway, for I can sooner get used to never hearing from him—the perfect reader—than to not being able to write for him at all" (198).[13] Leigh Gilmore offers this commentary on Kincaid's "unexpected conclusion": "It is as if Kincaid has switched the bodies and replaced the one we expected to bury and resurrect, her brother's, with another. Yet perhaps it is not surprising that her brother's death proves insufficient; after all, she admits that she does not love him. In her loss of William Shawn, Kincaid discovers a death that makes more of a claim on her, a death capable of replicating the conditions that spur her need to write for her life" (*Limits of Autobiography* 119).

Though Kincaid says that she found out about Devon's homosexuality only after his death, she could then look back and see the signs of it. She knew he had extraordinary friendships with other men, but many people who have such friendships with people of the same sex are not homosexual. She had been surprised that distinguished older men offered to take him on trips to other islands (*MB* 164), but Devon's flaunting of his elaborate courtships of women prevented her from suspecting his homosexuality or bisexuality. All of the author's explanations for her shock at discovering his homosexuality are certainly plausible, and yet one might wonder if this is not a part of her forgetting (or at least claiming to forget) so much of her family, her home, and her culture, even the fauna and the language (*MB* 8, 33). She had, after all, earlier indicated that she had "always" felt sad that he was not able to understand or let the world know who he was (*MB* 162). Further, as noted earlier, as soon as she received a telephone call about Devon, she knew that he had AIDS (Kin/Dance; *MB* 7).

The issue of Devon's homosexuality is a complicated one. Rabinowitz told me that she asked Devon in an indirect way about his homosexuality, and he said, vociferously, "No, I never . . ." (she did not finish the sentence—perhaps he didn't either). She shared with me something that I had noted during my visit, and that is a reluctance to acknowledge or even define homosexuality among some Antiguans. She talked about the fact that men who have sex with other men in Antigua do not consider themselves homosexuals and are sometimes not dubbed homosexuals by others. Joseph Drew seemed unaware of what I meant when I asked him about Devon's possible homosexuality, and when I asked if Devon loved and had sex with other men, he said he didn't think so. Admitted homosexuals were hated in the society. Rabinowitz shared with me an incident recounted in *My Brother* about a visit that she and Kincaid made to an admitted homosexual who was mercilessly taunted by passersby who yelled out hateful things such as "auntie-man, girlsy" at him as he sat on his veranda with his visitors (Kincaid writes about this in *My Brother* [146–48]). Reverend Lee told me: "I don't think the idea of homosexuality ever entered [Annie Drew's] mind. She just feel that he was promiscuous. And I think she feel that he loves girls. He was a very nice-looking fellow. . . . She said that he got it [AIDS] from a tourist on the beach, a *woman.*" One of Mrs. Drew's friends also recalled that "Annie said Devon got AIDS from an Australian woman on a tourist boat. Devon was a prostitute. He scored men and women for money" (January 21, 2009). Splif, a childhood acquaintance, said: "Devon was a very macho person. I don't think he was a homosexual." He assumed Devon might have contracted AIDS while in prison; however, since he was in prison when he was fourteen or fifteen, and the disease did not manifest itself until he was thirty-one, this is unlikely.

On the cover of *My Brother* is a photograph of Devon holding Annie Shawn with Annie cut out.[14] Even with this editing, it is noteworthy that this is the only Kincaid book with a picture of her actual subject other than *Among Flowers,* which has a picture of her in the Himalayas. The picture on the cover of *Mr. Potter* is, she told me, actually a picture of her grandparents (Ma Chess and Pa Chess) and her Aunt Mary.[15] (There is no picture, no sketch, no drawing on the cover of *See.*)

Devon's death, like so many deaths Kincaid has portrayed, brought the author a sense of relief and release. It was Devon and not she who had died. It was she who survived to tell the story. When she heard of Devon's illness, she writes that she knew right away that to comprehend his dying and to survive, she would have to write about it (*MB* 196). She relates even more to Devon than to other family and friends who died. Devon had all of the intellectual and creative talent that she possessed, talent and creativity that could never have blossomed in Antigua; unfortunately, he never left Antigua (168). He shared Jamaica's love of books; he did well on his exams; he was brilliant (39) and had great promise (59); he was a talented musician; he was a promising athlete, a great cricket player (190); he might have written a book on gardening (11). Kincaid is relieved and grateful that his is the life she managed to escape (176). Had she not escaped Antigua she might have lived Devon's life, in which case, she writes, she, too, would have died young or lost her sanity (90). Further, had she not been fortunate, her own "dangerous" youth might have left her with a sexually transmitted disease (see "Putting" 100–101). At one point, horrified by pictures of people suffering from AIDS, she proclaims, "I felt I would never have sex again, not even with myself" (*MB* 38).

9

ANNIE DREW'S LAST YEARS

When thou passest through the waters, I will be with thee;
and through the rivers, they shall not overflow thee.
—Isaiah 43:2

During the last years of her life, with her daughter's help, Mrs. Drew enjoyed a number of the modern conveniences the family did not have when Jamaica was growing up. She had electricity, a telephone, running water, indoor plumbing, a modern gas stove, and a television set that got better reception than Kincaid got in America because, Kincaid told me, the prime minister's son owned the cable company, "and so everybody got cable so that they could pay for it." Despite the fact that Kincaid had considered it a "great injustice" to have been sent away at sixteen to support her family and had soon thereafter stopped sending money, she told me that after having her own children she "grew up" and resumed regular support to her mother: "As I see it, it was just a form of growing up." It is interesting that while Kincaid often writes and talks about her decision when she was a teenager to stop sending money to her mother, she never says anything publicly about her support of her mother in later years. She did not volunteer any comment about the money she regularly provided Mrs. Drew in our conversations and only acknowledged it when I asked her about Annie's indication that she took care of her.

Connie Rabinowitz also confirms Kincaid's support of her mother:

> Rabinowitz: [Jamaica] did a great deal for her mother. She put on an addition to the house—oh, there were so many things. And when Annie showed me the additions of the new this and the new that, Annie was very *proud*. And it got to the point, "Well, what did you do for me yesterday?" Annie was never [satisfied], and she did a sort of a con job eventually on Jamaica—which to me was very sad, though we never talked about it after she told me about it. She said she needed so many thousands of dollars (first of all, not true) to have gall bladder surgery—that I don't think she ever had.
>
> Dance: But she got the money from Jamaica?

> Rabinowitz: I don't know. She asked. But Jamaica said, "I'm *not* going to send it." Of course Jamaica's saying she's not going to send it. . . . She was so bound up with her mother. A lot of her life was about it.

Reverend Lee recalled that Mrs. Drew told her Kincaid sent about three hundred U.S. dollars a month: "She was regular in her support. She would help her. But the writing of the books! Seems like that—whatever she was doing didn't matter." The point clearly was that the books hurt more than the money helped.

At some point around 1993 (during Devon's severe drug addiction but before he became ill with AIDS (see *MB* 72–73), Annie Richardson Drew travelled to her native Dominica to visit distant relatives for the first time since before Jamaica's birth, a trip I discussed with Jamaica Kincaid, Joseph Drew, and two anonymous sources. All of her immediate family had died by that time, according to Kincaid. Kincaid does not know why she returned after staying away so long. Perhaps she intentionally waited until her parents' and her sister's deaths. Perhaps she wanted to make one last visit to the place where it all began now free of the conflicts she suffered with her family. Though there were no loved ones to embrace her, she enjoyed her time in a land that she remembered for its beautiful landscape, its green hills, its golden fields, and its magnificent sea, her unforgettable birthplace.

On December 27, 1996, Annie Drew welcomed Mariana Cook, who came to her home with Kincaid and Annie Shawn to interview her and take pictures of the family for *Generations of Women: Women in Their Own Words.* This was a significant meeting because if Kincaid's comments in "The Estrangement" that she did not speak to her mother for three years before her death (40) are anywhere near accurate, it is likely that this meeting, which took place two years and five and a half months before Annie Drew's death, was the last time Annie saw Jamaica.

The pictures and comments of grandmother, daughter, and granddaughter in Cook's *Generations* are poignant reflections of their complex relationships. In a picture of Annie Drew, Annie Shawn, and Jamaica Kincaid in *Generations* (21), Kincaid is on the left, and holds her daughter, Annie Shawn, who is in the center, close to her, almost as if she is trying to pull her away from Mrs. Drew. Annie Shawn holds on to her grandmother's right hand, but the grandmother seems set apart from the other two; yet she looks resigned and strong with her Bible in her left hand. This picture seems so different from all of the other family groups in *Generations,* who seem to have a bond, but none as exaggerated as the close grasp that Kincaid has on Annie Shawn, almost pulling her into herself with her head resting on her daughter's head. In another picture of only Annie Shawn and Kincaid in *Generations* (8), Kincaid seems even more needy, nestling her head under Annie's neck and on her shoulder, as if she's trying to recapture the fetal position she relished when she lay like a little comma in Ma Chess's embrace (*AJ* 125–26; Cook 10) and as if she is trying to inhale her smell as she did when she sniffed at Annie Drew's neck in *Annie John* (22) or leaned into Ma Chess to enjoy her "amazing female smell" (Kin/Dance; see also Cook 10). In both pictures, Annie Shawn seems much less passionate and clinging than her mother, showing a rather cool reserve, even aloofness. In these pictures she and the grandmother seem to be going along with the program without any real excitement about or commitment to it. Kincaid, on the other hand, seems determined to project a loving mother-daughter image of her and Annie Shawn, though Kincaid appears more the child figure than Annie.

During my visit with Rabinowitz, she pointed to the picture of Annie Drew in *Generations* and declared of her: "You see the way she's dressed though. The sneakers—this is *all* an *act!* . . . just for effect." Annie Drew had on a housedress, a plain headwrap, and tennis shoes.

In her brief statement in Cook's *Generations,* Annie Drew mentions her difficult childhood and reinforces her role in Kincaid's development, noting that she protected her, allowed her time to read, and sent her for piano lessons. She concludes: "I didn't have anybody to raise me the way I did her, but it is to my own interest now that I'm old, because she's my support. All of us get on nicely. Jamaica looks after us and we love her. Even if sometimes she may say one or two things that are fiction, I'm never vexed. As a writer, what she will write is just fiction" (Cook 20). Given that her statement was made in the presence of Kincaid and her White American friend, and given her dependence on Jamaica for financial support, one suspects Annie was weighing her words carefully. We know she sometimes ranted against what she called the lies Kincaid wrote, but here she judiciously speaks of "*one or two* things that are *fiction*" (emphasis mine). She appears cautious to avoid offending her daughter. Of course, almost anything Mrs. Drew might do was likely to incense Kincaid, and her brief and circumspect comments to Cook indeed provoke a harsh retort. Kincaid declares in her introduction to *Generations* that her mother's "grand gestures" were empty: she sent her to a good school but couldn't get books for her; she sent her for piano lessons but did not provide her a piano. Her mother's stories, she claims, are amazing, dishonest, and blind. The fact is, she continues, that her mother sent her off to America to support the family when she was sixteen. She concludes with the accusation that her mother romanticized her life (Cook 20),[1] precisely the charge that is often leveled against Kincaid.

The pot a cuss kekle say im black.[2]

Gary Indiana, for example, describes her works as "memoirs of an entirely invented Caribbean girlhood" (156). One of Mrs. Drew's outspoken friends charges: "There is nothing about Kincaid's books that will tell you about Antigua. . . . Her descriptions of the schools she attended don't fit any of the schools in Antigua" (January 21, 2009). Jane King sarcastically suggests that "if Kincaid purports to be writing non-fiction about the Caribbean then in fairness she should at least attempt to tell the truth" (905).

The comments of then-twelve-year-old Annie Shawn in *Generations* begin with an expression of the love she and her mother have for each other (something that obviously her mother—indeed, any mother—would have wished her to say); she then declares that she is similar to her mother, "but I'm more forgiving." She says that when she acts mean, her mother accuses her of being like her grandmother. Her mother must have winced when she concluded by noting that her mother sometimes acts like her grandmother (Cook 20). As I read Annie Shawn's precocious statement, I was reminded of an incident in Trinidad at the second conference of the Association of Caribbean Women Writers and Scholars in April 1990, when I was waiting with Kincaid and Annie Shawn (who then must have been around five) for transportation from the University of the West Indies at St. Augustine back to our hotel in Port of Spain. Kincaid was indignant about the long wait, and griped over and over to several of the conference workers that she wanted to go back to the hotel *"now!"* Finally, Annie Shawn, apparently fed up with her mother, the diva, looked at her and, like a chastising parent, forcefully reminded her that she needed to understand that she couldn't have everything she wanted when she wanted it. I recall thinking that this little outspoken tot was her grandmother's revenge. And the accounts I have heard of Annie Shawn during my research for this work suggest that she is every bit as outspoken and as fearless as the three generations of women who preceded her (Ma Chess, Annie Drew, Jamaica Kincaid). Rabinowitz declared of Annie Shawn after repeating some sassy comments she made to her father: "That's a big mouth too, by the way. She and I get on very well."

Pawpaw no fall far from tree!

According to Kincaid, during the last years of Annie Drew's life none of her surviving three children was speaking to her, even though the two sons continued to live at her home. Even before that, according to Kincaid, the sons had begun to call her Mrs. Drew if they called her anything. Kincaid had called her Mamie until she got older and then started calling her Mother, and when they were alienated, Mrs. Drew. Though there certainly were some conflicts with Joseph and Dalma, the fact of the matter is that Mrs. Drew had much more interaction with her sons than Kincaid suggests, certainly with her eldest.

Kincaid says that she did not speak to her mother during the last three years of her life because her mother had denigrated her accomplishments and wished her dead ("The Estrangement" 40).[3] Obviously this was a painful conversation for both women, but it was not unlike all the other altercations throughout their lives in which these two unrelenting forces confronted each other, desiring love but inflicting as much pain as possible. The only thing different about this encounter was that it was apparently their last.

The anger Kincaid nurses from this last of what she views as many rejections caused her to declare in 2008, almost ten years after her mother's death, that she would prefer death than spending eternity with her ("The Estrangement" 43).

Pickney tangle yu feet when dey young an' yu heart string when dey ole.

There is no question that disappointments in her children and her relationships with them led an aging Annie Drew to feel lonely at times and drove her to focus more on her church family. Kincaid confirmed in our interview that during her waning years, her mother "came to rely more and more on [her church] and had a very close relationship with her pastor." This relation was indeed very important to Mrs. Drew, and she often confided to Pastor Lee her issues with her family. But she continued as well to enjoy the company of those longtime friends whom she saw and talked with regularly, including Jocelyn Reid. And there is no doubt that even in her old age Annie Drew continued to be Annie Drew—a forthright, assertive, active personality. She continued to love to walk, though she experienced some joint pain, as she noted in a letter written when she was almost seventy-nine to Sharon Chacko. Almost everyone I talked with recalled seeing her walking—all over town—Dr. Ramsey, Reverend Lee, Dr. Osoba, Dame Tonge, Splif, among others. And the noted Caribbean scholar Dr. Carole Boyce Davies, who saw her thirteen months before her death, said that she "was then sturdy on her legs and seemed quite strong as she navigated house, yard, steps, etc." Further, her son Joseph related that she continued to love young people's company: "She tried to be like a teenager—she even tried to run like a teenager."

She also continued to be a very sociable person. In May 1998 Davies was in Antigua for the Caribbean Studies Association's annual conference, and the idea struck her to seek out Mrs. Drew; she invited two other Caribbean American academics, Dr. Catherine John and Dr. Sharon Chacko, to join her, and they went to Mrs. Drew's home. Davies recalls that Mrs. Drew welcomed her "as though I were someone she had known as one of her daughter's childhood friends who had travelled abroad and started to indicate that she was so happy to see me after so long. She immediately invited us into the yard and then into the porch of the house" (e-mail). John, who found Mrs. Drew "warm and friendly and spirited," said she "seemed flattered that we had sought her out" (telephone interview, February 11, 2009), a fact reinforced in a letter that Mrs. Drew later wrote to Sharon Chacko in which she declared that she appreciated every minute of their visit with her, asked them to please return soon, asked Chacko to keep in touch with her, and promised to write again to Chacko. Chacko recalled "her wry sense of humor" and the "small, wry smile on her face" (telephone interview). They saw nothing of the Annie Drew who embarrassed Kincaid by pleading poverty and begging tourists for money. Davies insisted: "She was not the type who would do that. She was not poor or saw herself as poor as in the Caribbean context she was working-class with a house, grown children who would take care of her. Women like that would be humiliated to ask for money even if they were [in] need" (e-mail). Rather, they found her very generous to them. When she discovered that Chacko had to prepare her own meals because of allergies and had had trouble finding fresh greens in Antigua, she went into her garden and picked a generous amount of spinach for her. Like her daughter, she enjoyed showing her visitors the plants and vegetables in her garden. Mrs. Drew was very cordial and invited them into her living room for something to drink. They had garden-grown peppermint tea and water. John described the house as "humble by American standards, but a fairly nice home by Caribbean standards. It had a small living room. I don't know how many bedrooms" (telephone interview, February 11, 2009). Davies described the house as "a typical Caribbean house with about two or three bedrooms, a living room and a kitchen" (e-mail). She also took them across the street to Dalma's store and happily posed for pictures with them.

When they asked her about her daughter and about one of her books that had treated her negatively, she simply shrugged and said something like, "Well, she'll always be my daughter" (Chacko, telephone interview). John recalled:

> She seemed to have an emotionally generous way of viewing her daughter's choices. She didn't say anything with any bitterness, but I remember thinking that she knew her daughter well and had her own opinions about what influenced her to make the choices she made. I remember having the sense that she thought her daughter had become enamored with the world away from the Caribbean. [Mrs. Drew] had that old folks' way of communicating. People from that generation in the Caribbean community don't say negative things directly. It's understated. It's inferred. (e-mail)

Davies recalled:

> She was quite chatty, very proud of her daughter and repeatedly said to us that she was not sure why her daughter expressed complaints about how she had raised her. She was proud that she had raised her well and had made her study and not get pregnant early like some of the other girls around. She was very confident about herself, a kind of feisty Caribbean type who insisted that it was she who had allowed Jamaica Kincaid to be who she is today. She said things like: "I was the one who made her stay inside and study. I told her, 'You stay in and read your books.'" She was proud that her daughter was a famous writer in the United States, that she had done well after migrating and at each occasion took full credit for this success. She did not know why her daughter wanted to separate herself from that "constructed mother figure" which she seemed very aware of. She kept saying: "I don't know why she would blame me." (e-mail)

The women were also impressed with the warm interaction that Mrs. Drew had with neighbors in her community. Chacko noted: "I was also struck by Anne Drew's apparent good standing in her community and her integration into her habitat. Everyone knew her and [they] were quick to guide us to her home, and during our stroll with her from her house to her little shop [Dalma's store], she had jovial exchanges with her neighbors" (e-mail).

John summed up her impressions of Mrs. Drew: "She had a very sort of wise perspective. It was clear that she definitely was not a *bitter woman.* She seemed like a woman who was at ease with herself. She was slightly cocky" (interview).

Chacko added: "Miss Annie seemed quite familiar, evoking memories of older aunts who could be visited without warning, dispensing garden-grown peppermint tea, practical advice and reassuring endurance. While she was clearly a strong and worldly-wise woman, she was not the formidable persona crafted by her renowned daughter, and I was even a little surprised to see that she was not very large. She seemed in good health and I was quite startled to hear of her death about a year later" (e-mail). Chacko recalls their visit with Mrs. Drew as "a refreshing escape from the usual academic hot house of theorizing and maneuvering" (e-mail).

A review of Mrs. Drew's guarded comments to the visitors from America that she was seeing more and more of during her last years no doubt reinforces her awareness that despite whatever Kincaid might say otherwise, the writer's success was largely attributable to her mother's efforts.

Kincaid has maintained that her becoming a writer is a miracle: "There's really no reason in the world for me to be a writer. I have absolutely no credentials, no family backing" (Cryer B4). She often points to events that reinforce the lack of support she received from Annie. For example, when she was reading with her feet up on her windowsill, her mother complained that she was destined to be a shiftless person; the novelist gleefully declares that she was only destined to become a popular writer (*MB* 44). In the interview with Leslie Garis, reflecting on her achievements of which any parent other than Annie Drew might be proud, Kincaid declares, "It really is a mystery to me how I came to be the person I am" (70).

It was no mystery to Annie Drew. In fact, she came to realize that she had been creating the artist her daughter was to become from the moment she became pregnant. On a number of occasions, Kincaid recognizes that what she saw as abuse from her mother may have contributed to her success. This is suggested in a symbolic way when she writes about rosebushes that arrived at her home when it was still freezing and snowing: she notes that the roses did well despite the fact that they had been badly mistreated, proving that abuse contributed to their successful growth (*MG* 51). She certainly realizes, as she told Bonetti, "If I had had another kind of life I would not have been moved to write" (133). As Kincaid has herself indicated: "She's the source of literature for me. . . . Because of her, I'm able to articulate the pain she caused me" (Mendelsohn 23). Thus even when her daughter (and perhaps others) labeled Annie's influence as negative, it had a positive impact on the evolving writer.

Kincaid, of course, prefers to credit others for her development as a writer. She always applauds the men who introduced her to William Shawn and especially William Shawn for teaching her to write and giving her confidence to write. And though she often decries her colonial education, one which she insists was designed to make her feel inferior, she acknowledges, "If I have influences, it would be English literature, of the greatest kind, mind you" (Dilger 21–22). She frequently lists as influences on her writing the King James Bible, Shakespeare, Milton, and Charlotte Brontë. While all of these sources were certainly influential, the indisputable fact is that, as Colbert Nepaulsingh argues: "The naming and nursing of the writer, Jamaica Kincaid, was almost entirely matrilineal." He insists that "whatever technique she [Kincaid] applies and publishes had already been named and applied by her mother and grandmother, who, no doubt, reworked the stories of their ancestors" (205). And this includes even her technique, for Kincaid told me that packing and unpacking the trunk with her mother "was one of the main connections I had to her—a most profound experience, I think, in my life ground—a literary experience—I think it contributes to a lot of the ways in which I go about writing. It's an unpacking and a repacking. And that was what she would do with that trunk."

Mr. Potter is just one of the many illustrations from the Kincaid canon of her mother's influence on her writing. In that biography of an individual that Kincaid herself never really knew, it is clear that her source is her mother. For one example, Kincaid keeps varying the "I never knew his face" (*MP* 104) to suggestions that she saw him when she was four to finally acknowledging that any memory she has of his face came from her mother (*MP* 125–27). After presenting the family history in *Mr. Potter,* she admits that everything she recounts comes from what her mother told her, that the life she lives is one her mother told her (127). She embraces not only her mother's telling of the events that she (Jamaica) actually witnesses, but she is able to assure us (obviously because of her mother) that she has memories of Annie and Drickie before they became her parents (*MP* 137). The importance of a mother's memory is emphasized in that biography by the examples she gives us of others who were not so fortunate as to have the memories her mother provided her: her father, for one example, did not know about his father (56) and did not remember his mother's name (84). Kincaid ends *Mr. Potter* with a celebration of her giving voice to Mr. Potter's history in a series of sentences summarizing the stories of his life and everyone connected with him, each beginning with "Hear" (193–95). Surely this celebratory cataloguing of her achievements (obviously because of her mother) bespeaks Jamaica's pride in giving voice to what would otherwise be silenced.

On many occasions, however, Kincaid undercuts the significance of her mother's stories, noting that while her mother told her about her life and her family and their marriages and love, what she shared was more gossip and mythic than any traditional storytelling: "The great griots did not exist in my life" (Dilger 21).

Annie Drew was, I would argue (as has Tim Hector),[4] the *greatest* griot, and the significance of her stories and her influence on the Kincaid canon is the ultimate proof of that.

During my interview with Joseph Drew, he fondly recalled celebrating his mother's seventy-ninth birthday with her on September 15, 1998. He also talked about her last Mother's Day, Sunday, May 9, 1999, when he bought her shoes and "a dress with several beautiful colors, like your blouse" (I had on a very colorful blouse of bright lime, orange, red, and yellow). In response to my question about his relationship with his mother, he declared, "I treat her real good." He told me that before she died, "she said I treated her best."

Annie Drew did not suffer a lot from the decrepitude of old age. Though most people did not notice much deterioration in the condition of this active and vibrant woman until the last few months of her life, Reverend Lee dated her decline to three events, the first of them being "the daughter's books about her." The second was the incident in which Joseph threw her to the ground and injured her; though she "came around after a long hospitalization, she was never really herself, so to speak. She wasn't really down in bed, you know, but she wasn't as mobile as she used to be." The third factor that contributed to her decline was that "she never got over Devon's death. She never got over that."

Last pickney kill 'im mumma.

Jocelyn Reid insisted that Annie Drew continued quite healthy until a couple of months before her death, but then the heart condition, diagnosed shortly before her death, truly slowed her down in a way that everyone began to notice. Toward the end, Jocelyn recalled that she "had gotten a bit nervous and sometimes when there was a sudden noise as she sat on the porch talking with me, she might jump." Joseph said that toward the last she walked a little more slowly. In the last few months of her life, according to Reverend Lee, she was no longer able to walk to church and had to get a ride. She had begun to complain that she didn't feel well, but she was still active.

What is fi you can't be unfiyou.[5]

Mrs. Drew's diagnosis forced her to look death in the face, and it is very likely that she spent many a night reflecting on her estranged daughter. It is not hard to imagine some of her thoughts. She obviously regretted that she and her daughter were alienated. Yet there was much in her daughter's situation that undoubtedly gave her comfort. In this dangerous world of AIDS and other sexually transmitted diseases, a dying Annie Drew must have been especially relieved that the daughter whom she had once feared was on the way to becoming a "slut" was the proper married mother of two children.[6] Perhaps during those last days of her life, Annie Drew must have taken some comfort in the fact that despite all of Kincaid's issues and all of their conflicts, her daughter had escaped all the pitfalls she fought so hard to protect her against—poverty, teenage pregnancy, disgrace. Annie could rest content that her daughter was living the life she raised and prepared her to live: no matter what Kincaid may say, she is her mother's daughter—a proper mother and wife, an intelligent and strong-willed woman, sewing (occasionally), gardening, reading, writing, lecturing, speaking properly and eloquently, eliciting approval and compliments wherever she appears. How prescient were Annie's previously cited comments in the dictionary she gave her seven-year-old daughter: "To My Darling Daughter, who will one day make me proud of her" (NY 72)!

But no matter her consolation, the dying mother probably always came back to her daughter's traumas. So many contradictions, so much sadness. So much anger, so many fears. What release and relief was there for such anguish? What to do? What to do?

I expect the burdens of the world weighed heavily on Mrs. Drew's shoulders during her last days, especially her worries about her daughter. Perhaps she longed to cast off all her earthly encumbrances and plunge into the sea, feeling herself buoyed up by the clear Caribbean waters as she swam for one last time toward the horizon. But, as she always had, she probably characteristically yearned to first settle her Lainy into a safe cove, far from the reach of the perilous waves.

10

JAMAICA'S GOD IS STILLED

> She seemed to us not a mother at all but a God.... Her death was a shock... because I could not believe such a presence could be stilled.
> —Kincaid, "The Estrangement"

Mrs. Drew probably noted with little sympathy news of the death of her longtime foe, eighty-nine-year-old V. C. Bird, who died at the Holberton Hospital on June 28, 1999. There was much passion as Antiguans were caught up in the frenzy of planning a funeral scheduled for July 9 for the man who had been the leader of the longest-serving government in the Caribbean, having served as the first chief minister, the first and last premier, and the first prime minister of the nation (1981–94), and having been accorded the status of Antigua's first National Hero in 1994 (after having refused to be knighted by the queen). Mrs. Drew might have considered it poetic justice that she outlived him, perhaps remarking as she did upon the passing of Mr. Potter, "[V. C.] dead, 'e dead you know" (*MP* 185). As Tim Hector noted of V. C. Bird and Annie Drew, "between the two . . . there was no love lost" (13).

On July 7, 1999, the Wednesday before her death, Mrs. Drew went to her church's regular Wednesday services. She went straight to the altar to pray. After the services, she told Reverend Lee:

> "If you hear me dead, no frightened." But I thought she—because she had been talking strange things all along like she wants to die, better she dead because she feel people would be saying things about her because people are reading the *books,* and what not, so when she told me that night that, "Sister Lee, if you hear me dead, no frightened." I say, "Sister, you always talking nonsense!"
>
> "You hear what me say!"
>
> So I didn't say anything about it.

Mrs. Drew was referred to Dr. Ramsey a couple of days before her death, and he diagnosed congestive heart failure. She began taking a prescription he gave her. Dr. Ramsey said that she recognized the gravity of her illness, and he believes "she was relaxed and accepting to death," though "I didn't expect that she would go that soon either."

On Friday night, July 9, 1999, after V. C. Bird's funeral, Joseph went by his mother's house to take her some Phospherine she had sent him to get (it's not surprising that she was taking a folk remedy along with her prescription). He told me, "I spoke to her by the bedroom window." They had a pleasant conversation. It was to be their last.

The next morning Annie Drew lit the fire in her gas stove to prepare Joseph's breakfast, went outside to empty a small rubbish bin—and collapsed. A neighbor, Desiree Weston, saw her fall and raised an alarm. Joseph and Dalma rushed out, lifted her up, put her on the seat of Dalma's red pickup truck, and called an ambulance. They got no response from her. They tried to open her eyes. Joseph wiped off an area under her eye that had been cut in the fall. They now know her heart likely stopped beating right away, but Joseph had no idea at the time that she was probably already dead. Dalma called Reverend Lee to let her know they were taking their mother to the hospital. Reverend Lee rushed to the hospital, and when she did not find Mrs. Drew there, she hurried to their home. In the meantime, three policemen came; one took her pulse and declared, "The woman dead." Joseph was shocked. Reverend Lee arrived at the home, saw Mrs. Drew lying on the front seat of the pickup and went to her, entreating, "Sister Annie, Sister Annie!" She was shocked to be told she was dead. But she immediately took charge:

> Well, the police were there, because when it's a sudden death, they have to call the police. Well then I told them, "I didn't think this was a police case because she had told me she went to the doctor and if I hear she's dead, don't be surprised. So since she went to the doctor recently, look inside and see if you see any medication." So that's what they did: they went in and they saw the medications and saw the name of the doctor; they called the doctor, and the doctor said yes he was expecting it.

Mrs. Drew died on Saturday, July 10, 1999, shortly before her eightieth birthday in the yard of her house on Charlesworth Ross Street, formerly known as Nelson Street, the yard where so much of her life had taken place, where she had cooked meals for her family, washed their clothes, tended her garden, been thrown to the ground by her son Joseph, posed for the pictures for Cook's *Generations,* and seen her daughter Jamaica and her granddaughter Annie for the last time. Joseph was shocked. He cried for the whole day. He couldn't eat.

Kincaid's account of her mother's death is a bit more dramatic and continues until the end her image of Annie as often confrontational, even demonic:

> What happened is that she woke up one morning, a Saturday morning, I think, and got out of bed, not gently, just *got* up, and got into, apparently, a fight (my brothers could hear it) with the different animals in the yard, you know the cats were in her way, the chickens, and she was just in a *fury*, and she opened the gate to her yard and stumped her toe and fell down.[1] I think her heart gave out. But apparently, the doctor said, "If she had just gotten up *gentler* . . ." or something. She died in a kind of fury.

Kincaid's account incorporates behavior on her mother's part that was consistent with her character, as illustrated in what a close relative told me when I asked her what she remembered most about Mrs. Drew. Her ready reply: "She liked throwing things at dogs to run them out of her way" (January 16, 2009).

Looking back over Annie's last months, Reverend Lee understands that she was preparing for her death: "She would always go to that altar to pray. It's hardly a time that she comes to church that she would not come to the altar, so I think she knew. She was trying to get as close to God as she possibly can. I believe she really made her peace with God. I believe she felt better to go [die] than to stay [live]."

The cause of death on her death certificate is "cardiac failure, congestive heart failure as per cert. #7958 from Dr. Ramsey." The undertaker was E. Saunders; the funeral program indicates "Professional Services by Straffies Funeral Home." Her death was registered on July 13, 1999.

The funeral was held on Friday, July 16, 1999, at 3:00 p.m. at the Villa Church of the Nazarene (also known as the Beacon Light Church of the Nazarene), and she was interred at St. John's Public Cemetery. Scriptures were read by Jamaica Kincaid and by Natasha Drew, Dalma Drew's daughter. Senator Tim Hector, a good friend, delivered the eulogy at her funeral, and Rabinowitz remembers that he focused on Mrs. Drew's political career. A tribute was offered by Reverend Rosa Lee. Several women of the church offered commentaries on Mrs. Drew, all of which, according to Rabinowitz, reflected brutally honest assessments of a contradictory woman:

> What I remember most vividly: the pastor was the only person who moderated what [s]he said about her. There were various women [with whom she worked and took classes in the church] who spoke at her funeral. . . . The

> *very* first thing that everyone said was, "Annie was a difficult woman, *but* . . ." [They also said] That she was fun, she was fun, that they thought she was very dedicated and sincere—I would have to say that *they* thought she was sincere in the way that you speak of a good friend, but you also know where all her warts are, right? But she's still your very good friend—"Oh, shush, honey!" I had never heard *anybody* get up at *any* funeral with *everybody* saying [whispering and confident tone], "She was a difficult person."

Conversely, Kincaid recalls that everybody at Annie's funeral said what a nice person she was and detailed her unselfish and kind acts, shocking her children, who didn't know the person being described ("The Estrangement" 43).

Rabinowitz recalls Kincaid's nervousness during the services: "I was either sitting directly behind Jamaica or next to her. I can't remember, but I think I was right behind her. I was watching her tense up and relax and tense up and relax—but not really relax. And I was kind of, I had that, well, as Bud [Rabinowitz's husband] says to me, "you can't take care of the world's problems," so I do anyway after sixty and a half years—he just said it to me again today [laughter]."

Kincaid's husband did not accompany his wife to her mother's funeral. He never went to Antigua. He did not fly.

One of Mrs. Drew's dearest friends did not go to Annie's funeral "because Jamaica Kincaid would be there" (January 21, 2009).

The Antiguan prime minister, Baldwin Spencer, was in attendance.

The family buried Mrs. Drew next to Devon, but apparently not Mr. Drew. Kincaid indicated in *My Brother* that one of the first things she wanted to do when she first returned to Antigua in 1986 after her long absence was to visit Mr. Drew's grave, but no one would take her there, her mother believing that since they had not paid for the plot, someone else had probably been buried in it. Later, when Devon was dying, Kincaid insisted that her mother go with her to the cemetery to find the grave, and so they went and walked and looked, and looked and walked. Mrs. Drew looked for trees and other landmarks she recalled from the funeral, but she simply could not determine where he was buried (*MB* 120–23). However, Reverend Lee told me in 2009 that Joseph went to the cemetery to put flowers on his mother and father's graves, raising the possibility that he knew where both graves were. At any rate, according to Kincaid, she and her surviving brothers felt guilty about burying Mrs. Drew next to Devon, fearing that he would not have wanted to lie next to her throughout eternity ("The Estrangement" 43). She adds that they certainly would not wish to do so; they would all prefer death to spending eternity in her company ("The Estrangement" 43). Then she asks if she really means it, an equivocation that raises a question about her certitude. One has the feeling that if Mrs. Drew would only say she was sorry, Kincaid would happily spend eternity "curl[ed] up like a little comma" in her mother's embrace (see references to her symbolic return to the fetal position with Ma Chess, p. 50 of this book; and recall her longing for "the person in whose body I had lain curled up" when she is sent to Dominica [Cook 10]). In the story "My Mother" from *At the Bottom of the River,* the daughter fits perfectly in her mother's arms, on her back, in the hollow of her stomach; they eat and drink from the same utensils; they sleep on the same pillow; they merge (*AT* 60). Complete happiness! Her Eden!

The account Joseph gave me of his response to his mother's death varies from Kincaid's. Indeed, he seemed quite sentimental about her loss, poignantly describing to me the pictures of her he has on his wall, one of them with Jamaica, and declaring that he still goes up to the picture and kisses her—"It's a woman I love.[2] I still feel [the grief of her loss]—I spent forty-one years with her." He fondly recalled the last birthday he celebrated with her, her seventy-ninth birthday, on September 15, 1998, and the gifts that he gave her. His account is reinforced by Reverend Lee. When I asked her about the children's response to Mrs. Drew's death, the only response she mentioned was Joe's:

> Joe took it on, you know. I think he misses her quite a bit, quite a bit. She was always there for him. She always cared for him. Just the other day he was passing here. He say he was coming from the cemetery. He went to clean the mother's grave and his father's grave, you know. He's *always* talking about her. He remembers her birthday and he remembers everything. He *loved* his mother. They didn't get along too well, but he loved his mother. I believe she loved him too—it's just she can't get them to do what she wants them to, she gets upset. That was her personality.

Mrs. Drew's death was a victory for Kincaid, but one that she was too shocked to relish. Even after the funeral Kincaid could not believe that her mother was dead. She probably recalled an exchange that she recounted in *My Brother* when her mother complained about her health, and Kincaid quipped that her mother would bury them all. Her jovial mood ended when her mother laughed at the possibility of that. Kincaid did not find it funny, given that she was one of those whom Annie might bury (189). Earlier she had insisted that her mother would be exultant were she to outlive her children (*MB* 131). Often Kincaid expressed her fear that her mother would indeed outlive her. In *Mr. Potter,* as she looked at Mr. Potter's and Annie's graves, she recalls her fear that she would never experience seeing her mother dead: she had viewed it as a battle to see her mother dead, but she often feared she would lose that battle (192). Throughout her life, Kincaid, ever full of paradoxes, had vacillated between wishing her mother dead and fearing her mother might die, knowing that being motherless would be the worst thing that could happen to a child. Even as an adult, Kincaid admitted that it would be difficult for her to exist in a world without her mother's presence (introduction, Cook 20). When Mrs. Drew actually died, Kincaid wrote in "The Estrangement," it was difficult to believe her dead because she viewed her not so much as a mother but as a *God.* She remained shocked by her death, not because she grieved or missed her, but because she couldn't conceive of the fact that such a powerful person could actually die. Further, as she had reflected in *My Brother,* despite the certainty of death, death was always a surprise, leaving those left behind in a state of shock (193).

Rabinowitz reinforced Kincaid's inability to comprehend that her mother was really dead:

> And when she was standing right out there [gesturing toward the patio], after the funeral, she was saying [disbelieving, questioning voice], "She's really dead, she's really dead." Yes, it's very hard to convince yourself in one way, but it's as though she expected—I just hate myself for saying it. But it was as though, you know, "Is she really going to get up out of that grave and come back and haunt me again?" Yep! She just expected her to *rise* out of the grave. [She said that] right there [on the patio]. We all came back here after the burial.

This was a scenario that Kincaid had envisioned in her writing. One wonders if Kincaid shared Xuela's feelings upon her father's death: "I felt superior, I felt superior in the fact that I was alive and he was dead, and even though I knew and believed that death was my fate also, I felt superior to him, as if such a humiliation, death, would never happen to me" (*Auto* 213). The novel closes with Xuela declaring, "Death is the only reality" (228).

Indeed Kincaid, who is awed by death and reflects upon it throughout her writings, often recognizes a kind of power that accrues upon death, one that no doubt she continues to recognize with the death of her mother. In *My Garden (Book):,* she wrote that "death is just another way of being, and the dead will not stay put, and sometimes their actions are more significant, more profound, than when they were alive, and no square structure made out of concrete can contain them" (69). In *Mr. Potter,* she has the gravemaster declare that an individual cannot be known until he is dead and he can no longer change his actions, respond to his accusers, correct his errors, or seek forgiveness (51). And in *My Brother,* she insists that the dead never die (121).

One recognizes, too, the applicability of that other *Autobiography of My Mother* (by Rosellen Brown), where the daughter Renata, who is also a mother, speculates: "Will I have to die for [my daughter] to get free of me, free of the part of her history I carry around?" (241) She goes on to lament, "[My mother] is not my history only: my future. She won't die, she'll be waiting for me in the graveyard no matter what" (207). One wonders if these are Kincaid's sentiments as well. Even after Mrs. Drew was laid to rest in a grave next to her son Devon, she remains the demonic foe with whom her daughter wrestles.

After her mother's death, Jamaica Kincaid gathered together a few of her belongings to take with her back to America: Annie's thimbles, some pieces of her embroidery, and her Bible. These items, along with the wedding band Pa Chess gave Annie and the pictures Kincaid earlier demanded of Annie, are among the author's treasured mementos of her mother, some of which she shared with me during my visit with her on October 11, 2008. Kincaid smiled as she tenderly held the worn thimble that her mother used and started talking about things she remembered: the baby clothes her mother used to make, the little things she would embroider on them. As she recalled those days and fingered the items Annie had so frequently handled, the anger, pain and bitterness seemed for a moment to be replaced with sentimental recollections of a treasured Eden and a loving mother.

But not for long.

EPILOGUE *"I Married My Mother"*

> Listen. I am my mother. Aaahhh! Aaahhhh! [exasperation/laughter] And not only that, *I married my mother!*
>
> —Kincaid, interview with the author

> I am always thinking of my mother; I believe every action of a certain kind that I make is completely influenced by her.
>
> —Kincaid, "The Estrangement"

In 2013, fourteen years after Annie Drew's death, eleven years after Jamaica Kincaid's divorce from Allen Shawn,[1] and eight years after her last major publication (*Among Flowers*), Kincaid published *See Now Then: A Novel,* the story of the vicious cruelty of a short, ugly, unfaithful, impotent, unsuccessful, insecure, cowardly rodent of a husband toward his aging, hateful, overweight, loud, exaggerative, unsophisticated, insecure, and unattractive wife. The author, who had frequently insisted that *all* of her work was autobiography, primarily about her and her mother ("the central figure in my life" [*MP* 153]); that there was no reason to be a writer without autobiography; and that she did not know how to write a story about something that had not happened to her, suddenly was offended that this novel about the bitter dissolution of the marriage of an interracial Vermont couple was viewed as autobiographical. She declared that the book was "in no way my autobiography" (Haber): "*See Now Then* . . . isn't my own life. What I was describing wasn't my own life" (Alleyne). She expressed amazement that anyone would want to know about *her* life: "What do they think I am? A famous person? What is it about me that makes people want to know? I've written a book about my mother, and I don't remember anyone going to Antigua or calling up my mother and verifying her life. There is something about this new book that drives people mad with the autobiographical question" (Alleyne).[2]

In typical Kincaid fashion of making contradictory statements, she did admit to Hannah Levintova that she "suppose[d]" she was thinking about her own marriage when she wrote the novel. In that same interview, she says she never thought about how her former husband might react to the book because it never occurred to her that the novel was "about anybody." When asked in a *Time* interview if her former husband had read the book, she responded: "Since it's not about him, I don't know why he would" ("10 Questions" 60). In that same interview, she insists that when she wrote the book, "I wasn't thinking of myself" (60).

Kincaid, after bitterly denouncing those often racist critics who insist on reading the work as autobiography because she is not Norman Mailer and because she looks "different" (Headlee), contends that they miss the major focus in the novel as reflected in its title: *time itself.* While there is much to be said here, as well as in her other novels, about the significance of time, it would be hard not to read the title as a parody of the title of Lillian Ross's publication of *Here but Not Here,* the 1998 shocking revelations about her forty-year affair with William Shawn (Allen Shawn's father), who spent part of every day with her but always went home to have dinner with his legal family.[3] Alluding to that affair in *See,* Kincaid points to an idyllic period in her married life when her husband had not yet found "the note from his father, the note that told him how to lead his life: two households, two wives" (90). In Dwight Garner's review of *See,* he suggests that the works of the two spurned women might well be issued under one cover with a combined title: "Not Here Now, But Here Then, See?" ("The Marriage Has Ended: Revenge Begins"). Clearly it is not unlikely that Kincaid is also signifying on the title of Allen Shawn's memoir *Wish I Could Be There,* which is certainly a play on Ross's book, *Here but Not Here.* Perhaps the three books might make an interesting trilogy about abandonment titled *I Now See You Didn't Wish to Be Here Then.*[4]

The title *See Now Then* is only the beginning of the hints that the author here, as in the rest of her canon, is writing autobiography—or at least autobiographical fiction.

Immediately noteworthy is the fact that her protagonist's name is Jamaica Sweet, a combination of the name Kincaid chose for herself and by which she is known (Jamaica) and a variation of Sweetie, Allen Shawn's pet name for her,[5] though Kincaid suggested in one interview that she chose the name to reflect the irony that their garbage man in Vermont was a Mr. Sweet (Haber).

Also significant is the fact that the author seemingly merges Mrs. Sweet and Jamaica Kincaid in the narration or at least makes it difficult for the reader to distinguish between them. The story employs an omniscient narrator and is largely presented in the third person with Kincaid writing about Mrs. Sweet, revealing her thoughts and actions, and sometimes providing a lengthy quotation of Mrs. Sweet's writing (28–32) or her thoughts (137–39, 166–67, 176–78). Occasionally we are given Mrs. Sweet's thoughts and memories from the first person without quotation marks (110–12, 152–57), but for the most part Kincaid maintains the third person. In one instance when Mrs. Sweet is being quoted, we are told that she read to her son a chapter from a book called *See Then Now* (it is not clear from the context whether that variation of *See Now Then* was written by the protagonist Mrs. Sweet or perhaps the omniscient narrator Kincaid [111]). On one occasion there is a suggestion that it is Mrs. Sweet who is writing this book, *See Now Then* (132). Mrs. Sweet is credited with writing a verbatim sentence that appears in *Annie John* (*See* 130). There are also times when the omniscient narrator/Kincaid takes us into the minds of the other principals in the story, and often Mrs. Sweet is not privy to those thoughts and actions.

Jamaica Kincaid provides a series of particulars that force us to read the work as autobiographical. Her protagonist, like Jamaica Kincaid, was born in Antigua on May 25, the daughter of an illiterate man named Potter, who never was a father to her, and a mother who, like the mother in several of Kincaid's other writings and interviews, was so beautiful that her daughter was ashamed (176), grew up in Dominica where she had to cross a river to get to school, made clothing and sheets for her baby with her own hands (58, 61, 64), made her daughter eat breadfruit (74), which she hated, made sure her daughter ate items she considered good for her health (including uncooked cow's liver and fresh carrot juice [75]), loved her greatly as a child, at least until the age of seven (*See* 28), taught her to read (29), took her to the Antigua Library (29), sent her to school when she was only three and a half and told her to tell the teacher that she was five (30), and sent her to the Moravian School in Points when she was five or six (20, 137).

Like the Kincaid character in almost everything Kincaid has written, Jamaica Sweet was a tall and skinny child with Negroid features (dark, flaring nostrils, thick lips, flat nose [48]); she was afraid of the larger girls and boys (91); she was forced to copy books 1 and 2 of *Paradise Lost* (32, 132, 136, 154–55)[6] as punishment for misbehavior in class; she wet her bed every night until she was thirteen (67); she experienced an illness during "the Long Rain" (110); she did not know about washing machines when she grew up (93); and she was sent to the United States to make money to send home to her family (97).

In the United States, Jamaica Sweet, like Jamaica Kincaid, dyed her hair blonde, shaved her eyebrows, and painted them green or gold or some other unusual color; survived a youth that "was a carnival of sexual activity" (89; see similar descriptions in *Lucy* and "Putting Myself Together"); thought daily of the Caribbean; began writing in a New York apartment where she had a used desk, chair, and typewriter (71); married the Manhattan-bred White, Jewish classical-musician son of her *New Yorker* editor (not named in *See*); lived briefly in New York (72);[7] spent her time writing books about her past and her mother; married a husband who (as he notes in his own memoirs) when he was six asked his playmate, a six-year-old girl, to undress (14), and treasured memories of Paris (14); had a perfect, beautiful, and godlike daughter and son (Annie/Persephone and Harold/Heracles). The ages of the Shawn and Sweet children are the same, approximately four years apart (*See* 119); Annie Rosamond Shawn was born in 1985 and Harold Shawn was born in 1989. Mrs. Sweet's husband, like Kincaid's, left her for a younger woman (a musician) when she was fifty-two years old. Mrs. Sweet, like Kincaid, infuriated her children by being late picking them up at the bus.[8] On one such occasion, Persephone angrily assumes it is because she is trying to decide how to end a sentence: "my mother would kill me if she got the chance, I would kill my mother if I had the courage" (130), the verbatim sentence that appears in *Annie John* (89).

Like the usual Kincaid character, Jamaica Sweet loves the word *amazing* (22),[9] hates winters (11), loves taking hot baths in the winter, and buys medication for a person dying of AIDS.

Like the usual Kincaid character, Jamaica Sweet is enthusiastic about her garden and hunts for flower seeds in Asia (92). On one occasion Mrs. Sweet is disturbed that her tulips were eaten by deer (*See* 142, 143; when I interviewed the author, she had just returned from Seattle and was disturbed to find that deer had eaten several of her plants).

Like the usual accounts of Jamaica Kincaid as a mother, Jamaica Sweet worries that her children hate as well as love her, may wish her dead, and resent her writing, her being away from them on her trips to read or to collect flower seeds, and the hours she spends tending her garden (*See* 5).

Like the usual Kincaid character, Mrs. Sweet pays tributes to her friends and associates at the *New Yorker:* George (George W. S. Trow, whom Kincaid often credits with her development as a writer) and Sandy (Ian Frazier, one of Kincaid's best friends at the *New Yorker,* whom she has called her "true, true brother" [foreword, *Gone to New York* xi]). Here these two, referred to only as George and Sandy, are plotting ways to save the young Jamaica (no last name is given, though we are told that her father is Mr. Potter; she is not yet Sweet) from deportation (112). In that same section she also alludes to Veronica, likely the *New Yorker* writer Veronica Geng.

Numerous geographical points in *See* are familiar to readers of other accounts of Kincaid's beloved Bennington, Vermont, though the commentary on the Bennington Monument (128) is the only time Bennington is actually named. The home of the Sweets is the home of the famous writer Shirley Jackson, one never inhabited by any previous Kincaid characters. However, Shirley Jackson's life offers too perfect a parallel to Jamaica Kincaid/Jamaica Sweet to resist using her home. Jackson, too, was an overweight writer who was self-conscious about her appearance, who was an outsider, who chauffeured her Jewish husband and his colleagues at Bennington College, who attended to her role as a writer while raising her children, who was discouraged by her husband (Stanley Edgar Hyman, who was reportedly not only unfaithful but jealous of his wife's superior talent), and who often was criticized by contemporary critics and readers, some of whom attacked her for witchcraft and perversion. Jackson's famous short story "The Lottery" appeared in the *New Yorker* and provoked more mail than the magazine had ever received in response to a story, the vast majority of it negative. That Jackson was, like Allen Shawn, agoraphobic offers the final parallel that must have made it irresistible for Kincaid to choose her house as the setting for *See.*

The Jackson house, at 12 Prospect Street in North Bennington, is right across the street from a home in which Jamaica Kincaid once lived, referred to by the name of the actual people from whom she bought it, the McGovern House, and also called the Yellow House by Kincaid's children.[10] In *See* she mentions many of the details of the McGovern House and its gardens (especially the peony garden and the daylilies) that she also writes about in *My Garden* and *Among Flowers.* The only difference is that in *See,* Mrs. Sweet digs up flowers from the McGovern House and plants them in her garden in the Shirley Jackson House since Kincaid must provide Mrs. Sweet her own garden even though she has given her a different house. Here, too, Mrs. Sweet, like Kincaid in *My Garden* and *Among Flowers,* constantly looks out from her house at Mount Anthony. Jamaica Sweet's description of her journey home with her children from the bus stop (Silk Road across Walloomsac River, rounding Matteson Road, making a left on Harlan [131]) omits only the turn off Harlan onto College Road, where the Shawn family later lived, and then less than two blocks to Prospect Street, where the Sweets live.

See, like Kincaid's other works, depicts the Jamaica character enjoying perfect love and harmony in an Edenic garden with her loved one. The beginning of the Kincaid story is almost always the garden (even if the story begins in medias res and we have to be taken back to that beginning). The garden of the relationships in *See Now Then* is pictured even before this novel, as Kincaid writes in *My Garden, Among Flowers,* and *My Brother* with great delight of her enchanting Eden that is Bennington, describing the beauty of her actual garden and her delight in her home, her husband, her son and daughter. In *My Brother,* she is miserable when she visits her dying brother in Antigua, constantly longing to return to Bennington, the place where she has found love (149). Frequently, despite all the issues in *See Now Then,* she recalls how much she loved her husband (12, 39,42, 68, 72, 82, 83, 93, 111) and admired his knowledge, his talents, his music masterpieces (72, 81–82, 111); she points out that he once was "a very good person" (111), who felt with his wife that their love was perfect and their lives were perfect when their beautiful daughter was born (120); a good person who loved his wife (10, 12, 79, 87, 170), loved her long legs (15), loved her height (97), loved her eyes (19), loved the way she exaggerated everything (15), called her sweet names and pampered her (11), and thought her young and beautiful (89). Unfortunately, Mrs. Sweet recounts many later moments when she concludes that he never loved her (92).[11]

See provides only the shortest picture of the Edenic life (and much of this in medias res), for by the time this story reaches its second page, we are overwhelmed with accounts of deaths and told that Mr. Sweet hates Mrs. Sweet and wishes her dead, reinforcing what Kincaid told us in *My Garden (Book):* "When sorrow comes, I can never remember that I had once been glad" (*MG* 210). But as we suffer through the long list of painful events in the life of Mrs. Sweet, we are occasionally reminded that there was once an Eden, there was once love.

Throughout her works, the Kincaid character idolizes the object of her affection for characteristics that she herself lacks. In most of them she idolized her mother's classic beauty, lovely hair, fragrant aroma, orderly and efficient ordering of her household, expert sewing, delicious cooking, and loving devotion to her. Similarly in *See,* Mrs. Sweet idolizes the way her husband looks when she has ironed his shirts and trousers and made him look like a prominent American "to whom she was actually and legally wedded" (93–94), and when he wears his elegant double-breasted camel-hair jacket, the kind of coat a prince such as he should wear (9). She also idolizes her husband's knowledge of classical music and the great composers. Clearly this person who views herself as an unattractive, overweight, person who just got off a banana boat[12] and is "fortunate" enough that this eminent American married her to save her from being deported is as awed by his intelligence, his Americanness, his Whiteness,[13] his Jewishness,[14] his family background as she was by her mother's light skin, straight hair, and classic beauty.

Both of the Kincaid character's idols wanted her to become what they wanted: her mother wanted her to "become her" (*See* 29); and her husband, though he had initially been taken with her difference and delighted in teaching and cultivating her (170),[15] wanted her to be a slim, cultured, sophisticated, quiet lady who played Brahms, like the woman for whom he finally left her (155); he wanted her to be of his culture and not someone who "would be of the people who waited on us" (170). Furthermore those idols came to detest the Jamaica character's greatest passions: her mother came to loathe her reading to the point that she burned her books, one of the most painful events in the author's life. Her husband hated her "enthusiasms," which included (at the top of the list) her gardening (*See* 92; see also 5 and 9).

Both of her Edenic relationships are also adversely affected by money issues, with Kincaid and/or the Kincaid character resenting the expectation that she must make sacrifices to support her family. Perhaps two of the most infuriating events in Kincaid's relationship with her mother were that she had to drop out of school and care for her baby brother to allow her mother to work and that she was ultimately sent away to make money to support her family. Once the love goes out of Mrs. Sweet's relationship with Mr. Sweet, we are reminded that they sometimes have difficulty paying their utility bills (64, 77, 156), their bills for her long-distance calls to Antigua, the expenses of her gardening,[16] and his fee for the copyists who work with his musical compositions (65). Unfortunately, it seems to be Mrs. Sweet who has to pay all the bills (77, 156), something she sarcastically notes that she is able to do thanks to the writing and the traveling that her family hates for her to do and the resulting checks made out "to that Charles Laughton–like entity" (77).[17]

See, like Kincaid's other works, treats the Jamaica character suffering what she describes as "the worst humiliation": abandonment (166). Having enjoyed the perfect love and harmony in Eden, that ideal garden, that Paradise, the Kincaid character seems fated to endure the loss of that idyllic existence when she is abandoned by the source of her love (usually her mother, but here her husband [who is also her mother: "I married my mother"]), who transforms into a hateful brute who hated her (6, 10, 11, 18, 24, 40, 62, 63, 65,

87, 92, 99, 100, 111, 157), wished her dead (39, 63, 79, 143), and constantly views her as dreadful (7, 23), a horrible bitch (9, 10, 15, 17, 164,), a "monster" (170), "a shit" (77), and an old and ugly woman (160). He cannot even abide her voice (45–46, 84–86, 87), declaring at one point, "I wished she minced words, I wish she would bite off her tongue" (171).[18]

One of the major indications of the mother's abandonment in earlier accounts occurs when her mother insists that the Kincaid character is getting too old for the mother to continue to make their dresses out of the same fabric (*AJ* 25–27). From this point the Kincaid character agonizes that she is no longer the central figure in her mother's life, regards everything her mother does to allow her more independence as a rejection, and becomes more aware and more jealous of the time the mother spends with the father. The births of the three brothers, of course, represent the ultimate abandonment. She never gets over the cruelest cuts and compulsively rehashes them in book after book and interview after interview: the mother's calling her a slut, taking her out of school to care for her baby brother, burning her books, and sending her away to work in America.

Similarly Mr. Sweet's abandonment of Mrs. Sweet begins with his pernicious comments about her appearance, commencing, it seems, with the births of the children;[19] with his refusal to spend time with her and the children and escaping to his hideaway (a space above the garage where Mrs. Sweet was forbidden access [14]), where he composed nocturnes such as *This Marriage Is Dead* (24);[20] and with his many attractions to his attractive young, white students (16, 23, 98), until finally the ultimate abandonment when Mr. Sweet tells her he is in love with a young and beautiful woman who comes from a different culture than hers and who plays Brahms (155) and can talk with him about Mozart (159). Persephone declares that Mr. Sweet "dumped her" for a younger woman (100).[21] Mr. Sweet "gently" explained to his son that he is leaving because he loves another woman: "I don't love your mother, you know, we were always so incompatible, for she did emerge from a boat whose main cargo was bananas, and she is strange and should live in the attic of a house that burns down."[22] As when her mother abandoned her, the Kincaid character in *See* is absolutely devastated at her "Paradise Lost": she "now broke in two" over and over again (159–60): there were no words to express the agony, suffering, and pain that this rejection caused her (156). Mrs. Sweet's only consolation in this horrific event was that her mother was not alive to rejoice in her abandonment (170).

One of the consequences of the loss of her Eden is the Kincaid character's sense that she is ugly, that her body is unattractive. The disgust of her idols with her was more than reflected in her negative view of herself in all instances. In *Annie John*, after her mother refused to make their dresses out of the same fabric, she didn't recognize herself because she looked so strange and unattractive with her black skin, her unruly hair, her long neck, her big head (*AJ* 25–27): she lamented that she looked old and miserable (*AJ* 94). In *See*, after the birth of her son, she complains that her body looks like a garden shed (74). She frequently notes her height (10), her poor posture (10), her large, flat nose (10, 48, 122), her large lips (71, 76, 97, 123), her big feet (86), and the fact that her body, as her husband accused, looks like Charles Laughton (23, 74, 75, 119, 122, 125) with its expanding waist (139) and thickening arms and ankles (63, 139).

The Kincaid character does not, however, suffer abandonment quietly. She bitterly attacks both of her idols once they have destroyed her Eden. Throughout the Kincaid canon (including *See*), the Annie Drew character is assailed as a horrible person, a monster, a demon, a serpent, a hypocrite. In *See*, Mr. Sweet is bitterly attacked for his small size (7, 10, 18, 34, 48, 52–53, 55, 89, 90, 99, 155), his infantilism (90), his balding (20), his old age (55, 111), and his impotence (Mr. Sweet recalls a time when his son grabbed his testicles and "threw them away . . . and [they] were never heard from again" [46; see also 34 and 111]). He is frequently described as a rodent (7, 24).[23] He is ridiculed for his lack of success as a performer, for writing music that no one cared about or came to hear (6–7, 12, 34, 35, 82), for his hateful compositions (such as *This Marriage Is Dead* [24, 27, 28)], which is sometimes called *Husband Left Her* (27); for his inept compositions (the jumbled notes that Mr. Sweet "said was music" [65]), for his inability to express himself (7), for his jealousy of his wife's success (20–21, 77), and for his lack of concern for his wife (81). He is also ridiculed for his agoraphobia (13, 111), his tendency to become ill whenever he was to perform (49, 51), and his reclusiveness in his dark studio above the garage (14, 22, 23, 24, 25, 26, 27, 37, 45, 52, 82). There is none of the scientific and sympathetic treatment of this illness that Shawn provides in *Wish* or *Twin*; rather, Mrs. Sweet's sarcastic commentaries are relentless: speaking of the fears evoked by his agoraphobia, she declares that he "would not cross the street if he knew his shadow would accompany him" (98).

A particularly malicious barb by her original love with whom she once lived in Paradise is constantly recalled with much pain by the Kincaid character. Her mother's denouncing her as a "slut" finds a parallel in Mr. Sweet's castigating her as a backwater islander who arrived on a banana boat (9, 11, 16, 17, 18, 97). In fact, for Mrs. Sweet the banana boat accusation was "the seat of her diminishment, ah" (11). How painful it was to have each of her idols diminish her with a cruel affront that seemed to become more painful with each repetition!

It is clear that in *See,* Jamaica Kincaid's ongoing battle with her mother has not ended. Mrs. Sweet realizes that her efforts to bury her past cannot succeed (93), and she is not so much fated to "See Now Then" as she is to continue to "See Then Now." The Annie Drew figure is not only recalled throughout the novel but might be said to be resurrected in the person of Mr. Sweet, who is not only Jamaica Sweet's/Jamaica Kincaid's husband but also, alas, her mother.

NOTES

Introduction

1. Several critics have suggested that *My Brother* and other works in the Kincaid canon might more accurately have been titled "My Mother" (see Braziel 167–68). In an interview with Lauren K. Alleyne, Kincaid declared, "I've written a book about my mother," but it is not clear what book she has in mind; it is probably not *Autobiography* since she goes on to suggest that the book about her mother is set in Antigua—perhaps she was referring to *Annie John*.

2. This need to validate discredited knowledge is, of course, a goal of much African American and African Caribbean literature, especially of the writers often described as "magical realists," and it is nowhere more vividly addressed than in Erna Brodber's "One Bubby Susan," where the scholarship of Western anthropologists is discredited in favor of the oral folktales stemming from the appearance of the long-dead Susan (others might incorrectly designate Susan's reappearance a dream vision).

3. For a helpful discussion of "false memory," see Gilmore, *The Limits of Autobiography*, esp. 24–33.

4. Though Kincaid often insists that this 2013 novel is not autobiographical, there is no question that the Sweets are replicas of Allen Shawn and Jamaica Kincaid in physical appearance, family, history, vocation, geography, education, personality, health issues, etc.

5. Qtd. in Marshall, *Triangular Road* 148.

6. Kincaid told Alleyne that the traditional European classification of genres, such as fiction, history, etc., are "not useful."

7. Gilmore, who informs that "in autobiography and trauma studies veracity is always at issue," concludes: "Once fiction's truth is preferred to fact's, the authority of both trauma and autobiography that derives from the eyewitness's credibility is thrown into a crisis of legitimacy" (*Limits of Autobiography* 47).

8. Many similarities between these two books titled *The Autobiography of My Mother* will become obvious as this study develops. Both Gerda and Renada feel the other has offended, and neither can apologize. There are often standoffs such as those in *Annie John:* at one point Renada, the daughter, thinks: "I can't afford to be the soldier who puts down his arms to stare into the eyes of his brother enemy—he gets

a bayonet for his sympathy. There's no moral lesson here. Probably she was looking at me thinking, I shouldn't have expected anything better from you in the first place, how dare I be disappointed in you. And she's right, of course: I've made a profession of being unacceptable" (266). Mother and daughter agonize over having to share one life, with Renata reflecting: "This woman is my fate, that's all. Not my history only: my future. She won't die, she'll be waiting for me in the graveyard no matter what" (137). We shall hear eerily similar lines from Kincaid throughout this study.

9. Commentaries by a host of other writers reinforce this point: in response to one person who asked about postcolonialism at the 1990 Second International Caribbean Women Writers Conference in Trinidad, one writer exclaimed, "I'm not post anything." In like manner, in a panel ("Conversations with West Indian Writers") at the Virginia Museum of Fine Arts in Richmond on 10 June 1994, Velma Pollard declared her disdain for "all of these isms." Erna Brodber called me in desperation in 1994 and said: "Daryl, I've been invited to a conference in the U.S. on magical realism. They say I'm a magical realist. Please tell me what on earth I am." (Brodber alludes to this conversation in her "Beyond the Boundary.") At one session, "The Daughters of Anacoana Speak: Haiti and the Caribbean," of the 2006 Conference of the Association of Caribbean Women Scholars and Writers, many of the women rejected the term "magical realism," with Evelyne Trouillot asserting that magical realism is "not a literary scheme or literary choice, but a way of looking at life." Edwidge Dandicat averred: "If things seem out of the ordinary, it is not magical realism, but something that has been in our realities. We wrestle with a shifting reality. Feeling brave enough to write it is magical realism" (all of the above quotations are from my notes). In "Caligula's Horse," Derek Walcott mocks the French poststructuralists and deconstructionists as "dead fish," adding: "Mostly the fish are French fish, and off their pages there is the reek of the fishmonger's hands. I have a horror not of that stink, but of the intellectual veneration of rot, because from the far-off reek which I get from the stalls of the Academy, there is now a school of fishermen as well as schools of fish, and these fishmongers are interested in examining the disemboweled entrails of poetry, of marketing its guts and its surrounding conversation of flies" (141).

1 Beginnings in Dominica

1. In this chapter with constant references to "Antigua Crossings" and *Annie John,* I use Annie Victoria to distinguish Mrs. Drew from Annie John. She is actually called Victoria in "Antigua Crossings" and Mrs. John in *Annie John,* while the daughter, whose name is also Annie John, is really a portrait of Jamaica Kincaid.

2. Kincaid, who always refers to her only as Ma Chess, could not remember her real name during our interview. In "Antigua Crossings," she gives her the name Josephine Claudette, but there she gives fictional names to herself, her grandfather, and her stepfather, and she uses her aunt's and her mother's middle names rather than

their first names. Thus, there is no reason to assume that Josephine Claudette is Ma Chess's real name. It is interesting (and possibly significant), however, that she gives the name Claudette to Xuela Claudette Desvarieux Richardson in *The Autobiography of My Mother.*

3. The sea figures prominently in Caribbean literature. Austin Clarke ends his story "Leaving this Island Place" with a description of what he sees as he flies away from Barbados: "the architect-models of houses and buildings, and the beautiful quiltwork patches of land under the plough . . . and then there is the sea, and the sea, and then the sea" (227). In *The Pleasures of Exile,* George Lamming, describing the West Indies and its varied people and crops, concludes with this phrase written as a full sentence: "And always the sea!" (17). In his "Hymn to the Sea," Frank Collymore declares, "Like all who live on small islands / I must always be remembering the sea" (264). Kamau Brathwaite writes in "South": "By these shores I was born: sound of the sea / came in at my window" (56–57). Derek Walcott provides the response to an important question in "The Sea Is History": "Where are your monuments, your battles, martyrs? / Where is your tribal memory? Sirs, / in that gray vault. The Sea. The sea / has locked them up. The sea is History" (*Star Apple Kingdom* 25). Similarly, Édouard Glissant writes in "Ocean": "The ancestor speaks, it is the ocean, it is a race that washed the continents with its veil of suffering" (*The Collected Poems* 50). In "Tears of the Sea," Olive Senior's magical seashell informs: "All who came from the sea . . . continued to carry a part of the sea with them forever and ever" (*Arrival of the Snake Woman* 82). In *The Repeating Island,* Antonio Benítez-Rojo declares that "the culture of the Caribbean . . . is not terrestrial but aquatic" (11) and classifies Caribbeans as "Peoples of the Sea" (16).

4. In the course of my research for this book, I interviewed many people who preferred to remain anonymous. While my communication with informants who granted me permission to use their names is documented in the "Personal Communications with the Author" section of the bibliography, for those informants who chose anonymity, I document the date of our conversation parenthetically in the chapter text.

5. A detailed account of one variant of this story is given on page 90 of this book.

6. The possibility that Mary Elizabeth was jealous of Annie is reinforced in *The Autobiography of My Mother,* where the man Mary Elizabeth marries actually preferred Xuela, the Annie/Kincaid character.

7. This gesture is commonplace among African American and African Caribbean women who wish to distance themselves from stereotypes of the loud Black woman with her raucous laughter; for a fuller discussion, see Dance, *Honey, Hush!* xxii–xxv. One example of a similar gesture can be found in Rita Dove's *Through the Ivory Gate,* where the grandmother of the protagonist explains to her how a proper lady should laugh: "Hold your hand over your mouth . . . hold it straight and a little to the side, like you're going to whisper something to someone next to you" (58).

8. In this study I treat Annie's arrival in Antigua as occurring when she was sixteen, since that is the age most frequently given. However, Joseph's memory is never

to be discounted, and his placing of her arrival at twenty-three might be more consistent with the fact that her first child was born when she was thirty (see Kincaid's reflections on this issue on p. 38 of this book) and might make even more understandable her desperate efforts to escape her domineering father.

9. As previously noted, Annie Drew told Mariana Cook that she was raised by her father and not her mother (20).

10. As the Kincaid character in *Annie John* prepares to leave Antigua, she similarly catalogues things she never wants to see or do again (134–45).

2 Free and Single in Antigua

1. Hereafter, until there is the possibility of confusion, the young Annie Victoria Richardson will be called Annie.

2. Kincaid gives the size of Antigua as 12 miles by 9 miles (*A Small Place* 9, 80), or 12 by 8 miles (*Lucy* 134), or 12 miles by 10 miles (Ferguson, "A Lot of Memory" 180); and Paul Buhle describes it as 9 miles by 12 miles (8); but I have used the measurements from the Antigua and Barbuda homepage.

3. Dame Tonge is a highly honored person. Plaques and pictures on her walls and tables reinforce the recognition she has received. After teaching from the age of seventeen to fifty-something, she became the head of Antigua's Women's Affairs and was in charge of the Women's Desk. Eighty-four when I interviewed her in January 2009, she had visited every continent. When her technician arrived late to tape her weekly television show, she gave him a tongue-lashing (pun intended), reprimanding, "Don't you go for another appointment when I'm waiting unless it is for the prime minister. Otherwise you treat *me* as a priority!"

4. "I used to love mi rum," is the kind of statement one would hear from former bad johns who hung out in bars and bragged about their drinking and their womanizing, something comparable to the "bad niggers" such as Stagolee and Shine in African American folklore. Rum is the most popular alcoholic drink in the Caribbean.

5. Recall the previously quoted comment in the Vanessa Jones interview in which she insists she did not do research for *Mr. Potter* because it would have made the book too conventional.

6. The reference is to the line drawn through the space on Mr. Potter's and Jamaica's birth certificates where there should be the name of a father. See *Mr. Potter* 101.

7. Mindie Lazarus-Black indicates that only indigent women used this Magistrate's Court because the amount of child support awarded was so low and "'Carrying a case' to one of these courts entails many inconveniences and a willingness to endure an invasion of family privacy and community gossip" (195). It's not unlikely that Annie, like one of the women Lazarus-Black interviewed, took her baby's father to court less for money than for "justice": "I carry my case up there for justice. I complain him for justice" (193).

8. Kincaid alludes to the money that Annie took from Mr. Potter on pp. 20 and 142, but she never specifies the amount (*Mr. Potter*).

9. Among the similarities to Annie are the fact that Xuela has Annie's maiden name and the name Kincaid gives to her grandmother in "Antigua Crossings." Several of Annie's issues with her sister are treated here, with the sister in the novel having the actual married name of Annie's sister, Elizabeth Richardson Pacquet.

10. Moira's first name is that of one of the earliest Kincaid critics, Moira Ferguson.

11. Given the obsession with abortions in *The Autobiography of My Mother*, the numerous references to abortions in several other Kincaid works, the fact that Kincaid writes that she was intimate with so many men during her youth in New York that she cannot remember their names ("Putting Myself Together" 100), her vow never to give birth to a child without a legal father (*MP* 101), her insistence that she would rather die than have her mother see her with an illegitimate child (*Lucy* 70), the fact that she gave birth to her first child when she was thirty-six (though "women where I am from have children very early"), and her numerous claims that everything she writes is autobiographical, the reader might contemplate the same conclusions about Kincaid that she reached about her mother's not having a child until she was thirty.

3 Raising an Only Child

1. Though Annie is usually described as light or fair, Dr. Carole Boyce Davies, who met her thirteen months before her death, recalls her as "a brownish woman, about the same color as Jamaica Kincaid" (e-mail).

2. In "Jamaica Kincaid's New York," she says she learned to read before she was seven" (72).

3. Joseph Drew told me they married on 11 March 1967, but I have used the date on the marriage certificate.

4. In *My Garden (Book):*, Kincaid observes that none of the plants in the Botanical Gardens were native to Antigua, a kind of irony that Kincaid and other Caribbean writers often note: no matter how desirable something may be in the Caribbean, there is usually a preference for imports from the Western world.

5. The United States Military Base was established in Antigua in 1941.

6. Some of the details of the early morning routine are taken from Garis, "Through West Indian Eyes"; *Annie John;* "On Seeing England," "Biography of a Dress," and Kincaid's "Notes and Comment" piece in the 17 October 1977 *New Yorker.* Mr. Jarvis becomes Mr. Ephraim in *Annie John* (131).

7. I have taken some of the details of the uniform from "Jamaica Kincaid's New York," 72.

8. A crushed eggplant dish often served with salt fish.

9. People who live in tiny one-room houses in the Caribbean generally do everything outside, except sleeping.

10. Cold is almost always associated in Caribbean literature with the alien, but prosperous, lands of Canada, Europe, and the United States.

11. Similar stories of teaching children ownership and responsibility by giving them their own animal are commonplace. Oftentimes in these stories the child cannot contemplate killing and eating that animal. Jamaica, however, seemed to have had no such qualm.

12. The schools Tonge mentions do not seem to be the ones Kincaid listed for Cudjoe or me, though what she calls St. John's Girls Government School may be what Kincaid called Antiguan Girls School. Further, it appears from all accounts that she was constantly changing schools.

13. When she was reporting these violent actions of Ms. Annie, Jocelyn Reid called her "ignorant," a term that Joe also used in talking about her burning him (see p. <o> of this book). Velma Pollard explained that "Caribbean 'ignorant' means angry enough to do something terrible. . . . Nothing to do with the English meaning of 'not knowing'" (Pollard letter to the author).

14. Tales of the sexual exploitation of women are to be found in scores of Caribbean novels and stories, but of particular interest are Velma Pollard's "Bitter Tales," a section of eight stories of poor Jamaica women who suffer sexual exploitation in her *Considering Woman I and II;* and Erna Brodber's *The World Is a High Hill: Stories about Jamaican Women,* stories that treat more intelligent, better-educated, and/or more independent women who also endure sexual exploitation.

15. The soucouyant, who frequently appears in folklore throughout the Caribbean, is a supernatural woman who sheds her human skin at night and takes on another form; however, she must slip back into her skin before dawn. Kincaid often suggests that she or her Kincaid character, like the soucouyant, plays a part, lives a lie, puts on a mask. No wonder that one woman she met during her trip to the Himalayas made it clear that Kincaid was wearing a mask, that she was not revealing her true face (*AF* 100).

16. Kincaid writes in *My Brother* that when Mr. Drew died he was not active in any church, but she indicates that the reason the Methodist minister would not bury him was that her mother had no money to pay him (122).

17. At this point in our interview, Kincaid proudly showed me her unusually high instep.

18. Because Kincaid has spent part of the year in California since taking a position in 2009 at Claremont McKenna College, this Vermont garden probably is not as carefully tended as when I saw it; it's now like an unfinished book, she told Leigh Haber.

19. This account is taken from *AJ* 5–6. It is also treated in *MB* 4–5.

20. In "The Red Girl," Kincaid does not say she played marbles under the house but rather that she hid her marbles under the house.

21. Reid said of her portrait in "The Red Girl": "Some is true and some is not true. I laughed it off, and when she came, I told her, 'Elaine, how come you write such and such and you know it's not true?' She said, 'Well, some of it is true and some is fiction.'"

4 After Eden

1. Joseph told me in our interview that he was born on 5 March 1957, but I have used the year listed on his birth certificate. His birth was registered on 8 April 1958.

2. Kincaid gave Devon's birth date in *My Brother* as 5 May 1962, but his birth certificate says 4 May 1962, the date that he confirmed to me. One can only speculate about the confusion of dates. Information on birth certificates is copied from the official birth registry by hand, and errors are possible. In fact, when I was given my first copy of Kincaid's birth certificate, the date given for her birth was wrong. Furthermore, given that the birth is registered several days after the delivery, it is not unlikely that errors in reporting the date can occur. Finally, it is possible that Kincaid simply did not remember the correct date or that she chose to change it.

3. As previously noted, they were *not* married, though it is possible that Kincaid did not know this when Joseph was born, and perhaps didn't know it at the time of our 2008 interview.

4. Despite Annie Drew's independent and often rebellious spirit, she was still the traditional Caribbean woman of her time who expected her male children to be the doctors and lawyers and the female children to be the wives and possibly nurses and secretaries. Reverend Lee emphasized in our interview that despite Annie's activism, she was not a feminist. The Annie Drew characters are consistent in these respects throughout Kincaid's canon.

5. Paravisini-Gebert incorrectly asserts that Kincaid wrote of "the fictional mother's efforts to abort her third child" in *Annie John* (19). In fact, there is no mention of the conception, abortion, and/or birth of any of the boys in *Annie John*.

6. Paravisini-Gebert mistakenly asserts that this incident is fictionalized in *Annie John* (18). There Annie John is tricked by a playmate into sitting naked on a red ants' nest, but there is no mention of the brothers in that novel.

7. This event is recounted in many of her interviews and in several places in the Kincaid canon, but the most extended account is in *My Brother* (128–37).

8. Benna refers to Antiguan folksongs, similar to calypsos, which "nice" girls weren't expected to sing because of their sexual connotations and/or forbidden topics. They often were a signifying way of spreading rumors. For a girl to sing benna in her Antiguan Sunday school would be comparable to an African American girl singing raunchy blues or rap lyrics in church.

9. This is one of many instances in Kincaid's childhood where Mrs. Drew taught her the power of words and no doubt provided the inspiration for storytelling.

10. Later she would imply that dropping him was not an accident, declaring, "Murdering a brother you don't like, what could be so new about that?" (Snodgrass 9).

11. For an extended treatment of these figures, see Giselle Anatol's *Things That Fly in the Night: Female Vampires in Literature of the Circum-Caribbean and African Diaspora.*

12. Those females who "jumped up" and entered into the street revelries risked being "interfered with" by males: "it is a common Carnival custom for men to 'interfere' with the women—this interference being little more than a touching or pinching of the more outstanding parts of the female body" (Powrie 99–100). One can understand that, like Mrs. Drew, parents in general would not wish their daughters subjected to this "interference." Further, though any generalization about the attitudes of Caribbean people to Carnival is risky, many historical and literary sources make it clear that during the nineteenth and twentieth century, many proper Caribbean families throughout the islands forbade their children to participate in Carnival, which was and still is often viewed as a lower-class hedonistic abandonment to sexuality, erotic dancing, risqué costumes, obscene singing, violence, and boozing. Even by the last quarter of the nineteenth century, Carnival had become a Black, lower-class event, often called Jamette Carnival ("Jamette" referring to "people below the diameter of respectability" [Pearse 31]; see also Campbell). Barbara E. Powrie declares in her 1956 "The Changing Attitude of the Coloured Middle Class towards Carnival," "In a true sense, Carnival 'belongs' to the black, lower class" (95; see also Campbell). For literary treatments of the "objectionable" elements of Carnival (as well as some of its positive elements), see Michael Anthony, *The Games Were Coming;* Marion Patrick Jones, *Pan Beat* and *J'Ouvert Morning;* Ismith Khan, *The Obeah Man;* Merle Hodge, *Crick Crack, Monkey;* and Earl Lovelace, *The Dragon Can't Dance.* Throughout the history of Carnival since long before emancipation, when Carnival was mainly a White event, numerous laws have attempted to deal with the "objectionable" issues of Carnival, including the participation of Blacks; and at certain times Carnival has been outlawed. There have always been some upper-class people who have participated in Carnival; in some instances, upper-class Whites and Blacks have had their own private, exclusive fancy-dress balls to celebrate Carnival rather than participate in the street parades (see Pearse); in some instances, the elite have been mere spectators; in others, they simply have had nothing to do with Carnival. It is certainly clear that there has been more open participation of the upper classes since the latter years of the twentieth century. Indeed, as early as 1956 Powrie declared, "Today, there is little disapproval [of Carnival]" (106); however, many later commentaries (such as the above-cited novels) reinforce the continuing objection of many to Carnival. While one hears complaints that Carnival today has become mainly a tourist attraction, there is no denying the continuing appeal of Carnival to many in the Caribbean—of both the upper and lower classes.

The best-known Caribbean Carnival is held in Port of Spain, Trinidad, but other parts of Trinidad and most of the other islands, including Antigua, hold their own Carnivals. Indeed, annual Caribbean Carnivals are held in Canada, the United States, and Great Britain as well.

13. Restrictions upon going to movies have been commonplace in African American families as well, sometimes simply because of the concern about the safety of the movies and other times because of religious views of movies as the works of the devil (the latter prominently treated by James Baldwin in works such as *Go Tell It on the Mountain* and *The Devil Finds Work*). In the Caribbean many parents worried about the negative influence of American films on their children.

14. Another of what Rabinowitz describes as "the weirdest things [Jamaica and I have] in common" is the fact that Mr. Potter was her family's first driver when they came to Antigua. Rabinowitz also clearly believed that the Drews were legally married when their sons were born.

15. Joseph Drew, who has a phenomenal recall of dates, told me that they married on 11 March 1967. This is a small discrepancy, but I would place my money on Joseph and not the marriage certificate.

16. The school, founded by Mrs. Davis, mother of Dr. Osoba, is now run by the founder's children.

5 In America . . . Finally

1. Elaine Potter is her given name on the birth certificate. The last name would be the same as that of the parent listed on the birth certificate—Richardson.

2. Kincaid's use of "finally" seems overstated given that she arrived in the United States in December 1965, but in her excitement to see New York, even a few days or weeks could seem a lifetime. As noted earlier, in *Lucy* the arrival is moved up to January.

3. This account of Mr. Drew's death in *Lucy* actually moves his death to an earlier period in Jamaica's life. He did not actually die until 14 December 1975, at which time she was living independently in New York.

4. Kincaid also writes of her anger at being forced to memorize Wordsworth's poem on daffodils in *My Garden (Book):* (141). The poem was likely "I Wandered Lonely as a Cloud."

5. While Lucy is attracted to distinctive and pleasant aromas associated with her mother, she also often raves about the "amazing female smell" of Ma Chess, who did not bathe very often (Kin/Dance; Cook 11).

6. As previously noted, Lucifer's smile in the painting *The Young Lucifer* is only a "front" to cover the fact that he is indeed forlorn (*AJ* 94–95).

7. Kincaid wrote a story about the mouse running over her, but Mr. Shawn (her editor and mentor) never mentioned the story (*Talk Stories* 13). If he didn't like something, he simply ignored it, and Kincaid did not question his opinion.

8. As noted previously, the account of Mr. Drew's death in *Lucy* moves it to an earlier time.

9. Kincaid borrows the name Ovando from Fray Nicolás de Ovando, whose rule of Hispaniola from 1502 to 1508 was marked by excessive barbarities that wiped out most of the Indians under his domain. Her Ovando is a reprehensible representative of European colonialism who considers all of his own actions divine (76) and who loves himself so much that he views other beings as nothing (83). Ovando reminds us of many colonials in her works, such as Dr. Zoltan Weizenger in *Mr. Potter* and *A Small Place,* who despises all the natives of Antigua, who both serve him and afford him a livelihood; John Richardson, Xuela's Scottish grandfather in *The Autobiography of My Mother,* who probably abandoned his mixed family to return to Scotland; and Alfred Richardson, Xuela's mixed father, who acts as a colonizer toward his fellow Dominicans and despises all who acted like Africans (186–87).

10. She was accustomed to this ridicule in Antiqua. Even at the same time that Jamaica must have seen herself as the rebel who left home and determined to be everything her mother rejected in this new land, it must have been difficult to be treated as a ludicrous object of ridicule, contrasted with her mother, who had been an attractive figure who inspired admiration and envy when she migrated to Antigua. And yet she seemed to relish outlandish attire. A *New Yorker* colleague, Ian Frazier, tells of her wearing her hospital-issued pajamas and paper slippers to several events, including movies and a *New Yorker* event uptown (*Talk Stories* xv). Such outré behavior clearly served as a compensation—she is an object of ridicule because *she* chose to be.

11. For more detailed accounts of these meetings with O'Donoghue, Trow, and Shawn, see Kincaid's introduction to *Talk Stories;* Cudjoe 216; and Bouson 19–22.

12. *Talk Stories* is a 2001 anthology of Kincaid's writings for the *New Yorker* from 30 September 1974 to 14 March 1983.

13. It is clear that Mrs. Drew enjoyed signifying on these ladies just as she enjoyed, in Jocelyn Reid's words, "rubbing it into Elaine."

6 The Silent Years and the Reconnection

1. By my count, based on information from accounts of Shawn and Kincaid, the marriage lasted only twenty-two or twenty-three years. They were married in 1979 and divorced in 2002.

2. Shawn vaguely alludes to this when he lists the things he was unable to do in his life because of his agoraphobia: "Did I get to important family funerals in the West Indies, Chicago, Arizona?" (*Wish* 15).

3. Readers of Kincaid's works will recall the numerous references to the other women of her father and her stepfather, though none of those relationships seemed lasting.

4. On one occasion, Shawn suggests that there may have been more than one visit some years before he was twenty (*Twin* 11). However, throughout both autobiographies there is a constant emphasis on the *annual* visit.

5. In *Wish* and *Twin,* Allen Shawn refers to his twin as Mary when he uses a name at all (he rarely used names in the two works). Jamaica Kincaid told me that their daughter was named Annie Rosamond after her mother and Allen's twin sister. I have found no other indication that the twin's name was Rosamond; however, I assume from Kincaid's comment that her name was probably Mary Rosamond.

6. Both of these figures are, like Bessie, remarkable: "exceptionally beautiful young black woman, Cicely" (214); "another lovely African American woman" (218).

7. Shawn says he has had "a checkered sexual history, with some highs and some extraordinarily bad lows" (*Wish* 199).

8. Illness and mental disintegration are, Shawn tells us, frequent themes in his brother's work as well (*Twin* 97–98).

9. Kincaid's fictionalized account of his death in *Lucy* suggests that he died earlier, when she was still living with the Arlens-inspired family.

10. The professors who spoke to me about their visit with Mrs. Drew insisted that this description of her was inconsistent with the proud and generous woman whom they visited (see p. 88 of this book).

11. Jane King mistakenly declares that after leaving home when Devon was three, "Jamaica would never see him again until he was thirty and dying of AIDS" (893).

12. Clearly the novel that she has Annie John reading in "Somewhere, Belgium," where she feels the need to heap even more suffering on the girl who had suffered at the hands of a step-parent and then found herself without any parents at all is *Jane Eyre* (*AJ* 85–86).

13. Kincaid frequently criticizes Antiguans and Antigua in her other works and interviews. In *Lucy,* the Kincaid character discloses that the smallest and most natural gestures of Antiguans evoked such rage in her that she wished them all dead (6). She told Vorda, "Back home they talk about the nation of Antigua, but it's *only* a stupid little island" ("An Interview" 21).

14. Kincaid tried to repeat his comment in patois but finally gave up and gave a rather standard paraphrase of it.

15. Walter Jekyll was a close friend and patron of Claude McKay, helping him to publish his first two volumes of poetry.

16. Ross indicates that William Shawn's brother's name was Harold (168).

7 Annie Drew and Her Boys

1. Dub poetry, which is influenced by Rastafarianism, is a form of creole poetry designed for oral delivery and accompanied by reggae music. Like American rap music, it has its origin in the ghetto communities.

2. Joseph did not remember his sister ever coming back to Antigua to Carnival. He did note that he saw her in October 2006 when she came to Antigua to receive the First Annual Antigua and Barbuda Literary Award.

8 A Brother's Death / A Sister's Fears and Fury

1. When she prepares to leave him, knowing that she will never see him again, he asks if she is leaving without even giving him a hug, and she simply says, "Yes" (*MB* 108).

2. This proverb from Watson is translated by him: "For the good I have done, this is the thanks I get!" (124).

3. Jana Evans Braziel, like Kincaid, is unfairly critical of Mrs. Drew: "Annie Drew insensitively chops down the lemon tree, which for Kincaid would have persisted postmortem as a living death remainder and as palpable trace memories of Devon on earth . . . ; for the mother, however, the tree is merely a nuisance" (148; see also 169). This is only a small part of Braziel's "examin[ation of] Annie Drew as a destructive and elemental force of nature, a 'natural disaster,' who brings ravage, ruin, wreck, destruction. She is a divine maternal force who annihilates through death" (159).

4. While Ross briefly notes a friendly family relationship with Jamaica Kincaid, it is surprising that in the several lists she provides of William Shawn's colleagues, writers, and associates at the *New Yorker,* this is the only time she mentions Kincaid's relationship with him as an editor.

5. Her most extensive detailing of a relationship with her children is her fictional representation of Mrs. Sweet's interactions with her perfectly beautiful and godlike son Heracles and her similarly beautiful and musical daughter Persephone (*See*).

6. Mrs. Sweet does make sheets and tunics for her babies (*See* 58, 61, 64), and she knits stockings for her children (though they are too big before they are washed and too small after they are washed (*See* 129).

7. Here and elsewhere (especially in *See*) Kincaid's or the Kincaid character's greater emphasis on and attention to her son leave her open to the accusation she leveled against her own mother of preferring the male child. In *See,* it is the daughter, rather than the son, who sometimes confronts her and who seems less sympathetic toward the mother when she is spurned by the father.

8. See Hemingway, *For Whom the Bell Tolls,* chap. 19, esp. 250–57.

9. Throughout the novel, Kincaid seizes every opportunity to parody African Diasporic images of the power of the penis (such images are found especially in African American Black Arts/militant literature, toasts, and raps). Well-known images in the Caribbean include the calypso "Big Bamboo" and Earl Lovelace's Axe Man (*The Dragon Can't Dance*). We are reminded here, too, of Milkman's confidence in Toni Morrison's *Song of Solomon,* that his "magnificent joint" had driven his cousin and lover Hagar

wild (301), and of his sister Lena's scornful reminder that his presumed power came from that "hog's gut that hangs down between your legs" (215).

10. Tim Hector is also much admired and acclaimed by Kincaid, but he has been given no prominent role in any of her novels and memoirs. Before his death, she often said that she would return to Antigua only if he became prime minister (Buhle 3; Ramsey interview by Dance).

11. Kincaid uses the word "tapestry" here because it is in the context of her explanation that Devon was called "Patches" because he liked to put patches of different-colored fabrics on his clothes); and Devon called Joseph "Styles" because he dressed stylishly (*MB* 171–72).

12. Antonia MacDonald-Smythe says that Kincaid's constant retelling of the story of Mrs. Drew's burning of her books is a way to "retaliate against her great and terrible mother. She uses the monetary privileges that come from writing these books to play the Lady Bountiful to the two people who were responsible for the burning of the books. Now both the mother and Devon depend on her for their deliverance" (178).

13. Lillian Ross noted that all of the writers with whom he worked declared that they wrote for him: "'I write for *you,*' his authors would say to him. They all said the same words: 'I write for *you.*' He would look embarrassed when they said it to him" (14).

14. According to Giovanna Covi, Opal Palmer Adisa and she speculated that the cover picture is Kincaid (133n4), but Kincaid told me it was Devon. I expect that Kincaid had Annie Shawn cut out to allow the cover picture to focus on the subject of the book, her brother. Furthermore, she protects the privacy of her children, allowing for the publication of their pictures only rarely, as in Mariana Cook's *Generations of Women.*

15. The picture does not conform to Kincaid's descriptions of Ma Chess and Pa Chess, however. The woman has a much smaller frame than the Ma Chess Kincaid describes and does not look like a native American, nor does she look blacker than any other black person Kincaid might have ever seen (AC 50); neither does Pa Chess look as Nordic as some of the fiction suggests he was.

9 Annie Drew's Last Years

1. In our interview, Kincaid made a similar charge, calling her mother a "great dissimulator."

2. The pot calling the kettle black.

3. As previously noted, Kincaid obviously visited her mother with Cook approximately two and a half years before her death. We must assume then that the vexatious telephone conversation that she recounts in "The Estrangement" took place less than three years before Mrs. Drew died.

4. See p. 59 of this book, where Hector argues that Drew was more of a "guardian of the memory of the clan" than Kincaid and concluded, "Annie Drew was a griot" (15).

5. Velma Pollard translates this as, "What is yours cannot be unyours" (*Considering Woman* 125).

6. The only indication I have found that Mrs. Drew suspected the problems looming in Kincaid's marriage, which would dissolve in 2001 (according to Shawn, *Wish I Could Be There* 116) or 2002 (according to most other sources, such as Haber, Weisberg, and Ciabattari), two or three years after Annie Drew's death, was a statement from one source, who requested anonymity, that Annie had made a despairing comment about the marriage.

10 Jamaica's God Is Stilled

1. Note that Joseph Drew's account suggests his mother collapsed and did not experience the *accidental* fall Kincaid describes.

2. He later showed me those pictures in his home.

Epilogue

1. In *Wish I Could Be There,* Shawn indicates that they were divorced in 2001 (116). In fact, the final divorce decree was issued on 19 February 2002, according to the Vermont State Archives and Record Administration. This is consistent with the time frame in *See,* where Mrs. Sweet is fifty-two years old (18); she was born on 25 May (176); assuming the same year as Kincaid's birth (1949), she would have turned fifty-three three months after the divorce. (The names as they appear on the divorce decree are Allen Shawn and Jamaica Kincaid.)

2. This comment about her mother is puzzling given that Kincaid told me in 2008, eight years before this 2013 Alleyne interview, about people who went to Antigua seeking out her mother; furthermore, she knew that I went to Antigua seeking information "verifying her [mother's] life" in 2009.

3. Allen Shawn dedicates a chapter to his father's relationship with Lillian Ross in *Twin:* "Finding Words," 152–69.

4. Not unrelated to these titles is the comment that Lillian Ross frequently tells us that William Shawn often made about his married life: "I am there, but I am not there" (10, 11, for example).

5. See *MB* 99. During the good times, Mr. Sweet often called Mrs. Sweet "Sweetie" (*See* 11).

6. The impact of having to copy books 1 and 2 of *Paradise Lost* was such a traumatic event in Kincaid's life that she alludes to it over and over in her works and even read

from it instead of her own writing at PEN's World Festival of International Literature in 2013, explaining, "as a 7-year-old it formed very much my feelings about tyranny and about injustice. . . . I just wanted to read something that would not be what was expected. . . . I was almost sure people wanted me to read from my writing, but I never give people what they want" (Loh).

7. In *See* she provides the specific address: 284 Hudson Street (72).

8. Kincaid told Hannah Levintova that her children said she was always late picking them up at the bus.

9. Kincaid often alludes to her grandmother's "amazing" smell (Kin/Dance; Cook 10); she used "amazing" four times in my interview with her.

10. Kincaid later moved from the McGovern House on Prospect Street to a home on College Road that she and her husband purchased from a Dr. Woodworth. The Woodworth House is where she lived when I interviewed her in 2008.

11. Throughout the Kincaid canon, Kincaid and the characters in her works wrestle with the fact that love and hate are always closely intertwined and difficult to distinguish.

12. A common stereotype of Caribbean people and a slight Mr. Sweet often uses to refer to Mrs. Sweet.

13. Kincaid does not mention race, but Mrs. Sweet's focus on Mr. Sweet's blue blood and aristocratic family and background (*See* 94) contrasted with his emphasis on Mrs. Sweet's Third World, backwater origins (he constantly reminds her that she came on a banana boat) reflect the same ambivalence about race that I discussed earlier in this study.

14. She does convert to Judaism, but, as noted earlier, the Shawns were not devout Jews.

15. From the time in his childhood that Allen Shawn invited a six-year-old girl "known for wildness and indecent exposure" to his house "for the express purpose of suggesting an exchange of anatomical explorations," he "gravitate[d]" toward women who were "'foreign' to the milieu of my childhood" (*Wish* 101).

16. Kincaid often speaks in interviews and several books of the money she spends on her gardening, noting in *My Garden* that this passion has often brought the family "to the brink of bankruptcy" (226).

17. Mr. Sweet often ridicules Mrs. Sweet for looking like Charles Laughton.

18. Kincaid has often reported her husband's appeal to her to "mince words."

19. When Mr. Sweet compares Mrs. Sweet's body after the birth of their son to Charles Laughton, she was moved to tears while he thought he had said something very funny (75), reminding of Kincaid or the Kincaid character's pain when her mother made jokes at her expense. Later Mrs. Sweet tells us it was after the birth of her daughter that the husband started joking about her looking like Charles Laughton (119).

20. While this is probably a fictional addition, it is interesting to note that Kincaid's husband, Allen Shawn, has written: "My better, darker music represents some-

thing truer about me. . . . A Japanese psychiatrist . . . put it this way: 'His music and his phobias are the same'" (*Wish* 191).

21. Annie Shawn's bitterness about this issue was discussed by Connie Rabinowitz in our interview.

22. This allusion is to Jean Rhys's *Wide Sargasso Sea,* the story of Bertha Mason Rochester, the mad West Indian woman who is concealed in the attic in Charlotte Brontë's *Jane Eyre,* a source that Rhys, Kincaid, and many other female Caribbean writers cite as the only character to whom they could relate in the literature they studied; they all are motivated to provide some reality to the "mad woman."

23. This association of Mr. Sweet with a rodent may allude to what appears to be one of the most traumatic events in his life, the death of his beloved hamster when he was seven (*Wish* 45; and *Twin* 4, 67).

BIBLIOGRAPHY

Personal Communications with the Author

Brodber, Erna. E-mail. 18 November 2008.

Chacko, Sharon. E-mail. 13 May 2009.

———. Telephone interview. 20 February 2009.

Davies, Carole Boyce. E-mail. 10 August 2009.

Derrick, Vincent (Tubby). Interview. 21 January 2009.

———. E-mails. 12 February 2009 and 14 May 2009.

Derrick, Winston. Telephone interview. 18 January 2009.

Drew, Joseph. Interviews. 15 January 2009 and 19 January 2009.

———. Telephone interview. 22 January 2009.

George, Gordon. Interview. 18 January 2009.

John, Catherine. E-mail. 4 April 2009.

———. Telephone interviews. 11 February 2009 and 20 February 2009.

Kincaid, Jamaica. E-mail. 30 March 2009.

———. Interview. 11–12 October 2008. (Cited as Kin/Dance)

———. Telephone interview. 5 August 2008.

Lee, Reverend Rosa. Interview. 19 January 2009.

Luke, Conrad. Telephone interview. 20 January 2009.

Mayers, Phyllis. Telephone interview. 20 January 2009.

Osoba, Ermina. Interview. 16 January 2009.

Philip, Ivor (Splif). Interview. 16 January 2009.

Pollard, Velma. Letter. Undated, received December 2010.

Rabinowitz, Connie. Interview. 17 January 2009.

Ramsey, Dr. Sir Prince. Interview. 19 January 2009.

Reid, Jocelyn. Interview. 16 January 2009.

———. Telephone interview. 26 April 2009.

Tonge, Dame Gwendolyn. Interview. 16 January 2009.

Books, Articles, and Other Sources

"About Dominica." http://offshoresimple.com/dominica_about.htm.

Abrahams, Roger D. *African Folktales.* New York: Pantheon, 1983.

Abruna, Laura Niesen de. "Dreams of Leaving: Mother and Mother Country in Jamaica Kincaid's Fiction." *The Woman, the Writer and Caribbean Society.* Ed. Helen Pyne-Timothy. Los Angeles: Center for African American Studies, 1998. 164–75.

———. "Family Connections: Mother and Mother Country in the Fiction of Jean Rhys and Jamaica Kincaid." *Motherlands: Black Women's Writing from Africa, the Caribbean, and South Asia.* Ed. Susheila Nasta. New Brunswick, NJ: Rutgers UP. 257–89.

Adisa, Opal Palmer. "I Must Write What I Know So I'll Know I've Known It All Along." *The Woman, the Writer and Caribbean Society: Essays on Literature and Culture.* Ed. Helen Pyne-Timothy. Los Angeles: Center for Afro-American Studies Publications, 1998. 102–17.

Alexander, Simone A. James. *Mother Imagery in the Novels of Afro-Caribbean Writers.* Columbia: U of Missouri P, 2001.

Alleyne, Lauren K. "Does Truth Have a Tone?" *Guernica: A Magazine of Art & Politics* 17 June 2013. www.guernicamag.com/interviews/does-truth-have-a-tone/.

Anatol, Giselle Liza. "Speaking in (M)other Tongues: The Role of Language in Jamaica Kincaid's *The Autobiography of My Mother.*" *Callaloo* 25.3 (2002): 938–53.

———. *Things That Fly in the Night: Female Vampires in Literature of the Circum-Caribbean and African Diaspora.* New Brunswick, NJ: Rutgers UP, 2015.

The Antigua and Barbuda Homepage. www.geographia.com/antigua-barbuda/.

Baugh, Edward. *Derek Walcott.* New York: Cambridge UP, 2006.

Benítez-Rojo, Antonio. *The Repeating Island: The Caribbean and the Postmodern Perspective.* Durham: Duke UP, 1992.

Bernard, Louise. "Countermemory and Return: Reclamation of the (Postmodern) Self in Jamaica Kincaid's *The Autobiography of My Mother* and *My Brother.*" *Modern Fiction Studies* 48.1 (Spring 2002): 113–38.

Birbalsingh, Frank. "Jamaica Kincaid: From Antigua to America." *Frontiers of Caribbean Literature in English.* Ed. Birbalsingh. New York: St. Martin's, 1996. 138–51.

Birnbaum, Robert. "Robert Birnbaum Talks with Jamaica Kincaid." *The Believer Book of Writers Talking to Writers.* Ed. Vendela Vida. San Francisco: Believer, 2005. 159–74.

Bonetti, Kay. "Jamaica Kincaid." *Conversations with American Novelists: The Best Interviews from the "Missouri Review" and the American Audio Prose Library.* Ed. Bonetti et al. Columbia: UP of Missouri, 1997. 26–38.

Bouson, J. Brooks. *Jamaica Kincaid: Writing Memory, Writing Back to the Mother.* Albany: State U of New York P, 2005.

Brancato, Sabrina. *Mother and Motherland in Jamaica Kincaid.* New York: Peter Lang, 2005.

Brathwaite, Edward. "South." *Rights of Passage.* London: Oxford UP, 1967. 56–57.

Braziel, Jana Evans. *Caribbean Genesis: Jamaica Kincaid and the Writing of the New Worlds.* Albany: State U of New York P, 2009.

Brodber, Erna. "Beyond the Boundary—Magical Realism in the Jamaican Frame of Reference." Conference paper dated April 1994. Published in *Annals of Scholarship* 12.1–2 (1997): 41–47. Ed. Edward K. Brathwaite and Timothy J. Reiss; and in *Sisyphus and Eldorado: Magical and Other Realisms in Caribbean literature.* Ed. Timothy J. Reiss. Trenton: African World P, 2002. 15–24.

———. "One Bubby Susan." *The Penguin Book of Caribbean Short Stories.* Ed. E. A. Markham. London: Penguin, 1996. 48–53.

———. *The World Is a High Hill: Stories about Jamaican Women.* Kingston, Jamaica: Ian Randle, 2012.

Brooks, Gwendolyn. "The Mother." *A Street in Bronzeville.* New York: Harper and Brothers, 1945. Rpt. in *Selected Poems by Gwendolyn Brooks.* New York: Harper and Row, 1963. 4–5.

Brophy, Sarah. "Angels in Antigua: The Diasporic of Melancholy in Jamaica Kincaid's *My Brother.*" *PMLA* 117.2 (March 2002): 165–77.

Brown, Rosellen. *The Autobiography of My Mother.* New York: Dell, 1976.

Brown-Hinds, Paulette. "'Can't Leave Home without It': The Paradox of Memory in Jamaica Kincaid's *Lucy.*" *Postcolonial Perspectives on Women Writers from Africa, the Caribbean, and the US.* Ed. Martin Japtok. Trenton: Africa World P, 2003. 133–49.

Buckner, Brittnay. "Singular Beast: A Conversation with Jamaica Kincaid." *Callaloo* 31.2 (Spring 2008): 461–69.

Buhle, Paul. *Tim Hector: A Caribbean Radical's Story.* Jackson: UP of Mississippi, 2006.

Campbell, Susan. "Carnival, Calypso, and Class Struggle in Nineteenth Century Trinidad." *History Workshop* 26 (Winter 1988): 1–27.

Christian, Barbara. "The Race for Theory." *Cultural Critique* 6 (Spring 1987): 50–75.

Ciabattari, Jane. "'See Now Then' by Jamaica Kincaid." *Boston Globe* 16 February 2013.

Clarke, Austin. "Leaving This Island Place." *The Oxford Book of Caribbean Short Stories.* Ed. Stewart Brown and John Wickham. New York: Oxford UP, 2001. 220–27.

Clarke, Edith. *My Mother Who Fathered Me: A Study of the Family in Three Selected Communities in Jamaica.* London: Allen and Unwin, 1957.

Collymore, Frank. "Hymn to the Sea." *Voiceprint: An Anthology of Oral and Related Poetry from the Caribbean.* Ed. Stewart Brown, Mervyn Morris, and Gordon Rohlehr. Essex, England: Longman, 1989. 264–65.

Cook, Mariana. *Generations of Women: Women in Their Own Words.* San Francisco: Chronicle, 1998.

Covi, Giovanna. *Jamaica Kincaid's Prismatic Subjects: Making Sense of Being in the World.* London: Mango, 2003.

Cryer, Dan. "The Unlikely Success of Jamaica Kincaid." *Newsday* 8 January 1996: B4-5.

Cudjoe, Selwyn R. "Jamaica Kincaid and the Modernist Project: An Interview." *Caribbean Women Writers: Essays from the First International Conference.* Wellesley: Calaloux, 1990. 215-32. Originally published in *Callaloo* 12 (Spring 1989): 396–411.

Dance, Daryl Cumber. *Honey, Hush! An Anthology of African American Women's Humor.* New York: Norton, 1998.

———. Review of *My Brother. Art and Understanding* 7.2 (February 1998): 59–62.

Dilger, Gerhard. "'I Use a Cut and Slash Policy of Writing': Jamaica Kincaid Talks to Gerhard Dilger." *Wasafari* 16 (Autumn 1992): 21–25.

Donahue, Deirdre, "Kincaid Calls on Antigua's Influence." *USA Today* 8 November 1990: 05D.

Dove, Rita. *Through the Ivory Gate: A Novel.* New York: Pantheon, 1992.

Draine, Betsy. *Substance under Pressure: Artistic Coherence and Evolving Form in the Novels of Doris Lessing.* Madison: U of Wisconsin P, 1993.

Drew, Annie. Letter to Sharon Chacko. 21 July 1998.

Edwards, Audrey. "Jamaica Kincaid Writes of Passage." *Essence* May 1991: 87–90.

Edwards, Justin D. *Understanding Jamaica Kincaid.* Columbia: U of SC P, 2007.

Ellison, Ralph. *Shadow and Act.* 1964. New York: Vintage, 1972.

Emecheta, Buchi. "Feminism with a Small 'f!'" *Criticism and Ideology: Second African Writers' Conference.* Ed. Kirsten Holst Petersen. Uppsala: Scandinavian Institute of African Studies, 1988. 173–85.

Ferguson, Moira. *Jamaica Kincaid: Where the Land Meets the Body.* Charlottesville: UP of Virginia, 1994.

———. "A Lot of Memory: An Interview with Jamaica Kincaid." *Kenyon Review* 16.1 (1994): 163–88.

———. "A Small Place: Glossing Annie John's Rebellion." *Colonialism and Gender Relations from Mary Wollstonecraft to Jamaica Kincaid: East Caribbean Connections.* New York: Columbia UP, 1993. 116–38.

Frazier, Ian. Foreword to *Talk Stories* by Jamaica Kincaid. New York: Farrar, Straus and Giroux, 2001. xi–xx.

French, Patrick. *The World Is What It Is: The Authorized Biography of V. S. Naipaul.* New York: Knopf, 2008.

Garis, Leslie. "Through West Indian Eyes." *New York Times Magazine* 7 October 1990: 42, 44, 70, 78, 80, 91.

Garner, Dwight. "Jamaica Kincaid: The *Salon* Interview." 13 January 1996.

———. "The Marriage Has Ended: Revenge Begins." *New York Times* 12 February 2013. 13 November 2013. www.nytimes.com/2013/02/13/books/see-now-then-jamaica-kincaids-new-novel.

Gilmore, Leigh. "Autobiography's Wounds." *Just Advocacy? Women's Human Rights, Transnational Feminisms, and the Politics of Representation.* Ed. Wendy S. Hesford and Wendy Kozol. New Brunswick: Rutgers UP, 2005. 99–119.

———. "Endless Autobiography? Jamaica Kincaid and Serial Autobiography." *Postcolonialism & Autobiography.* Ed. Alfred Hornung and Ernstpeter Ruhe. Amsterdam: Rodopi, 1998. 211–31.

———. *The Limits of Autobiography: Trauma and Testimony.* Ithaca: Cornell UP, 2001.

Glissant, Édouard. *The Collected Poems of Édouard Glissant.* Ed. Jeff Humphries. Trans. Jeff Humphries with Melissa Manolas. Minneapolis: U of Minnesota P, 2005.

Goldfarb, Brad. "Writing Life": Interview with Writer Jamaica Kincaid. *Interview* 27.10 (October 1997): 94–99.

Goveia, Elsa V. *Slave Society in the British Leeward Islands at the End of the Eighteenth Century.* New Haven: Yale UP, 1965.

Haber, Leigh. "Fiercely Original Jamaica Kincaid in Her First Novel in a Decade." J. K. Interviews. Oprah.com. 17 February 2013. Originally published in *Oprah Magazine* March 2013.

Halperin, David. *Saint Foucault: Towards a Gay Hagiography.* New York: Oxford UP, 1995.

Hazelle [Goodman]. "I Not Going to Stop Til I Make It to de Top." *Honey, Hush: An Anthology of African American Women's Humor.* Ed. Daryl Cumber Dance. New York: Norton, 1998. 10–14.

Headlee, Celeste, interviewer. "Time Rules in Jamaica Kincaid's New Novel, 'See Now Then.'" *All Things Considered.* National Public Radio, 3 March 2013.

Hector, Tim. "The Matriarch of Matriarchs." *Tim Hector Anthology.* Spec. issue of *CLR James Journal* 8 (Winter 2000/2001): 12–21. Reprinted from *Outlet* 23 July 1999.

Hemingway, Ernest. *For Whom the Bell Tolls.* 1940. New York: Scribner's Sons, 1968.

"In the Main Ring with the Literati: Joe Cuomo, Master of Ceremonies. *CUNY Matters* (Spring 2001). http://www1.cuny.edu/events/cunymatters/2001_spring/joecuomo.html.

Indiana, Gary. *Resentment: A Comedy.* New York: Doubleday, 1997.

Jacobs, Sally. "Don't Mess with Jamaica Kincaid: Author and Gardener, She Withers as Well as Creates (Just Ask Tina Brown)." *Boston Globe* 20 June 1996: "Living" section, 57.

Jackson, Tommie Lee. "The Symbolic Implications of the Portmanteau in Jamaica Kincaid's *Annie John.*" *CLA Journal* 50.3 (March 2007): 298–311.

Jay, Julia De Foor. "'What a History You Have': Ancestral Memory, Cultural History, Migration Patterns, and Dreams of Freedom in the Works of Jamaica Kincaid." *Middle Passages and the Healing of History: Migration and Identity in Black Women's Literature.* Ed. Elizabeth Brown-Guillory. Columbus: Ohio State UP. 263–93.

Jones, Vanessa E. "Jamaica Kincaid Explores a Father of Her Own Invention; Kincaid Writes Her Own Truth in 'Mr. Potter.'" *Boston Globe* 20 June 2002: "Living" section, D1.

Kaufman, Joanne. "Jamaica Kincaid." *People* 15 December 1997: 109–14.

Kincaid. Jamaica. *Among Flowers: A Walk in the Himalaya.* New York: Farrar, Straus and Giroux, 2005.

———. *Annie John.* New York: Farrar, Straus and Giroux, 1985.

———. "Antigua Crossings: A Deep and Blue Passage on the Caribbean Sea." *Rolling Stone* 29 June 1978: 48–50.

———. *At the Bottom of the River.* New York: Farrar, Straus and Giroux, 1983.

———. *The Autobiography of My Mother.* New York: Farrar, Straus and Giroux, 1996.

———, ed. *The Best American Travel Writing.* Boston: Houghton Mifflin, 2005.

———. "Biography of a Dress." *Grand Street* 43 (1992): 92–100.

———. "The Estrangement." *AARP Magazine* May and June 2008: 40, 43.

———. "A Fire by Ice." *New Yorker* 22 February 1993: 64–67.

———. Foreword. *Gone to New York: Adventures in the City.* By Ian Frazier. New York: Picador, 2006. ix–xvi.

———. Introduction. *Generations of Women in Their Own Words.* Ed. Mariana Cook. San Francisco: Chronicle, 1998. 8–11.

———. "Jamaica Kincaid's New York." *Rolling Stone* 6 October 1977: 71–73.

———. "Just Reading." From "In the Garden." *New Yorker* 29 March 1993: 47–51.

———. *Lucy.* New York: Farrar, Straus and Giroux, 1990.

———. "Mariah." *New Yorker* 26 June 1989: 32–38.

———. *Mr. Potter.* New York: Farrar, Straus and Giroux, 2002.

———. *My Brother.* New York: Farrar, Straus and Giroux, 1997.

———, ed. *My Favorite Plant: Writers and Gardeners on the Plants They Love.* New York: Farrar, Straus and Giroux, 1998.

———. *My Garden (Book):.* New York: Farrar, Straus and Giroux, 1999.

———. "On Seeing England for the First Time." *Transition* 51 (1991): 32–40.

———. "Ovando." *Conjunctions* 14 (1989): 75–83.

———. "Plant Parenthood." *New Yorker* 19 June 1995: 43.

———. "Putting Myself Together." *New Yorker* 20 and 27 February 1995: 93–101.

———. *See Now Then: A Novel.* New York: Farrar, Straus and Giroux, 2013.

———. *A Small Place.* New York: Farrar, Straus and Giroux, 1988.

———. *Talk Stories.* New York: Farrar, Straus and Giroux, 2001.

———. "This Other Eden." *New Yorker* 30 August 1993: 69–72.

Kincaid, Jamaica, and Eric Fischl. *Annie, Gwen, Lilly, Pam and Tulip.* New York: Knopf, in association with the Whitney Museum of American Art, 1989.

King, Jane. "A Small Place Writes Back." *Callaloo* 25.3 (Summer 2002): 885–909.

Laforest, Marie-Hélène. "Ages of a Woman: Jamaica Kincaid's *My Brother.*" *MaComère* 6 (2004): 19–25.

Lamming, George. *The Pleasures of Exile.* 1960. Ann Arbor: U of Michigan P, 1992.

Lang-Peralta, Linda, ed. *Jamaica Kincaid and Caribbean Double Crossings.* Newark: U of Delaware P, 2006.

Langston, James. "Women at War: A 'Falling Out' Is How the Writer Jamaica Kincaid Refers to Her Row with the Formidable Tina Brown, Editor of *The New Yorker.*" *Sunday Telegraph* (London) 13 October 1996: 6.

Lazarus-Black, Mindie. *Legitimate Acts and Illegal Encounters: Law and Society in Antigua and Barbuda.* Washington, DC: Smithsonian Institution P, 1994.

Lee, Felicia R. "At Home With: Jamaica Kincaid; Dark Woods, Light Being." *New York*

Times 25 January 1996: C-1. http://query.nytimes.com/gst/fullpage.html?res=9B06E0D71639F936A15752C0A960958260.

Levintova, Hannah. "'Our Sassy Black Friend' Jamaica Kincaid." *Mother Jones* January/February 2013, 60.

Listfield, Emily. "Straight from the Heart." *Harper's Bazaar* October 1990: 82.

Loh, Alyssa. "A Conversation with Jamaica Kincaid." *American Reader.* http://theamericanreader.com/a-conversation-with-jamaica-kincaid/.

Lorde, Audre."The Master's Tools Will Never Dismantle the Master's House." *Sister Outsider: Essays & Speeches by Audre Lorde.* Freedom, CA: Crossing, 1984. 110–13.

Lovelace, Earl. *The Dragon Can't Dance.* London: André Deutsch, 1979.

MacDonald-Smythe, Antonia. *Making Homes in the West Indies.* New York: Garland, 2001.

Mangum, Bryant. "Jamaica Kincaid." *Fifty Caribbean Writers: A Bio-Bibliographical Critical Sourcebook.* Ed. Daryl Cumber Dance. New York: Greenwood, 1986. 255–63.

Marshall, Paule. *Triangular Road: A Memoir.* New York: Perseus, 2009.

Mendelsohn, Jane. "Leaving Home: Jamaica Kincaid's Voyage Round Her Mother." *Village Voice Literary Supplement* 89 (October 1990): 21.

Mistron, Deborah. *Understanding Jamaica Kincaid's "Annie John": A Student Casebook to Issues, Sources, and Historical Documents.* Westport: Greenwood, 1999.

Morrison, Toni. *Playing in the Dark: Whiteness and the Literary Imagination.* Cambridge: Harvard UP, 1992.

———. "Rootedness: The Ancestor as Foundation." *Black Women Writers: A Critical Evaluation.* Ed. Mari Evans. New York: Doubleday, 1983. 339–45.

———. *Song of Solomon.* New York: Knopf, 1977.

Mother Love [Jo Anne Hart], with Connie Church. *Listen Up, Girlfriends!* New York: St. Martin's, 1995.

Moyers, Bill. "Chinua Achebe." *A World of Ideas.* Ed. Betty Sue Flowers. New York: Doubleday, 1989. 333–44.

Murdoch, H. Adlai. "Severing the (M)other Connection: The Representation of Cultural Identity in Jamaica Kincaid's *Annie John.*" *Callaloo* 13 (1990): 325–40.

Nasta, Susheila, ed. *Motherlands: Black Women's Writing from Africa, the Caribbean, and South Asia.* New Brunswick, NJ: Rutgers UP, 1992.

Nepaulsingh, Colbert. "The Names of Elaine Potter Richardson." *MaComère* 5 (2002): 204–21.

Nnaemeka, Obioma, ed. *The Politics of (M)Othering: Womanhood, Identity, and Resistance in African Literature.* New York: Routledge, 1997.

O'Conner, Patricia T. "Paradise with Snake." Review of *Annie John, by Jamiaca Kincaid. New York Times Book Review* 7 April 1985: 6.

Paquet, Sandra Pouchet. "Death and Sexuality: Jamaica Kincaid's *My Brother.*" *Caribbean Autobiography: Cultural Identity and Self-Representation.* Madison: U of Wisconsin P, 2002. 243–56.

Paravisini-Gebert, Lizabeth. *Jamaica Kincaid: A Critical Companion.* Westport: Greenwood, 1999.

Pearse, Andrew. "Carnival in Nineteenth Century Trinidad." *Trinidad Carnival: A Republication of the Caribbean Quarterly Trinidad Carnival Issue* 4.3–4 (1956). Port of Spain, Trinidad: Paria, 1988. 4–41.

Perry, Donna. "An Interview with Jamaica Kincaid." *Reading Black, Reading Feminist: A Critical Anthology.* Ed. Henry Louis Gates Jr. New York: Meridian-Penguin, 1990. 492–509.

Piontelli, Alessandra. *Twins in the World: The Legends They Inspire and the Lives They Lead.* New York: Palgrave Macmillan, 2008.

Pollard, Velma. "Bitter Tales." *Considering Woman I & II.* Leeds, England: Peepal Tree, 2010: 83–109. (*Considering Woman* (I) was first published by the Women's Press in London in 1989.)

Powrie, Barbara E. "The Changing Attitude of the Coloured Middle Class towards Carnival." *Trinidad Carnival: A Republication of the Caribbean Quarterly Trinidad Carnival Issue* 4.3–4 (1956). Port of Spain, Trinidad: Paria, 1988. 91–107.

Prince, Mary. *The History of Mary Prince, A West Indian Slave, Related by Herself with a Supplement by the Editor. To Which Is Added, The Narrative of Asa-Asa, a Captured African.* 3rd ed. London: F. Westley and A. H. Davis, Stationers' Hall Court; Edinburgh: Waugh & Innes, 1831.

Rice, Anne P. "Burning Connections: Maternal Betrayal in Jamaica Kincaid's *My Brother.*" *Autobiography Studies* 14.1 (Summer 1994): 23–37.

Rich, Adrienne. *Of Woman Born: Motherhood as Experience and Institution.* New York: Norton, 1982.

Roberts, Brian. *Cecil Rhodes: Flawed Colossus.* New York: Norton, 1988.

Ross, Lillian. *Here but Not Here: A Love Story.* New York: Random House, 1998.

Rowell, Charles H. "An Interview with Olive Senior." *Callaloo* 36 (Summer 1988): 480–90.

Ruas, Charles. "Archéologie d'une passion." *Magazine Littéraire* 221 (July–August 1985): 100–105.

Saunders, Patricia Joan. *Alien-Nation and Repatriation: Translating Identity in Anglophone Caribbean Literature.* New York: Lexington, 2007.

Senior, Olive. *Arrival of the Snake-Woman and Other Stories.* Essex, England: Longman Caribbean, 1989.

Shawn, Allen. *Twin: A Memoir.* New York: Viking Penguin, 2011.

———. *Wish I Could Be There: Notes from a Phobic Life.* New York: Viking Penguin, 2007.

Shawn, Annie Rosamond. Résumé. 2 April 2009. http://www2.massgeneral.org/allpsych/arp/local_images/CV%20Annie%20Shawn%206-11-07.pdf.

Simmons, Diane. *Jamaica Kincaid.* New York: Twayne, 1994.

———. "Loving Too Much: Jamaica Kincaid and the Dilemma of Constructing a Postcolonial Identity." *Postcolonialism & Autobiography.* Ed. Alfred Hornung and Ernstpeter Ruhe. Amsterdam: Rodopi, 1998. 233–45.

Simon, Louis. "Triumph of Ambivalence: Jamaica Kincaid's *The Autobiography of My Mother.*" *Journal of Caribbean Literature* 4.1 (2005): 31–37.

Smith, Derik, and Cliff Beumel. "My Other: Imperialism and Subjectivity in Jamaica Kincaid's *My Brother.*" *Jamaica Kincaid and Caribbean Double Crossings.* Ed. Linda Lang-Peralta. Newark: U of Delaware P. 96–112.

Smith, Sidonie. *A Poetics of Women's Autobiography—Marginality and the Fictions of Self-Representation.* Bloomington: Indiana UP, 1987.

Snodgrass, Mary Ellen. *Jamaica Kincaid: A Literary Companion.* Jefferson, NC: McFarland, 2008.

Soto-Crespo, Ramon E. "Death and the Diaspora Writer: Hybridity and Mourning in the Work of Jamaica Kincaid." *Contemporary Literature* 43.2 (Summer 2002): 342–76.

Splif. See Philip, Ivor.

Taylor, Jenny. *Notebooks/Memoirs/Archives. Reading and Rereading Doris Lessing.* Boston: Routledge and Kegan Paul, 1982.

"10 Questions." *Time* 4 February 2013: 60.

Tiffin, Helen. "Cold Hearts and (Foreign) Tongues: Recitation and the Reclamation of the Female Body in the Works of Erna Brodber and Jamaica Kincaid." *Callaloo* 16.4 (Fall 1993): 909–21.

Vorda, Allan. "I Come from a Place That's Very Unreal: An Interview with Jamaica Kincaid." *Face to Face: Interviews with Contemporary Novelists.* Ed. Vorda. Houston: Rice UP, 1993. 77–105.

———. "An Interview with Jamaica Kincaid" (1991). *Mississippi Review* 20.1–2 (1991): 7–26.

Wadler, Joyce. "A Life Lived in Fear, but Not Half Bad." Review of *Wish I Could Be There: Notes from a Phobic Life,* by Allen Shawn. *New York Times Magazine* 25 January 2007: 1. http://query.nytimes.com/gst/fullpage.html?res=9C02E2DC163FF936A15752C0A9619C8B63.

Walcott, Derek. "Caligula's Horse." Opening address delivered at the Eighth Conference on West Indian Literature, Mona, Jamaica, May 1988. *After Europe: Critical Theory and Post-Colonial Writing.* Ed. Stephen Slemon and Helen Tiffin. Sydney, Australia: Dangaroo, 1989. 138–42.

———. *Star Apple Kingdom.* New York: Farrar, Straus and Giroux, 1977.

Walker, Alice. *The Color Purple.* New York: Harcourt Brace Jovanovich, 1982.

Walker, Susan. "Jamaica Kincaid, Master Storyteller." *Toronto Star* 27 May 2002: E04.

Watson, G. Llewellyn. *Jamaican Sayings: With Notes on Folklore, Aesthetics, and Social Control.* Gainesville: UP of Florida, 1991.

Weisberg, Jessica. "Jamaica Kincaid Is Still Jewish." *Tablet Magazine* 5 February 2013.

Weiss, Philip. "Nothing for Lillian Ross in William Shawn's Will." *New York Observer,* August 31, 1998.

INDEX